THE WINDS OF HAVOC

THE WINDS OF HAVOC

A MEMOIR OF ADVENTURE AND DESTRUCTION IN DEEPEST AFRICA

Adelino Serras Pires

AS TOLD TO

Fiona Claire Capstick

ST. MARTIN'S PRESS
NEW YORK

www.stmartins.com

Illustration on title page: *Town of Tete from the North Shore of Zambezi,* by Thomas Baines (April 1859), reprinted with permission from the Royal Geographical Society, London.

BOOK DESIGN BY CASEY HAMPTON

ISBN: 0-312-27003-8

First Edition: January 2001

10 9 8 7 6 5 4 3 2 1

IN LOVING MEMORY OF LOLI,

a most admirable, gallant, and noble lady
I was so privileged to have known.

She Understood

CONTENTS

Acknowledgments

The genesis of this book goes back to November 1986 when my late husband, Peter Hathaway Capstick, conducted a series of extensive tape-recorded interviews with Adelino concerning his life and the book they wished to write together. They first met in 1968. The time was not right and these tape recordings and relevant documentation were placed in safekeeping until the wind shifted and this story could at last be told. The bedrock of this book lies in those recordings and we should like to acknowledge Peter's role all those years ago in gathering together the threads of Adelino's life.

Our warm appreciation and thanks go to the following people: Lucinda Feijão, Adelino's sister, for her prodigious memory and Moises Feijão, her husband who is now eighty-seven and who provided many of the historic photographs featured in this book; the Serras Pires clan, now scattered over four continents; Richard Curtis in New York City, our literary agent, for his unfailing support, shrewd advice and skills in a very difficult business; Brad Wood, our editor, and all at St. Martin's Press in New York for their exemplary work; Bertus Floor and Jan van Graan of Pretoria, South Africa, information technology whiz kids whose expertise proved to us that there is indeed a generation gap; Bernard Clark of Pretoria for his professional photographic assistance; Marisa Fenderl of Pretoria, valued friend and voracious reader, whose first-hand experience of political turmoil in several African countries made her the ideal person to read the raw manuscript; Laurian Coughlan, my sister, in Pietermaritzburg, South Africa, whose encyclopedic knowledge and attention to detail made her the other ideal person to review the manuscript; Pierre van der Walt of Johannesburg, whose experience and knowledge as a hunter and firearms expert proved invaluable; Steve Comus, Director of Publications of Safari Club International, in Tucson, Arizona, for the splendid exposure accorded the manuscript in *Safari*, the flagship publication of Safari Club International; Harriet Hedley of Christie's in Johannesburg, for her assistance concerning the Royal Geographical Society in London; the Royal Geographical Society in London for permission to reproduce the painting by Thomas Baines which is featured on the title page; Robert M. Lee of Reno, Nevada for permission to quote from his historic book, *Safari Today*, published in 1960 by The Stackpole Company of Harrisburg, Pennsylvania; Bert Klineburger of San Antonio, Texas, a pioneer in the international hunting safari industry, for agreeing to write the Foreword; and friends in several countries who have requested anonymity.

Author's Note

You are about to read the extraordinary story of Adelino Serras Pires, which straddles almost sixty-five years of pre- and postcolonial Africa. Based on many hours of tape recordings, voluminous quantities of documentation from overt and covert sources, and research in several countries, this story concerns one of the most controversial members of the international safari-hunting industry.

Set against the backdrop of sun-seared savannas, swamps, and triple-canopy equatorial forests, the text is peopled by European aristocracy, heads of state, astronauts and captains of industry, World War II heroes, wine barons, pioneers of the African safari, intelligence operatives, and guerrilla fighters, as well as by those who bore the brunt of the savagery which has swept through Africa in the past few decades—the bush Africans and the wildlife whose world they shared.

Laughter and excitement, political intrigue, cowardice and treachery, interspersed with periods of high achievement, intense happiness, gut-mauling fear, and sadness color this tale. It is unapologetic in its directness, unashamed in its emotion as it traces Adelino's remarkable life from the time he arrived as a child on the banks of the Zambezi River in Mozambique, on Christmas Eve in 1936, to the sound of church bells and the roar of the Benga man-eating lions, until the dawning of the new millennium.

This book goes far beyond the confines of a mere tale of hunting adventure in the African bush. It is a social history, a eulogy of passionate remembrance which will, at times, shock and anger you. Nobody will remain indifferent to the events or the man as you follow his tracks. The wildlife Eden of Mozambique until it erupted into revolution, Angola on the eve of civil war, the Rhodesian bush war, Kenya and the end of hunting, the Central African Empire/Republic and ivory scandals, Sudan and its human misery, Zaire and the Mobutu kleptocracy, aided and abetted by the West, Tanzania and one of the most disgraceful episodes in the annals of the African hunting safari, game ranching in South Africa, and subsequent hands-on involvement in Mozambican resistance politics—this is an intense story with few parallels. All events described are authentic, as are the names appearing in the text.

The first person has been employed throughout as the narrative device in order to retain the personal impact of this disturbing testimony.

—*Fiona Claire Capstick*
Waterkloof, Pretoria
Republic of South Africa

Foreword

I first set foot on the continent of Africa in 1962. It was an instant love affair. Africa was in my blood and, for the next seven years, I was very active in Uganda, Tanzania, and the Central African Republic. In both Uganda and Tanzania, I helped start excellent tourism and conservation programs. For me, it was both fun and business. In 1969, after having met hunters and travelers who had been to Mozambique and who spoke with such enthusiasm of that beautiful, peaceful, game-rich country with magnificent habitat, I decided that I had to pay a visit there and explore hunting-safari opportunities.

One of the first people I met in Mozambique was Adelino Serras Pires. He was born in Portugal and came out to Mozambique as a child of eight to the remote town of Tete on the Zambezi River. Adelino clearly remembers hearing church bells and lions roaring on the night that he arrived in Tete. Almost immediately, he would be hunting man-killing lions with his father. He was a natural hunter, raised among the animals and learning at an early age that this renewable resource held great value for Mozambique. His feelings can but be imagined many years later, when he would witness the destruction of so much of Africa's wildlife through wars and greed.

With his natural charisma and professional hunting background, Adelino was the right person to be asked to head what would become Africa's largest safari company, the fabled Safrique. A major Portuguese bank had incorporated huge hunting areas which stretched from the Zambezi down to the Indian Ocean, covering four distinct habitats teeming with game. Fine camps were built and a vigorous program was launched to attract an ever-increasing number of international sport hunters to Mozambique.

Adelino and I hit it off right away and established a lifelong friendship. My brothers, Chris and Gene, and I were operating the world's largest taxidermy and hunter-booking service out of Seattle, specializing in Africa and Asia. Adelino appointed me as an advisory director of Safrique. The years that followed were very successful. Hunters came to Mozambique from all over the world, thereby helping fund game management and creating sustainable jobs for hundreds of Africans. The country was peaceful and entirely integrated.

All this came to a pitiful end by 1975, when the Portuguese government turned loose its colonies. They would join many other African countries on the path of strife and destruction. After the fall of Mozambique, Adelino was stripped of all he possessed and left the country he loved with only the shirt on his back. Pioneer hunter, game-management expert and safari organizer, Adelino went to Angola, Rhodesia, and Kenya. Europe was not for him.

In the meantime, I had gone to the Central African Republic to sign an agreement with President Jean-Bédel Bokassa. Soon I had some of the finest hunting concessions in Africa, where I built up a huge and successful safari-hunting company. My wife, Brigitte, and I ran the company for three years. When we left, most regrettably the company was run into the ground in less than a year. The Americans asked me to help find an appropriate person to resurrect and run the company. I told them that if Adelino Serras Pires would accept their offer, they would have the best man on the continent, someone who spoke the languages and had the experience and integrity. Adelino took up the challenge once again.

In 1973, I was on the last safari in Zaire with the astronauts Captain James Lovell of *Apollo 13* fame, Stuart Roosa of *Apollo 14*, and Charles E. Wilson, the son of the former president of General Motors. At the suggestion of Prince Abdorreza, the renowned hunter and brother of the last shah of Iran, President Mobutu of Zaire had closed hunting, so that a new company could be appointed and a fresh start made in Zaire. Adelino and I kept working with President Mobutu to get hunting reopened in that giant heart of Africa. This was accomplished in 1983, a contract was concluded with the government of Zaire, and Stan Studer was our main shareholder. After huge expense and a major investment in time and effort, the company was fully equipped and ready to go into operation. Overnight, the government of Zaire reneged on the contract. I was forced to agree with Adelino: There is nothing new out of Africa.

Much of what you will be reading will disturb you, but it is the truth, told by a man of uncompromising directness. History is history and, like wars, famine and other natural disasters, it can be very unpleasant. This book encompasses over six decades of personal experience in nine African countries, spanning a time of triumph, turbulence, and tragedy.

Fiona Capstick is the widow of the famous American writer, Peter Hathaway Capstick, whose thirteen books on African hunting and adventure continue to play a pivotal role in promoting Africa as a hunting safari destination. As you will discover, she is well equipped to share this unique and riveting story from Africa.

Bert Klineburger

Bert Klineburger
San Antonio, Texas

The wind of change is blowing through the continent. Whether we like it or not, this growth of nationl consciousness is a political fact.

—Harold Macmillan, Prime Minister of Great Britain,
Speech in the South African Parliament,
Cape Town, February 3, 1960

HAVOC: devastation, destruction, ruination, rack and ruin, holocaust, demolition, wipe-out, debacle, ruin, spoliation, despoliation, ravage, pillage, plunder, sack, robbing, plundering, gutting, ransacking, vandalizing, wasting, rapine, ravishment, predation, depredation, desolation, waste, wreckage, ravagement, extermination, extirpation, obliteration, annihilation, disaster, calamity, catastrophe, cataclysm (*The Synonym Finder*, Rodale Press, 1981).

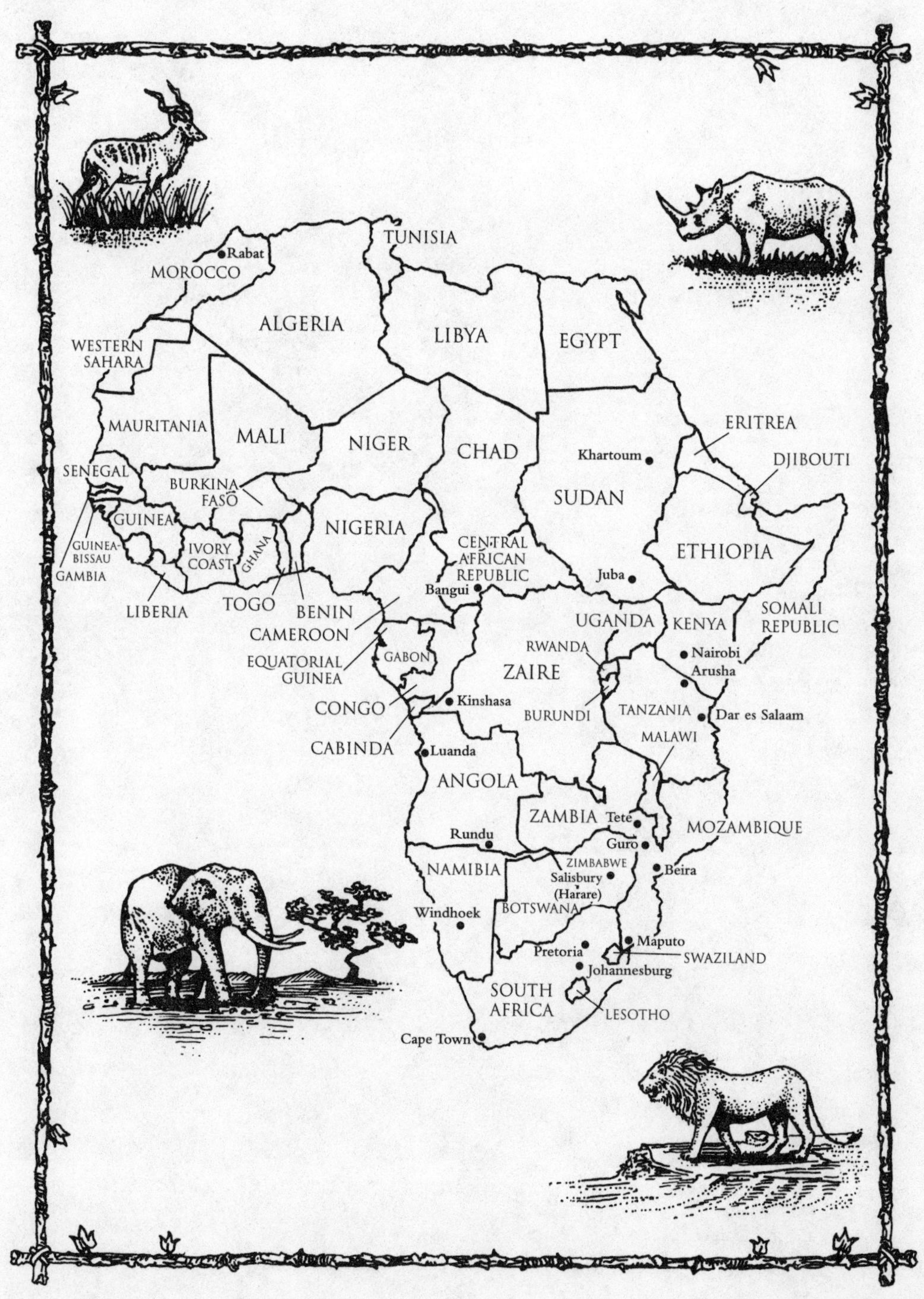

TUNISIA
Rabat
MOROCCO
ALGERIA
LIBYA
EGYPT
WESTERN SAHARA
MAURITANIA
MALI
NIGER
CHAD
ERITREA
Khartoum
DJIBOUTI
SENEGAL
BURKINA FASO
SUDAN
GUINEA
NIGERIA
GUINEA-BISSAU
IVORY COAST
GHANA
CENTRAL AFRICAN REPUBLIC
ETHIOPIA
GAMBIA
Juba
Bangui
LIBERIA
TOGO
BENIN
SOMALI REPUBLIC
CAMEROON
UGANDA
KENYA
RWANDA
Nairobi
EQUATORIAL GUINEA
GABON
ZAIRE
Arusha
CONGO
Kinshasa
BURUNDI
TANZANIA
Dar es Salaam
CABINDA
MALAWI
Luanda
ANGOLA
ZAMBIA
Tete
MOZAMBIQUE
Rundu
Guro
NAMIBIA
ZIMBABWE
Beira
Salisbury (Harare)
Windhoek
BOTSWANA
Maputo
Pretoria
SWAZILAND
Johannesburg
SOUTH AFRICA
LESOTHO
Cape Town

PRELUDE

I could not walk. My feet were fast-blackening balloons of swollen agony, the ankles tightly bound with the inner tubes of bicycle tires. My hands were two bulbous mounds of fire, the wrists also tightly bound with rubber strips. I was blindfolded and barefoot as I was shoved and dragged from a vehicle.

The sounds of jet engines told me that we were being taken to a landing strip. With Tanzanian secret policemen on either side of me, I was pushed up some steps into an aircraft and forced into a seat, where my blindfold was removed. In front of me sat my son, Adelino Jr., known as Tim-Tim; my nephew, Carlos Artur, known as Caju; and a fellow Portuguese hunter and relative, Rui Monteiro. The horror on their faces is something I wish I could efface from my memory of that terrible day, August 29, 1984, in Tanzania.

We took off from Kilimanjaro Airport. I was in such agony, yowling with pain at the ever-tightening rubber bands on my hands and feet, that I thought I was dying. My son and the others were able to persuade the thugs on the executive aircraft, provided by President of Tanzania Julius Nyerere, to cut off the rubber vises. As the blood started to flow back into my extremities, the pain increased and I teetered on the verge of blackout. My son started rubbing my hands in a desperate attempt to stave off what we feared most, gangrene.

The aircraft gained height and we all thought we were heading for the Tanzanian seaport of Dar-es-Salaam. What irony as I write this, to think that the name means "Haven of Peace," when we were all at the gateway to hell. I was facing the rear when we noticed that the sun was now in the wrong position. It was on my right, meaning the left of the jet. We were heading south, for Mozambique. That meant only one thing: We were about to be delivered into the hands of the Mozambican Secret Police.

My son, Caju, and Rui had been rounded up and arrested in the middle of a safari with an American couple from Texas. I had suddenly been detained at my hotel in Arusha, where I had been taking a brief break, having just completed a two-week safari in the Ugalla concession with Valéry Giscard d'Estaing, the former president of France.

No experience before or since has equaled what we endured. I could not have foreseen the savage safari into depravity and deceit which lay ahead for all of us. Nauseous with pain and shock, my mind traveled back in time, comalike, to that day in 1936 when we docked in Beira, Mozambique, now below the jet, and a lifetime away.

ONE

A ZAMBEZI CHILDHOOD

In this town and island they call Mocobiquy (Moçambique) was a Senhor they called Sultan, who was like a Viceroy . . .

—Eric Axelson, *Vasco da Gama: The Diary of His Travels Through African Waters* 1497–1499

The monthlong voyage down the west coast of Africa, round the *Cabo das Tormentas*, the Cape of Storms, into the Mozambique Channel and our new home left me with a lifelong aversion to boats because I had been so seasick. The entire trip, however, had been mercifully interspersed with such novel experiences that I was constantly distracted. We watched children diving for coins in the shallows off Madeira Island and were totally intrigued by the boat's resident parrot as it paraded its staggering vocabulary of ripe language, picked up from Portuguese seamen. Eventually, the bird started mimicking my very proper mother as she ordered my sister Lucinda to stay away from it for modesty's sake. Being the loquacious one in the family, Lucinda made friends in a flash with the parrot. I can also remember staring in disbelief as the adults pointed out shoals of flying fish flirting with the boat's foaming wake when any small boy already knew that fish had to live under the water and that only birds could fly!

When we finally landed in Angola, I thought most of the people were black because the scorching sun had burnt them that color. My child's logic also convinced me that the dreadful humidity we felt as we neared Beira was because the sun was crying hot tears. All this left me bewildered but energized. I could smell adventure in the air. It was grand to be eight years old and on a journey to the other end of the earth, seasickness be damned. Maybe the Gypsy lady who had read my palm as a little boy had cast a spell of wanderlust over me because, to this day, I have surely led a Gypsy's existence.

We thronged on deck that dawn as word spread that we were about to dock in Beira. A heat haze was already forming along the low-lying coast, which had been dominated by the Arabs and Persians from the ninth century A.D., perhaps even earlier. They once controlled the trade in slaves, gold, ivory, pearls, hardwoods such as ebony, tortoiseshell, iron, and animal skins. In fact, it is said that the name Mozambique is derived from the name of Musa ben Biki, the Muslim sheik of Mozambique Island, a small coral island lying in the channel, just south of the great natural harbor of Nacala. Sheik ben Biki was in power at the time of Vasco da Gama's visit in March 1498, after the Portuguese mariners had rounded the southern extremity of Africa, changing human history.

We were now about to set foot on the "Land of Sofala" ("the low-lying place,") that fabled region Vasco da Gama first visited in 1502 when he put in to the Bay of Sofala, just south of Beira, on his way back from his second voyage to India. The Arabs referred to Sofala as *Sufalat edh-dhahab*, Sofala the Golden, because of its prominence in the coastal Arab kingdom as a trading station for gold from the interior. My sense of excitement and anticipation that dawn was acute. We were entering a new world, a new life, and our family was to be reunited.

My world until then had been the village of Ponte de Sor and the surrounding low-lying hills of central Portugal, where my father used to take me on hunts for hare, green pigeon, and partridge, our retriever dogs in tow. Our family had lived for generations in the whitewashed villages of the Alentejo, where the deep pink terra-cotta roofs punctuated the arid beauty of the surrounding cork and olive groves. This was a land where nobody challenged his place in the order of things, where the narrow ways of village life and a deeply traditional people continued with claustrophobic predictability. Change was discouraged with the fatalism which permeates Portuguese *fado* folksong, that unique musical tradition known for its melancholic view of life where humans are portrayed as the hapless victims of an overpowering fate.

It was a world where the women started dressing in black from an early age to show respect for family members as they succeeded one another in death, a world ordered by the rituals of the Catholic church. The menfolk would gather at the café for their daily wine and gossip, some playing *damas*, draughts (checkers). Pig farming, chickens, cork, and olives dominated the conversation, the womenfolk dutifully at home. News from the outside world had little impact on the seasoned rhythms and aromas of my village childhood.

A profound change came over our family when my father's three brothers, who had all emigrated to Mozambique around the time of my birth in 1928, wrote, urging him to come out with his family and join them in a land bursting with opportunities, wide open to enterprise and needing skills. Although we had a coffee mill which processed beans from the Portuguese colonies and we lived a secure life, my family decided to emigrate. The mill was sold, and my father preceded us by three years in order to establish a base for his family.

I can remember the day we left for Africa. My sisters Lucinda and Maria-José, my brother Jacinto, and I left our home with our mother, the car bumping along the cobblestoned village street and past the anchors of all our childhood memories and securities to the railway station and a place called Lisbon. There, we boarded the *Quanza* one cold, wet day in November 1936.

The boat pushed out, beyond the Tagus estuary, and into the gathering night. We were following the path of the flimsy Portuguese caravels of the fifteenth century in their quest for a sea route to India. Ours was a quest for a life of greater opportunity and reward, where the horizons were broader than anything we had ever known in cramped Portugal, with her matching ways. It would be a month before we reached Mozambique.

It seemed an eternity before we were allowed to leave the boat and step onto the quayside, where my father was waiting for us amid a host of Black dockworkers handling baggage as customs officials in their crisp naval uniforms directed us where to go. My father was as I remembered him, a darkly handsome man with thick, curly hair whom we mobbed in our excitement as our stories of the voyage tumbled out of our mouths in noisy celebration. But my little brother, Jacinto, was unimpressed and started wailing. He did not know who this man was; he had been only a few months old when my father left for Mozambique. In the furnace heat of that day in late December 1936, we children bridged the gap of three years as if it were a day. We had no concept of the emotional strain and sacrifices our parents had made for us.

The ground rolled with every step I tried to take, making me feel queasy all over again. I never quite found my sea legs, and now my land legs seemed to have deserted me. As we made our way through the wide sandy streets of the port, two things made an early impression on me: the flamboyant trees lining the streets, looking as if they were on fire with their vibrant colors, and then the quaint two-seater, white-hooded carriages, like rickshaws, running on narrow tracks in the sand, being propelled by smartly turned out Black attendants. My senses were freshly courted by these novelties, memories of Portugal ebbing like the tide of a receding world, ready to be replaced by another.

It was nightfall on Christmas Eve when we finally arrived in Tete, the ancient Arab port on the Zambezi River, settled just over four hundred years previously by the Portuguese. It was reputedly the oldest continuously inhabited inland town in Africa south of the equator. My Uncle João and my namesake, Uncle Adelino, were there to welcome us into our new life. Uncle Jacinto had already died of blackwater fever. It had been an exhausting trip of about 375 miles in a black "Terraplano" motorcar over dirt roads which snaked their way across vast areas of rough, undulating bush country scarred by stony, dry riverbeds baking in unrelenting heat. The car broke down on a couple of occasions and my father had to put in oil, to the accompaniment of muttered irritations which my mother was quick to counter with "Pires, please! The children are listening!" She always addressed my father by the last part of our surname.

Church bells were pealing that night in Tete, calling the few hundred inhabitants to midnight mass. During an interval in the ringing, a fresh sound drifted toward us, a muted tone which rose and fell, followed by two or three staccato grunts. There it was again, only this time more distinct. Fatigue forgotten, I remember turning to my father and asking, *"Pai, o que foi aquele barulho?"* "Dad, what was that noise?"

"Leões! Lions! The man-eating lions of Benga, across the river, son. You have heard the lions. That is a sign. When you grow up, you will be a hunter. You heard the lions tonight."

Now I *knew* I was in a different world.

The woman's badly decomposed and mauled body was found on the fringes of the *posto,* the administrative headquarters at Benga, which was situated on the northern bank of the Zambezi River, just east of Tete. My Uncle Adelino, who was also my godfather, was the *Chefe de Posto,* the head of station, a position of considerable authority in those days. He was judge, arbitrator, medic, scribe for the illiterate, intercessor with the faceless, distant Portuguese bureaucracy and chain of command, father confessor, counsellor, and defender in a region covering thousands of square miles of raw bush which had seen little change in centuries. He was known to be a fair man who never took sides, who listened well, and who was trusted in the harsh, unforgiving world of the tribal people.

He and a handful of *sipaios,* the tribal policemen, kept order in that vast region with remarkably little effort. If a serious crime occurred, such as a killing, my uncle would dispatch one of his men to the village in question and put the word out that the perpetrator of the crime had better hand himself over at the *posto* forthwith. In the meantime, the entire family of the suspect was escorted back to my uncle's compound at Benga and kept there until such time as the alleged criminal gave himself up. The family was always very well treated and this "hostage-taking," for want of a better term, was hardly ever employed because the rules were well understood and applied without exception. The community nearly always rounded up the suspect beforehand because they knew the consequences. In the tribal culture, there was no place to hide.

My uncle was dedicated and generous, spending his own money to upgrade the *posto,* install and equip a simple clinic, and generally earn the respect and support of the tribal people in his jurisdiction. Portugal would take forever to attend to such needs in a backwater of the colonial empire. These are matters of official record, not the fond memories of a doting nephew. In many a tribal dispute, *o Senhor* Chefe de Posto was the last resort in efforts to restore peace. It was only natural, therefore, that the people would turn to him when the catastrophe of early 1937 hit them.

Sleeping sickness, caused by the bite of the tsetse fly, the ubiquitous malaria, and the scourge of leprosy had scythed through the local population by February 1937. Many of the sick and dying struggled into my uncle's compound, or were brought there by despairing relatives. They completely overwhelmed the rudimentary health-care facilities, exhausting medical supplies as they died by the dozens, like the proverbial flies which were attracted to the stench of human flesh decomposing in temperatures which waltzed into the 100s almost every day. The situation had become intolerable, but it would worsen.

A consequence of this epidemic was the sudden proliferation of man-eating lions in large parts of the Benga region. Such was the availability of weak, sick, and defenseless people of all ages that the lions abandoned their traditional hunting activities and turned man-eater because of the sheer volume of protein in their backyards. My uncle and his *sipaios,* without whom he could never have been as effective as he was, sent for my father and anyone he thought suitable to come over to Benga with whatever medical supplies they could muster as well as with their firearms for an all-out campaign against several groups of man-eating lions. The people were living in terror and something had to be done. They had tried placating their ancestors with sacrifices and other rituals conducted by the tribal soothsayers, the *cuchcucheiros* or witch doctors, but the ancestors ears were deaf that summer. They turned to my uncle who, in turn, called upon his family and the community for backup. Metropolitan Portugal and the comfortable bureaucrats in Lisbon who called the shots may as well have been on another planet, as my Father explained to me years later. In a crisis, we had to be largely self-reliant. I was to learn that lesson over and over again in Africa.

I had just recovered from my first attack of malaria and had started attending the local school in Tete, when my father took me along with a group of his friends on my first actual hunting experience. As an eight-year-old, cutting your hunting teeth on man-eating lions is a devil of a bush baptism, but I would have followed my father into Hades itself, such was my total trust in him. He was invincible in my eyes. I was apprehensive, however, as we boarded a boat to cross the Zambezi and go to my uncle's aid. No lover of sailing of any sort, I recall asking my father, as I watched the chanting Nyungwe paddlers fight the strong currents, dipping their oars in unison, if the deep and muddy waters of the Zambezi would ever engulf Tete, built on a rocky outcrop set back from the river. What I really wanted to know was whether we would reach the other side! My father laughed at my anxiety, telling me that there were two kinds of death I need never fear, one of which was dying of fright. The other had something to do with having babies. At the time, I did not quite grasp his meaning.

We arrived at the *posto* quite late that afternoon and were organized into two groups, each with a guide. Unless you traverse an area regularly and are familiar with its features, the African bush can kill you in a day, especially with the heat of the Zambezi Valley.

I was the only child on that obviously all-male expedition told to stick right behind my father, like a second shadow at all times, and not to speak at all unless spoken to. My duty was to carry a water bottle. I felt I owned the universe that day as I watched my father and his friends fit the famous old Winchester five-battery torches to their heads, pushed to the left, a battery pack fastened around their waists. This was no fair-chase stalk. This was a nighttime blitzkrieg designed to decimate the lion population in the region of the *posto* and scare off the rest. The lions had lost all possible fear of their traditional enemy and had become dangerously brazen as they lay in wait along paths to water, prowling the perimeters of the villages where the odor of the dying was the finest encouragement for them to pursue this change in diet.

My father was armed with a bolt-action Mauser 9,3 × 62 with open sights, which I eventually inherited. We set off into the gloom of a near-moonless night and headed for a thorn-scrub hillock overlooking a gully. Our guide had tracked a fair-sized male into the dense cover that day, judging by the pug marks, and it was thought that we would find lion there.

I can remember my father's fingers suddenly digging into my left shoulder and tightening with a viselike urgency as we crouched among scrub and rock. My mouth had gone dry. I could not swallow properly and my ears suddenly felt "fat" with silence. Then it came—a hissing, ominous rumbling, followed by a spitting sound rising up from the gully. I cannot remember quite what happened next—the hot night air just tore apart with an ear-splitting din, the burned smell of propellant everywhere and my father shouting, "They're down! They're down! Hold your fire!" I felt light-headed with shock and exhilaration. What a rite of passage! I had barely had time to register the malevolent yellowish stare of the lions when the Winchester headlamps picked them out in the gully.

Five lions died that night, lionesses among them. Man-eating was a family affair, and no distinction was made. In fact, we found two very young cubs in that gully. My father promptly took them back to Tete to my mother, with instructions to feed and nurture the little creatures until further notice! My sisters were ecstatic, and the cubs apparently equally so. They thrived in our large house with its huge veranda and swallows' nests in the eaves, so much so that my parents started becoming concerned after the cubs went onto a diet of chicken and were seen stalking, down in the gardens by the poultry run. Before they got ideas of stalking the Serras Pires offspring, the cubs were donated to the zoo in Lourenço Marques, the capital city of Mozambique. I can still hear our howls of protest at what we thought was an insane decision by adults out to spoil our fun. I was the only little boy at school who could invite his pals over to play with lion cubs.

The psychological effect on the local population as the carcasses of several lions were brought into the *posto* the next morning was utterly dramatic. Ululations shook the air as the people kept chanting *"Pondoro kufa! Pondoro kufa!"* "The lions are dead! The lions are dead!" in the chiNyungwe language. The shiver of panic which had gripped the region subsided, a certain normality returned to village life, people stopped dying in such numbers, and late rains came to ease the drought. The ancestors had heard. Whether he liked it or not, my uncle took on the aspect of miracle worker and became busier than ever. People felt that somebody gave a damn. Another crisis had been survived. Until the next time. There was always a next time in the African bush. The mercy was that we could not see ahead.

Sir Alfred Pease, Theodore Roosevelt's professional hunter, once said that no man could shoot one hundred lions and live. My father, who was the honorary game warden of Tete and no braggart, shot perhaps that number in the twenty years between 1933 and 1953. At that time, the Zambezi Valley was awash with the big five. Lion were considered vermin. There were no hunting regulations, and no licenses were required. In fact, people were paid a small bounty for bringing in the tails of lions, leopards, and elephant, but not of buffalo. Game often attacked tribal livestock and also destroyed the crops of villagers, this being especially true of elephant, the hunting of which was opened in Mozambique in 1937. They were also declared vermin. Some of the old-time ivory hunters were active in the region during my childhood, and it was my strange destiny to meet one of the most notorious before I was much older.

Before my teens, I entered a fantastic learning curve with my father about the African bush, hunting, firearms, and wildlife in general. He was a cautious man and an accurate shot, who was fortunate never to have had a serious mishap with dangerous game. The same could not be said of one of his trackers, who spent months in a hospital after a run-in with a lioness, in the days before antibiotics.

My father taught me practically everything I know about life in the African bush. Three things, in particular, remain engraved on my soul, precepts which apply to life in general: Stand your ground; never turn your back; face the danger! He also instilled in me a savage love of Africa, which fueled a subsequent and undiminished fury at the outrages my generation eventually suffered.

One animal my father refused to hunt was the rhino. We had healthy populations of black rhino in the Zambezi Valley and in Manica Sofala Province, but he always said, "Son, don't ever shoot a rhino! They're becoming extinct." This was an unusual attitude in the 1930s. I have never hunted a rhino for myself, although I recognize the South African success story in bringing the white rhino back from the brink of extinction to their robust status today. Unfortunately, black rhinos are quite another story.

Mozambique, a largely subtropical country on the southeastern coast of Africa, is nearly 298,000 square miles in extent and features mountains, plateaus, and dense forest. Vast savannas are crisscrossed by rivers which flow down to the humid coastal plain some 1,550 miles long, with incomparable beaches, lagoons, and lush vegetation. It is home to many tribes, speaking a great variety of languages and finding spiritual homes in animism, Christianity, and Islam. Portuguese remains the lingua franca. As a youngster, I picked up the two main languages of the region, chiSena of Manica Sofala, and chiNyungwe of the Zambezi Valley. Children soak up language like drought-parched earth drinking up the first rains. It all has to do with lack of inhibition and prejudice.

One thing we children noticed about the Nyungwe women around Tete was their curious habit of flattening the upper part of their bare breasts with strips of cloth or leather as soon as they were married. This was to designate their newfound, more elevated status. I could not figure out why they would want to disfigure themselves when repeated childbearing would soon do the job for them.

The local school was a very happy, entirely multiracial home from home where I played and learned alongside the sons and daughters of the Black *assimilados,* the educated Blacks, as well as those of the fairly large mulatto population, and of the Indians of Goanese origin. Portugal had captured Goa in 1510, and Goa retained a very special subsequent link with Mozambique, many Goanese eventually crossing the Indian Ocean to settle there. I do not remember being color conscious as a child and I recall no ugly racial incidents at all from my youth in Mozambique. That would come later, a foreign virus designed to contaminate and destroy. Mozambique was quite distinct from its rigid neighbor, the Union of South Africa, and from the British colonial possessions of our other neighbors, the two Rhodesias, Nyasaland, and Tanganyika. We were a much more relaxed, racially mixed, and tolerant society.

Those early school days are crowded with memories, one of which concerned the headmaster. We noticed how he would chase us out of the classroom during the morning tea break, when his tea was brought to him in an earthenware pot. We began to observe a sublime transformation in the old dog after those tea breaks. He would be less cantankerous, more jolly. The tea was laced with good old Portuguese *vinho branco*. In fact, the teapot, we suspected, was really an ersatz wine decanter!

In between playing soccer, having bicycle races, indulging in word games with siblings, preparing for carnival every year, looking forward to the torrid Christmas holidays and the annual arrival of the mobile cinema, and accompanying my father into the bush to hunt and explore, I used to revel in the docking of the riverboats. Those steamers came up from Chinde at the mouth of the Zambezi to Tete, bringing letters from Portugal, fine linens for the ladies, construction materials, consumer goods of all sorts and an infusion of worldly chic to the heat-soaked backwater of the colony.

We would hear the steamboat horn sounding and, when possible, charge off down to what passed for a jetty, where we would goggle at the comings and goings, the governor himself sometimes being present in his finery, surrounded by his entourage, as he greeted some important visitor. For centuries, Tete was a vital crossroad into Nyasaland and beyond for the ivory trade, to cite one example. It is even more so today, now that a fine bridge spans the river. Mozambique's only gunboat, which patrolled the Zambezi, was also an eagerly welcomed visitor. When I look at the yellowing photographs, I now see a rickety, scruffy little vessel which does not match my childhood recollections of the armed gunboat, staffed by dashing officers who were always fêted in Tete.

Malaria notwithstanding, I flourished. We were a large and happy family, my father having become a successful businessman and our home an open house. My youngest brother, José Augusto, was a late and joyous addition to our family, arriving fifteen years after my birth and growing up to join me in the hunting safari business. We were a pioneering family and had the distinction of importing the first innerspring mattress and refrigerator to Tete. When we arrived in 1936, there was no running water there. Water carriers would bring up water into the town every day from the Zambezi in five-gallon cans balanced on their shoulders. The power station, which was run by my father at one stage, was fired up with coal from the Moatize coalfields across the river. It was a tough life full of critical decisions, one of which had to be made about the Serras Pires children as we approached the end of primary school in Tete, which had no high school.

My family paid many business visits and occasional medical visits to Salisbury in Southern Rhodesia, a fairly long haul from Tete, but a journey which could be made in a day on the roads of the time. This exposure convinced my father that his children had to become proficient in English. Again, he showed a certain farsightedness which was uncommon then. Children either had to go down south to Lourenço Marques and boarding school or, as some parents elected, they had to return to Portugal. Neither option was remotely considered by my parents.

Southern Rhodesia was the once-fabled land of gold ruled by King Mwene Mutapa with whom the Arabs traded long before the arrival of the Portuguese. It was colonized by the British from 1889 onward and was named after Cecil John Rhodes, the British-born entrepreneur and politician. That country would become our second home, where we were to be educated at some of the best schools. My sisters attended the Dominican convent, and I went to Selborne and Allan Wilson schools before attending Prince Edward High School.

My education in Rhodesia began in January 1940. This exposure to a classic, British colonial school with its rigid code of school uniform and discipline was directly responsible for my meeting one of the most controversial characters in African hunting literature. I had just returned to Tete at the end of that year for the long Christmas summer holidays and was, in fact, walking past one of the more notorious bars in Tete, the Rapa, showing off in my school blazer and tie when a loud boozed voice called out to me in strangely accented English: "C'm 'ere, lad. Let's 'ave a look at ye!"

The foggy-eyed White man in a crumpled khaki shirt and shorts wore sandals and a grubby calico turban. He was lounging on the veranda of the Rapa Bar, an institution in Tete. The sun was like a freshly stoked furnace that day as this strange individual called me over in what I eventually learned was an Irish brogue.

I stopped, turned, and came over. The man asked how it was that an obviously Portuguese child, dressed in the Sunday-best uniform of a snooty Southern Rhodesian school and who, so he said, spoke almost the King's English, happened to be in a sweltering backwater like Tete, "for the Almoity's sake!"

Enter John "Pondoro" Taylor, son of an Irish surgeon, who had converted to the Islamic faith and who had gone "bush" after years as a professional ivory hunter. He is the subject of the landmark biography by my late friend, Peter Hathaway Capstick, in collaboration with another long-standing friend, hunter, and published author, Brian Marsh, who attended high school with me in Salisbury. Taylor was a well-known sight in Tete, where he would come in with his porters and sell his ivory to the local Indian merchants after lengthy absences spent hunting elephant in all-but-uncharted country. Now, what a convert to Islam was doing, much the worse for wear, in the Rapa Bar, is a matter for conjecture.

I never forgot that meeting. Taylor offered me a lemonade and asked me to sit down. I had, in fact, seen this strange and solitary man on one or two occasions in past years, and I had heard stories about his legendary bar brawls. In fact, one of Tete's two White policemen and a friend of my father, had to smack Taylor over the head with his truncheon one night to prevent him from firing his guns in town and endangering the population. Contrary to the stories about him, Taylor never learned to speak Portuguese. He was a high-born misfit who generally avoided Whites. I think he struck up that conversation with me not only out of curiosity but also, perhaps, out of nostalgia for his own distant youth.

I discovered that this rogue Irishman had known my Uncle Adelino, who had since been transferred to Zambezia Province on the Indian Ocean. In fact, Taylor told me how my uncle had helped him open a small trading store at Benga. It was run for the eccentric Irishman by a Black man, my uncle keeping an eye on things in general during Taylor's very lengthy absences. The opening words in Taylor's *Maneaters and Marauders* have a special ring for me: "I used to have a small trading store at Benga on the Revugwi not far from its confluence with the Zambezi, and had given the native who ran it for me an interest in the business so as to keep him on his toes."

Taylor asked me if my uncle had ever told me the story of the man-eating lions of Benga. That opened the floodgates of conversation. Taylor was clearly surprised at what I told him of my first hunting experience that tense night overlooking the near-moonless gully. I described the dead lionesses and the cubs which came back to Tete with us on the ferry and of the near-riot among the Nyungwe paddlers who could not fathom this fresh evidence of the *mzungu's* (white man's) madness in wanting to save the cubs of animals which had been killing their people at random in past months.

I remember sharing with Taylor my story of hearing the lions on Christmas Eve in 1936, and of my father's prediction about my growing up to become a hunter. I recall with equal clarity Taylor's ice-blue, booze-smudged eyes boring into me as he replied, " 'Tis a devil's life, me lad. 'Tis a devil's life."

I had occasion to remember those words years down the line. Taylor and I would meet again under sad circumstances, when I was already a grown man, living in Beira.

Profound culture shock, of course, awaited me when my parents took me into Southern Rhodesia to start school as a boarder at Selborne in Salisbury. I spoke no English at all and had no friends of my own age with me from Tete. This was also my first time away from the security blanket of a large and happy family. I felt less trepidation that night with the Benga man-eaters than I did on the first day of school, not understanding one word around me.

I had three fistfights on the first day. Several local boys, sniffing an outsider and imagining me to be just another *Dago*—the derogatory word used for Latinos—ganged up on me. Having spent the previous three years sharpening my wits and cultivating courage in the Mozambican bush left me fit and able to knock the townies flying. For the entire seven years I was at school in Salisbury, I hardly had to raise my fists again. However, this incident revealed a certain attitude toward foreigners in the British colonies. The rebel streak in me as well as the very nature of my upbringing never accommodated these limited individuals, and I certainly did not share their blinkered world.

My fists still sore, I promptly walked out of the school grounds and flagged down a Black man on a bicycle. I somehow made him understand that I wanted to go to the Frascati Hotel, near the station. I knew the name. Sitting on the crossbar, we pedaled through Salisbury's wide, tree-lined streets down to where my parents always stayed when in Salisbury.

My parents were stunned at the sudden arrival of their firstborn son, and they promptly took me back to Selborne—but not before I had had my say and consolidated my own arrangements with the hotel owners, great friends of my parents. They were the Merdjans, prominent members of the local Sephardi Jewish community, who originated from the island of Rhodes. Their son Zack, who attended high school with me later on, became a great friend, with whom I am in touch to this day. The Merdjans treated me like their own child, including me in their lives and, very often, in the Sabbath gatherings at the Sephardi Hall on Fridays where I would enjoy the wonderful Sephardi food and songs. I had an instant rapport with the community, as did my whole family. They understood what it meant to be an outsider, and we shared Mediterranean roots.

Desperation is the finest teacher. I learned English at top speed. Talent had little to do with it as I found my feet and plunged into the life of the school with the strict discipline and vigorous sports program of a typically British colonial primary school. It certainly wasn't all work because I found time to develop an aching crush on my teacher, an Irish beauty called Miss Mulligan. We boys also had the privilege of being taught by several outstanding men, foremost among them a Mr. Hathaway, who helped me enormously to adapt and do well.

Life is full of omens. One of the early ones in my life was the name of my school "house" where I boarded—Selous House, named after Frederick Courteney Selous, the legendary British big-game hunter with historic links to the entire southern African region, including Mozambique. In the 1890s, Selous wrote: "The trade of Tete is in ivory and gold dust." This was in *Travel and Adventure in South-East Africa*, a mere forty-five years or so before we arrived in Tete. But I digress.

It was inevitable that I would soon be straddling several cultures. There was my Mozambican home; there was the world of the tribal people in the Mozambican bush; the pukka world of English-speaking colonial Southern Rhodesia and, by no means out of the reckoning, the Sephardi community of Salisbury. This prepared me for an adult life where I would live in many countries and among many different cultures.

My sisters, Lucinda and Maria-José, and I would meet at the Catholic cathedral on Sundays. Religious fervor had nothing to do with it. It was simply a chance to get out, have a change of air, flirt, and catch up with news from home and elsewhere. We would also sometimes go to the beautiful park to hear the police band play. It was wartime, and there were major Royal Air Force training bases in the country; Belvedere and Cranborne air stations were on the outskirts of Salisbury. The profusion of lilac-colored jacarandas, the beautiful public parks and matching climate, peace, and an abundance of good food, meant that our school days there were far removed from the horrors of wartime Europe in the 1940s. What reminded us, however, was the presence of the trainee pilots from Great Britain, Australia, New Zealand, Poland, Yugoslavia, and other countries who always wore their distinctive uniforms in town as they prepared for a mission many would not survive. At night, we would hear the characteristic whine of the Tiger Moths as the young pilots practiced their circuits and bumps.

The Sephardi community provided my family with another insight into the distant war as we started hearing traumatic accounts, some from recently arrived Jewish refugees, of Hitler's "final solution," of places called concentration camps, of maltreatment and death on a scale we could not absorb or even remotely understand. I also learned quickly that my other school pals would greet such stories with disbelief and worse, so I kept to myself these early warnings of atrocities largely camouflaged from the rest of the globe.

My years at the prestigious Prince Edward High School, which celebrated its centenary in 1998, were very full and successful. Many of the boys developed into all-rounders. I had already enjoyed the hugely morale-enhancing honor, as a foreign scholar, of being awarded the dux (top) prize for academic and sporting achievements while at Selborne Primary School in 1941. At Prince Edward, I played first-team rugby and cricket, apart from water polo, field hockey, and tennis, as well as participating in boxing and soccer. We competed in away games and generally led healthy, varied lives. No British colonial schooling would have been complete without Gilbert and Sullivan operettas. I had a one-liner in *The Gondoliers* that I remember to this day.

As a foreigner, I was under no obligation to join the school cadet corps, but I volunteered anyway, happily giving up Saturday mornings to this activity. We learned to shoot the .303, the Bren gun, and the twenty-five-pounder cannon. In addition, we were instructed in driving and maintenance involving trucks and the Norton motorcycle. When I left school at eighteen, I was awarded a proficiency certificate as a cadet sergeant.

I was even persuaded to take piano lessons for one year, and was awarded a book, another powerful omen. It was written by Marcus Daly and was titled *Big Game Hunting and Adventure 1897–1936.* The die was cast! I read and reread that book with the gold-embossed head of a lion on the green cover until the binding started coming apart. Not for me the predictable life of a townie. I wanted to get back into the Mozambican bush to explore and hunt, to be free of rigid routine so that I could lead an adventurous life of challenge and danger. Who needed piano lessons after that? I had a whole symphony orchestra playing in my head as to what I wanted out of life.

All schoolboys have their heroes. Mine was "Jeeves" Hougaard, the rugby coach and Afrikaans teacher. He was an inspiration to us all. An evenhanded, profoundly decent and supportive person, he took a special interest in the welfare of the "foreign" boys: the Portuguese, Greek, and Jewish pupils. An Afrikaner from South Africa, where his people had fought a bloody war against the British Empire between 1899 and 1902, Hougaard understood the effects of prejudice and exclusion. He counterbalanced and outclassed the couple of unpleasant individuals I met during my schooling, and it was largely in honor of his memory that I crossed hemispheres in 1998 to attend the Prince Edward centenary, apart from my enduring links with the Merdjan family. Hougaard went on to become headmaster of Prince Edward and, eventually, of the renowned Churchill School in Salisbury, which my son was privileged to attend during Hougaard's term of office.

With a Cambridge matriculation in hand, I was at a fresh set of crossroads in life. My parents wanted me to attend university in South Africa, but it was proving extremely difficult to find a place. Preference was being given South African ex-servicemen. Quite frankly, I was weary of the academic life, and this turn of events simply reinforced my desire to return to Mozambique, my first love. The rugged wilderness, amazing animal life, gorgeous beaches, hospitable people, and atmosphere of general tolerance and harmony had long since ensnared my soul.

I wanted to go home.

TWO

A WILD LIFE

> *Soon after passing the mouth of the Ruenya we sighted the hill of Caroera, behind which, our boatmen told us, lay the town of Tete, or In-yung-wi, as the natives call it . . .*
>
> —Frederick Courteney Selous,
> *Travel and Adventure in South-East Africa*

It was cold that June night in 1949. I was in the rocky hill terrain around the village of Lundo, southeast of Tete, in the black-soil country of the cotton fields. I had already fallen asleep when something disturbed me and I woke up. Chiganda, my Sena assistant, who was the brother of a tribal chief, was standing in the doorway of the *palhota,* the typical grass hut of the region. The pungent smell of paraffin filtered into the hut from the lantern he was carrying, its blackened glass cover filtering the light before his eyes which were stretched wide with anxiety.

A runner had just arrived at our trading store post from a nearby village, where a woman had been in labor for two days and was now in danger of dying. The word had long since spread that my assistants and I had arrived to restock the trading post. It was known that I always carried a rudimentary medical kit with me, and it was common for the bush people to flock to the post for help with eye infections, malaria, burns, and wounds of one sort or another. On more than one occasion, I had arranged for tribesmen with fractured limbs to be treated elsewhere, and their eventual recovery had bolstered the faith of the people in our ability to help them. Obstetrics, however, was something new, and it scared me.

I pulled on my clothes, grabbed the first-aid kit and the 8 × 56 mm Mannlicher–Schönauer carbine my dad had given me, and followed Chiganda into the gloom, down a track to the woman's village. It was a solid hour's walk through dense bush which no vehicle could negotiate. All I could seem to hear was our anxious breathing, which shut out the night sounds. If snakes were curled on the pathway to absorb the warmth of the previous day's sun, we were unlikely to see them in time. That would include the lethal mambas. Chiganda preceded me, acting as our eyes and ears. This was where he had been born, and I trusted him totally.

The light of a *mopane* wood fire outlined the entrance to the village which we reached at about 2:00 A.M. A weak sliver of moon hung overhead as we emerged from the dense surrounding bush, where the obscene sooty songs of a pack of hyenas punctuated the night air. No doubt they had scented a kill. That meant lion. Any real medical help was a day's journey away, so the villagers had turned to me—a kid barely out of his teens—to help save a woman and her unborn baby.

I took one look at the hugely distended and exhausted bundle on a mat in a corner of the dark and musky hut, surrounded by old women, and realized that we had to get her to the first-aid post at Mungári farther south over bone-breaking bush tracks. A crude stretcher was fashioned out of poles and blankets to help carry her back the way Chiganda and I had just come. Villagers accompanied us as we struggled with the stretcher carriers to reach my Ford B truck at the trading store. It was an eternity before we reached the clearing.

We placed the woman and two members of her family in the back of the truck on a rough bedding of sacks and set off along a bush track. We battled over increasingly rough terrain, where I needed all my wits about me to keep the truck under control. It had faulty brakes, and I had to keep a murderous grip on the gears so that they would not jump and send us off into a gully, where we would be stuck forever.

An hour or so later, there was a sudden urgent banging on the cab roof. "Stop, *Patrão*, stop! The baby's coming!" I brought the Ford to a stop on a rise in the track and scrambled out with Chiganda. Speaking very rapidly in chiSena, which I knew, the women at the back of the truck said that the thudding ride over the bush track had done the trick. The baby had been shaken loose. With scissors at the ready, Chiganda holding my torch, the umbilical cord was cut and the baby boy wrapped in a makeshift receiving blanket of sacking, its first sounds not unlike those of a mewling kitten. We cleaned up the afterbirth, which the women helpers insisted on keeping, probably for some tribal ritual, gave the exhausted but triumphant mother water to drink and turned around to go back the way we had come.

It was extraordinary. In the space of not quite four hours, the sky starting to lighten as another day broke in the Manica Sofala wilderness, the bush telegraph was fully operational. When we eventually rattled back into the compound, a crowd of villagers had already arrived and were gathered about a couple of fires to await the arrival of the baby and its mother. How the news had spread so quickly through the chill bush country that night, I could not figure out. It was a phenomenon I was to witness over and over again in the ensuing decades I spent in the African savannas, forests and swamps, far from all possible modern forms of communication.

A steaming tin mug of coffee in hand, and to the sound of ululations by the women and banter by the menfolk, I returned briefly to my hut to digest the impact of the night's events. I had been thrust into the multiple roles of hunter, storekeeper, mechanic, medic, arbiter, and latter-day midwife at the very outset of what were to be some of the most absorbing years of my young life. I felt an odd sense of accomplishment that dawn. A woman had survived. A child had been born, and a whole village was rejoicing. In the years that followed, whenever I passed through that particular region, the villagers would always give me eggs, or thrust a scrawny village fowl into my hands. I could not help but make a comparison between the intrinsic value of such gestures and the value attached to the rare minerals being prospected at the time in Mozambique and in which I became briefly involved.

Fresh out of school and back in Tete in 1947, news came of a decision which would set in motion a multiplicity of events that would eventually influence millions of lives in many African countries, including Mozambique. India was granted independence from Great Britain that year. This did not seem to have any relevance for us at the time. We pursued our lives in the Zambezi Valley where my family had businesses in Tete and where we lived a comfortable life in cordial association with everyone. In fact, the Serras Pires family name became synonymous with Tete. I played lots of sports there, especially soccer and tennis, sport being fully integrated. It reflected our whole society where there was never any color bar. Like any other country on earth, Mozambique had social distinctions, but no formal, legislated racial segregation, as became the case the following year, in neighboring South Africa. That fateful decision by the Afrikaner National Party would also directly influence Mozambique and my family's destiny.

While awaiting replies from South African universities as to whether I would be granted a place, the mining giants in South Africa started to show increasing interest in prospecting in Mozambique. In 1948, I was approached by Goldfields of South Africa and offered a position in one of their major prospecting ventures in the Zambezi Valley. The English-speaking mining giant needed a man on the ground, fluent in both English and Portuguese, conversant in the main indigenous language, chiNungwe, able to hunt for the pot in order to feed the local workforce, someone who was bushwise, preferably single, young, and prepared to live for protracted periods far from all modern comforts in wild country to supervise the laborers.

It was a job made in heaven for me. I had grown up in the region and thirsted for action, adventure, and the freedom only the bush can give. I managed a workforce of about 800 volunteers from among the Nungwe people, at a time when a system of contracted labor was widely utilized and, unfortunately, sometimes abused. At Goldfield's, however, at no stage did I have to compel any of the men to stay on the job because they were given decent conditions by the mining giant and they were treated well.

With Tete as a reference point, I fanned out over a very extensive region across the Zambezi River, north of Tete and along the reaches of the Mavusi River, a Zambezi River tributary. Goldfields was particularly interested in a radioactive mineral called samarskite, a mineral oxide which is the source of a number of rare-earth metals. It resembled velvety lumps of coal and we began discovering significant deposits not far from the abundant Moatize coalfields. I traveled immense distances cross-country over treacherously rocky and often steep terrain in vehicles nobody would touch today. We eventually had the use of a company Willys Jeep at a time when four-wheel-drive vehicles were still a far-off luxury for most of us.

I had already had sufficient experience of the wooden bridges over rivers with their sometimes-suspect struts and gaps between the rough-hewn logs not to have further panic attacks as we drove gingerly over them. I can still hear the creaks and ominous cracking sounds as our truck inched forward, the structure frequently swaying under the load. Once one of these rough bridges sagged and then collapsed behind us just as we drove onto solid ground on the opposite bank. Enough of such experiences in the African bush make you into a fatalist. What will be will be. The sight through the rough-hewn logs of muddy swirling waters from a flash flood do nothing to feed your confidence, especially when you are transporting people as well as dry rations and cash money to sustain an entire prospecting camp for weeks.

Apart from carrying the wages in hard cash for the workforce, I hired and sometimes had to fire workers, in addition to helping feed them by hunting antelope and buffalo. The climate was rigorous. Most of us were struck down at one or other time with vicious bouts of malaria and sometimes dysentery. I remember the water in the region being so loaded with lime that even the filters did a poor job. This resulted in several South Africans being medically evacuated with kidney problems, some foreign workers even dying. It was a tough life, dominated by extremes in temperature, disease, terrible roads, and an utter lack of basic amenities. We learned quickly to sort out our priorities and to be content with very little. This was an enduring lesson for the rest of my life in Africa.

During that period, I used one of my father's 9,3 × 62mm Mauser rifles when shooting for the pot. This particular aspect of my work with Goldfields increased my physical endurance in very rough country and taught me valuable lessons. I understood with increasing clarity the value of hardy game over cattle, goats, and pigs, which were not bred for that tough terrain and which could not withstand disease in the same way as did game animals. In the process, I developed a greater insight into the lives and customs of the tribal people, the importance of patience, the willingness to absorb and adapt. I also learned a sobering lesson about international politics.

When it became clear that Goldfields had highly ambitious plans for exploiting mineral deposits in that part of Mozambique, and when it became even clearer that Mozambique's underground riches were starting to excite international interest, Goldfields was ordered out of the country. Antonio de Oliveira Salazar, prime minister and virtual dictator of Portugal from 1932 until 1968, feared a wholesale influx of foreign interests and lifestyles into Mozambique. He feared perturbation of what was a remarkably peaceful, overwhelmingly agricultural country through the introduction of foreign-bred needs, ambitions, and influences. Would our fate have been different had Salazar not been so closed to foreign influences, had he not been so fearful of the African colonies claiming independence as Brazil had done? He was a product of his time.

A shrewd man, Salazar is reliably reported to have said, when told of the discovery of oil in Angola, for example: "Poor Angola!" Today, as I write this, Angola's bloody civil war continues unabated, financed by the very oil discoveries which were supposed to enrich the country, fueled as well by the diamond wealth in the hands of Angola's opposition forces. The oil, in particular, is controlled by several international petroleum companies with scant regard for the suffering of the Angolan people. Profit or perish is the foreign conglomerate credo. Nothing at all will change this mindset in the new millennium. Plans are far advanced now for the exploitation of vast deposits of titanium, other minerals, and gas fields in Mozambique. Of course, there will be political consequences.

After a year of tough living and even tougher hunting under the burning blue skies of the Zambezi Valley, I came back to base in Tete, caught my breath and received my call-up papers. I was to commence the obligatory military conscription period of three months at a military base in Boane, far to the south, near the border with the kingdom of Swaziland. Before all of us from up north were transported by boat to Lourenço Marques in the south, we first called at a couple of other ports, going as far as Porto Amelia, today's Pemba. The stunning clarity of the peacock blue seas, accented by the string of exotic islets off that far-northern coast filled me with the urge to jump ship and disappear. We went ashore for a day on *Ilha de Moçambique*, Mozambique Island, and relived a dramatic time in Portuguese history. It had been the center of Portuguese authority in East Africa from the mid-sixteenth century and was a favored port of call for the ships on the India run, becoming the most important such port between Portugal and India. It flourished to such an extent that a massive fortress, the *Fortaleza São Sebastião*, was built to protect Portuguese interests. We rode into the fort on rickshaws, it being difficult to believe that that isolated and neglected pinprick on the map was once the pivot of an empire and a magnet to generations of people seeking their share of wealth and fame. Our looming military service was temporarily forgotten during those sun-seared, devil-may-care days of discovery.

Portugal had remained neutral during the Second World War, and Mozambique faced no actual threat of aggression in the immediate postwar years. Our military service was tedious, consisting of a bit of parade-ground drill basic discipline, and rifle practice. After my thorough cadet training at high school in Salisbury, there were no surprises for me, except, perhaps the ancient First World War weapons we were expected to master. We never fired a shot. The monotony was enlivened by frequent weekend passes to the capital, Lourenço

Marques—now Maputo—where I had relatives and where my pals and I enjoyed the break, luxuriating, amongst other things, in hot water, which we never once had back at camp.

One of our lieutenants was Alvaro Pereira de Carvalho, an old friend from Tete. In fact, on many occasions, I had taken him and a fellow officer named Casseano out hunting from the military base there. Our hunts for rations for the base served another purpose as well. Kudu were consistent and notoriously successful night raiders of the villagers' crops nearby, and it was very easy to pick them out at night using spotlights. This provided rations for the military base, a morale-enhancing service and some meat for the villagers as well as an exciting break from military routine. One night, it became a little too exciting for Carvalho. He was rather conscious of his military status and supposed metropolitan polish and eventually this annoyed the rest of us. It was time to take the envoy from Lisbon down a peg or three. It was time to take Carvalho on a hunt with a difference.

I had always urged him—and anyone else I ever had on safari—never to shoot until sure of the animal and that it was within close enough range. Our nighttime excursions after the crop-raiding kudu meant picking out the animals by spotlight; their eyes were a powerful giveaway. Well, out we went in my tough old Ford Model B to the outskirts of Tete, where we then went on foot into the sorghum fields of the locals. It was late at night, and we were skirting a small village along a footpath when I saw some cattle. Getting all excited, Carvalho picked out the shapes of the animals with his headmounted spotlight. Then temptation overcame me. I told him, "See those eyes to the far left? It's a kudu. Shoot, shoot before it moves!"

He shot. It was a plump cow. It was very quickly a dead plump cow.

And the village came awake as if dynamited.

Before Carvalho could gather his wits, villagers started swarming toward us. We were very near a cluster of huts and an area where the prized cattle of this tiny village were kept in an enclosure at night to protect them from predators, which infested the whole region. Cattle mean wealth and status to Black Africa and they are killed in such isolated areas only for special occasions such as a feast, a funeral or the arrival of a special tribal dignitary. Goats and chickens provide meat under normal circumstances, and not always frequently.

A village elder, with grizzled hair and hardly a tooth in his head, let fly in a stream of angry chiNyungwe, asking us what the devil we thought we were doing killing their cow. In a breath laced with *pombe,* the local brew the villagers made from millet, he told me that he recognized me and that I had better fix up the mess and compensate the whole village on the spot. I turned to Lieutenant Carvalho, who had become unusually quiet, and berated him for shooting a cow when he should have known better. I asked him if he had eye problems, and what was wrong with him to have made such an elementary mistake. He blurted out that I had clearly indicated the animal on the extreme left. I countered by saying that I meant the kudu, not a cow. Hadn't he seen the kudu in the gloom on the extreme left?

Carvalho forked out the required 400 escudos, the equivalent then of ten dollars, and calm returned instantaneously to the village. Our honor was salvaged, and the folk could look forward to a feast the next day, with sufficient money in the kitty to replace the cow. This was a dirty trick on my part, but the lesson was learned. Carvalho climbed down from his Lisbon high horse and became a good pal. But not before muttering to me, "I'll get you back for this!"

The point is this: Carvalho spotted me at the Boane military base, after not seeing me in over two years, and asked me, "What's your number?"

I gave it thinking that the dead cow would now truly come back to haunt me. It never did. In fact, I used to accompany the lieutenant on our trips to the bright lights, and he was great fun.

My three-month military stint over, much broader and more exciting horizons awaited me back in Manica Sofala, all thought of a university education in South Africa now abandoned. My father and mother were tremendously active and enterprising people, and they had decided to spread their wings and develop a large farm some 100 miles south of Tete, at a place called Guro in the very core of big-five country. We owned a sawmill in the region which processed timber for the Rhodesias, and my father would always stop near Guro on his way to attend to sawmill business.

Guro enjoyed the highest elevation on the road between Tete and Vila Pery. It was glorious country. Guro Mountain dominated the thickly wooded, sparsely populated bush country where wildlife abounded, where the black rhinoceros was royal game, where the cough of the leopard, the bold beauty of dark-maned lion, the heady scent of buffalo, and the admonishments of matriarch elephants keeping order in the herds were the daily counterpoint to our lives in that uncontaminated wilderness. There, in the shadow of Guro Mountain, as from 1946, we established our farm. Some 12,350 acres of untouched bush were transformed into a landmark in the region, an oasis of hospitality and, eventually, the headquarters of a superb hunting concession.

Almost every night, hyenas, and often leopards, fought with our big dogs, which roamed our huge property and which were sometimes found dead at dawn or badly torn up. Only when lion appeared did a chilling silence envelop the bush. Even the crickets would stop chirruping. Antonio, our Sena cook for almost thirty years, would sometimes find African wild cats in our chicken run.

Pioneering European-born women in Africa, such as my mother, became deft at organizing their lives and those of their families and staff around such invasions and potential dangers. Family retainers like Antonio played a pivotal role in helping us deal with the daily challenges in the wilds. We all became adept at coping with bush crises, such as the time a spitting cobra spat venom into the eyes of one of our staff. Quick as a flash, my mother obtained milk from a nursing mother down at the servants' compound and washed out the eyes of the poor devil, saving his sight in the process. Finding the pug marks of a full-grown male leopard right next to the farmhouse was not at all unusual, and we became quite used to damage to the orchards and crops caused by monkeys and bushpig. We were living, after all, in their world and these occurrences were a small fee for admission to that world and the quality of life it gave us.

Of course, isolation has its price. Toothache! Dr. Schnek, an Austrian doctor turned dentist, was based in Beira and would undertake annual "tours" to Tete and other far-smaller locations to bring relief. But this institution of rural life in Manica Sofala could not be everywhere, and

I once had to summon the urgent help of a male nurse, Tomé, sending a messenger to his outpost some 25 miles from the farm.

Tomé and his pliers finally arrived.

I asked him, "Tomé, how many teeth have you pulled?" The Sena's eyes rolled as he struggled to recall how many teeth he had extracted with no ill effects, over the years, the total absence of any anaesthetic notwithstanding.

"Right, Tomé. One pull! No mistakes, please."

The offending tooth was out in a flash. There is nothing humans cannot get used to when they have no choice.

Our farm took shape. From the early days of crude thatched structures and no running water emerged our whitewashed sprawling farmhouse, framed by golden rain creeper, with its breathtaking views of the savanna countryside. Citrus and apple orchards, an experimental vineyard, maize and sunflower fields, a huge vegetable garden and cotton fields gradually developed, like a multicolored butterfly breaking free of its chrysalis.

We kept no cattle because Guro was tsetse-fly country. Our farm workers as well as the mainstays such as the cook, his kitchen helpers, and the house servants were all housed in proper quarters on the farm itself. We were a large family, and we always kept an open-house policy. The nearest town was Vila Gouveia, over 50 miles away, and the *Chefe de Posto* was about 25 miles away at Mungári, with no facilities in between. It was wild country, uninhabited for many square miles.

We often used to see plains game such as kudu, sable, and hartebeest around the farm during the day as well as sizable herds of buffalo. Game would come to our farm dams to quench their thirst, especially during the all-too-frequent droughts which savaged the region from time to time. One of the exhilarating sights on our farm was the packs of wild dogs that would chase through the bush after game, especially kudu. I can see them now as they mobbed their prey, snapping at their legs, going for the throat, flanks, soft underbelly, or wherever they could get a hold, frequently disemboweling their victim in the process. Their white, black, and yellow blotched coats and their stiffened, bushy white-tipped tails would blur as they swarmed their victim, high-pitched twittering sounds and yelps of savage excitement washing over the countryside as nature took its course. Some die that most may live. Many is the time I saw packs of these "painted dogs" feasting on a kill, their huge round ears and dark muzzles buried in the gory delights of fresh meat which was devoured in a flash. I never thought I would live to see these misunderstood animals become the most endangered carnivore in Africa, after the Ethiopian wolf, having disappeared from most of its former sub-Saharan habitat.

Talking of big game in the backyard, one early evening there was a terrible din down at the staff quarters, where a black rhino had been charging the cooking fires. Miguel Guerra, a good friend and fellow hunter, was having dinner with us when our headman asked us to come down and chase out the rhino. Everyone knew I would refuse to shoot it, unless lives were directly threatened. By the time Miguel and I got there, the rhino had barged off into the nearby dense bush, smashing its way through the dangerously dry undergrowth. The night's festivities, however, were far from over. As Miguel and I scanned the bush with our Winchester headlamps, the beams picked out a hillock overlooking the staff compound. Silhouetted against the stunted growth on the hillock was a massive leopard. I brought the leopard down with what I thought was a well-placed shot. It tumbled off the mound and was swallowed by the night-blackened bush.

We stood for a short while, shoulder to shoulder, listening intently, when something absolutely chilling occurred. Miguel yelled a warning at me as the supposedly "dead" leopard suddenly materialized right next to my feet, actually getting hold of one of my boots. I rocketed backward and Miguel shoved the barrel of his rifle into the leopard, ending its life. My initial shot had hit it in the front legs and it had crawled, unseen and unheard, from the dense scrub at the base of the hillock to where we were standing.

My mother became surrogate mother to many orphaned wild animals on our farm. She had started off with the Benga man-eater's cubs and progressed to baby elephants, which bonded so closely with her that they shadowed her every move. She took charge of kudu, buffalo calves, and several other species of plains game, including a zebra foal which, unfortunately, got into one of our storage areas, knocking over some paint cans. One popped open and the zebra licked at the paint. It died of poisoning that day.

After that hugely upsetting incident, we decided not to bring home any other wild creatures for my mother to rear. Apart from the tremendously hard work and worry involved, they did not always thrive. We found, for example, that our farm staff adopted a passive resistance to their presence, seemingly objecting to the attention devoted to the orphaned wild animals. If we were not on the farm to supervise their care, there was always the risk that these youngsters would not be adequately cared for, so we ended our wildlife experiment. We placed the young elephant and other creatures with a private game park near Beira and came to the conclusion that man does more harm than good much of the time when he intervenes in nature. It has to be allowed to take its course, however harsh.

My father was a farmer at heart who loved to experiment, but I did not share his passion. We all did our bit in those tough early years, however, such as the time I was helping plow a field with the old steel-wheeled Fordson tractor. My Sena assistant fell off the tractor and was horribly cut up by the circular plow disks, blood spurting out of his left side where a deep gash ran like a crimson snake from his rib cage to his ankle. God, the shock! I leaped off the tractor and ran for help, returning with a sacking awl and coarse yarn with which I stitched up the wound, the poor man nearly in shock. I had no idea if any major damage had been done to veins or arteries, I just kept stitching, sluicing my handiwork with a household disinfectant. Giving him a stiff shot of booze, I bandaged most of the gash as best I could and prayed he would survive. Not only did my helper recover, the wound did not become infected, no major injury occurred, and he was back at work in a very short while. Such experiences toughen the nervous system and make you utterly self-reliant and coolheaded in a crisis. Not bad credentials for the African bush.

With our farm literally surrounded by big game, it was inevitable that we would have further unusual experiences. Once, when returning to Guro from Tete at night, Miguel Guerra and I came across no less than five full-grown tom leopards in the road at fairly short intervals. It was extraordinary. They were quite brazen about blocking the road before slinking off into the murk.

While speaking of leopards, I had an experience which remains unique in my life. One late summer afternoon in 1950/51 or thereabouts, in the heart of the rainy season, I happened to be on a very lonely stretch of rough bush track northeast of Guro. Suddenly a pitch black animal ghosted onto the track from the thick bush flanking the track. It was some 40 yards away. I stopped the vehicle, got out with my rifle at the ready, and approached this raven creature. Twilight was closing in, and dark storm clouds were scudding overhead as the wind picked up. The atmosphere became oppressive, ominous, as this ebony apparition smudged into the gloom, only its yellow eyes fixing on me like enemy searchlights.

I was well and truly spooked when I made out the shape of a large jet tom leopard, its tail tip raised, flicking menacingly as it sank into a crouch, its eyes never leaving me. It was an abnormal situation and something told me not to shoot, but to retreat to the vehicle, facing the leopard. As I reached the front of the Dodge pickup, my leg brushing against the canvas water bag, the leopard rose and eased back into the bush silently, like black ink pouring into the night.

I sat for a few moments, my heart thudding from the tension. It was the only black leopard I saw in forty years in Mozambique. Wally Johnson, that grand old man of the Mozambican bush and Robert Ruark's professional hunter at one time, saw only two such leopards in fifty-five years. Few other professional hunters in Mozambique—and I knew most of them—had ever seen a black leopard. It was the right thing not to have killed that highly unusual, magnificent feline.

In 1949, the authorities approached my father with a request to open trading stores in a region covering many thousands of square miles, with Guro as our base. There were no such facilities in that vast area. The idea was to establish, stock, and manage the stores, employing Indians to run them, as the local tribal people were disinclined to this sort of work. The need was there and it was growing, so we accepted the challenge and I was entrusted with the task of jump-starting a miniempire of trading stores in the Manica Sofala wilderness.

With my sturdy old Ford B model truck and a three-ton Chevrolet, my rifles, an assistant or two, water bags, personal rations and basic equipment, I prepared for the seemingly uncharted territory northeast of our farm. My first task in any area where we decided to open a trading store was to establish contact and foster cordial relations with the local chief. In the wilds, the chief's word was law. His cooperation was vital for any undertaking, and I had it drilled into me never to flout tribal etiquette by attempting to circumvent the niceties. In any case, the chief's subjects would never cooperate if they even suspected that their leader had not been duly consulted and his accord given for the project in mind.

The tribesmen cultivated cotton, millet, sorghum, and peanuts, which formed part of the goods traded. The little stores stocked such goods as salt, sugar, soap, brightly colored cloth for the capulanas worn by the women like a sarong, and much more. I would visit the stores to inspect and restock on a weekly basis and to solidify relations with the chiefs by providing game meat to feed them and their people. I had to carry a rifle at all times because the countryside was awash with game and predators. We nearly survived on game. The chiefs were not allowed to have firearms, but found ways of making their own traps for small game. This aspect of my work refined my skills as a hunter and did much to teach me how to interact successfully with the tribal people. I got on consistently well with the chiefs and with their subjects.

I quickly noticed one of the injustices that the tribal people were subjected to by the Portuguese authorities. They were not completely free to cultivate the crops of their choice, but were obliged to grow cotton, for example, where soil conditions were appropriate. They were then forced to sell it to specific state entities and at derisory prices. My parents were also victims of this corrupt system which hamstrung the entrepreneurial agricultural spirit. As a very young man, I sensed that we were heading for trouble in this regard. Portugal insisted on rigid control of life in the colonies. It was creating resentment—mute, but no less real.

It was an exceedingly lonely life at times. I would often not see my family or friends for weeks on end. It was particularly tough in the winter, when the icy nights seemed to seep into my bones, despite the blankets and fires. I would sleep right on top of the loaded Chevrolet in an effort to get away from the mosquitoes. In that unpolluted air, however, the night heavens were a spectacular riot of stars and whenever there was a full moon, it lit up the densest bush.

One day, we were busy negotiating a rough riverbed not far from the Zambezi River when the Chevrolet's battery decided to go on the blink. As we were battling to restart the vehicle, a black rhino bull and cow appeared as if out of thin air in the riverine growth just ahead of us. Notorious for their poor eyesight and even worse tempers, the rhinos started picking up speed as they headed for the truck. I froze where I stood, next to the cab, my two assistants clambering on top of the load of store goods, leaving me to face the rhinos.

What a circus! The rhinos churned up river sand and snorted as they screeched to a halt just short of the truck before swerving and making off in the opposite direction, only to turn around suddenly and charge the truck at full tilt! There were three or four of these mock charges, my numbed brain trying to gauge the chances of two rhinos overturning the Chevrolet when they sprayed sand and stone about them as they pulled up almost on top of the front grille, a mere couple of feet from me. They were so close I could study the blood-encrusted skin lesions on the bull's forelegs, caused by the filaria parasite. The rhinos both repeatedly loosened their bowels in between the charges, the acrid stench of their steaming ad hoc latrine smiting our nostrils whenever we dared take a breath. The few minutes' drama seemed interminable before the rhinos bolted back into the undergrowth ahead, barreling their way forward and away from the human intruders.

Back at the farm, my father told me that he had only heard of one case of a hunter having been killed by a rhino. Since those early days, however, I have heard of several reports of rhino gorings, most taking place in South Africa, which has the highest concentration of rhino in the world. My years in the bush, however, especially in Chete, Rhodesia in 1976, where I shared accommodation with no less than

250 black rhinos, taught me that rhinos are like locomotives without a driver and that they are usually more bluff than anything else. It is better to stand still and face the charge because the chances of outrunning a rhino are poor, unless a nearby tree is handy. Rhinos were royal game and, even had they not been, my father raised me never to even think of going after one.

There were many human dramas during those five years in the bush; the woman in labor had been one of my early ordeals. There were also natural phenomena which shook me up as well, such as the time I was nearly caught in a flash flood. With the Ford Model B and a full load, I was on my way to a store near the settlement of Mteme, northeast of our farm, just at the start of our rainy season in mid-October. The air was oppressive that late afternoon. The birds had become silent, the skies were blackening, and the wind was picking up. We were stuck in the sand of a bone-dry riverbed and had been sweating it for a couple of hours, trying to support the tires with wood and stone to stop the senseless churning each time we started the ignition.

We finally had enough traction and were able to get going again, heading for the opposite bank, when we were overwhelmed by a roaring sound that became louder and louder, drowning out the straining engine. Luiz, my Sena assistant, yelled for me to get out of the riverbed and onto the other side. His words were still being formed when a muddy wave roared into sight to our left, fully six feet high and stretching from bank to bank. We nearly lost the vehicle that day as the water tore at the back tires. With inches to spare, our truck reached the safety of the other side, which was not steep, the thundering water and debris of trees and rocks smashing past us in a world gone mad, a devil's deluge of mud and turmoil. Luiz broke the silence when the torrential rain stopped as suddenly as it had started, saying, "This is not a good sign, *Patrão*. I must go to the *cuchcucheiro*." Who was I to argue about witch doctors? Maybe Luiz had a point. I never belittled tribal superstitions and beliefs. The White man's world is full of them.

The time had come to move on. Five intense years of often grinding hard work, sometimes tricky human relations, isolation, and challenges had been negotiated. It was a steep learning curve in survival, ingenuity, and persistence. I also learned about real responsibility and courage, but I needed fresh horizons and more company of my own kind. Beira, on the warm Indian Ocean, beckoned. My whole existence was about to be channeled into a life-changing new direction.

In 1953 I was back in Beira, a solid fifteen years after our arrival there. I was now a grown man, confident and full of vigor and knowing very clearly what I did not want out of life. That meant declining lucrative job offers from banks, heaven forbid such a fate! My spirit had been permanently infused with the need to wander, to spend protracted periods in the wilds. The smell of the bush after the rains, the sight of distant horizons devoid of other human beings, the feel of a campfire's warmth after an exhausting day spent following elephant spoor on foot, the sound of lion in concert on a kill, and the taste of guinea fowl over the coals had turned me into a cultural hybrid with a permanent longing for change, for wild places and challenges.

It was inevitable, therefore, that I would be intoxicated with the unique beauty of the Gorongosa Game Reserve, some 100 miles north of Beira and over 2,000 square miles in area. It was bursting with game. In the space of a few hours, one could easily see elephant, lion, buffalo, hippo, croc, and a whole range of plains game as well as a tremendous diversity of bird life. Many established experts on wildlife concurred that Gorongosa was without doubt the most densely populated and the most scenic game reserve in Africa. The lushness of the bush, the icy clarity of the streams as they tumbled over granite boulders, and the towering, verdant beauty of Gorongosa Mountain bewitched me as surely as any beautiful but unattainable young girl would have done.

I fell in love with Gorongosa.

I joined a travel agency in Beira called Turismo, and my associates and I promoted Gorongosa vigorously. We became the concessionaires for the reserve, where I was directly involved in the building of Chitengo, the main camp. We ran Gorongosa, which was attracting an ever-increasing number of visitors from the Rhodesias and South Africa and, later on, from many other countries. In all my travels in Africa, including the famed Kenyan game reserves, I never saw its equal for scenic beauty, incredible richness of game, and a magical atmosphere. Gorongosa's fate two decades later devastated me. I certainly could never have foreseen the savage rape of that paradise, from which it cannot recover for generations—if at all—despite what politicians and assorted nongovernmental organizations would have the world believe.

I would return very frequently to our farm to assist my parents and to hunt with friends. It was at that time that my brothers and I began another passion—rally driving—which took us all over Mozambique, into Southern Rhodesia, Swaziland, and South Africa. At times we won against all odds, against much more sophisticated vehicles, our many thousands of miles of bush bashing having given us an edge, perhaps. We rallied for fun and excitement; winning was a bonus.

During those early days in Beira, Turismo acted as agents for Thomas Cook & Son and would meet the trains from the Federation of Rhodesia and Nyasaland to assist passengers in boarding boats and to meet passengers off the boats who were traveling inland. This aspect of my work resulted in a reunion with the legendary bush character, John "Pondoro" Taylor.

I received a voucher to assist a Mr. J. Taylor who would be arriving from Nyasaland by train to board a boat bound for Italy. In the years since my first meeting with Taylor as a schoolboy in Tete, he had ghosted in and out of local gossip, maintaining his frozen distance from other Whites, his reputation for belligerence and booze undiminished. I met Taylor off the train from Nyasaland, and we recalled our meeting all those years ago in steamy Tete. He was already fried at 8:00 A.M., and I am not sure just how truthful he was being when he said he had not forgotten me. Taylor insisted on being dropped off at the nearest bar, where he promised he would be when I picked him up that afternoon to take him to the docks.

Came the appointed hour, no Taylor. With a sense of panic, I began a zigzag search among the favorite human watering holes, looking for the Irish rogue, until I came across a small group of Blacks clustered together in a side street, all staring down at their feet at the side of the road, as if at an accident victim. Naturally, I stopped to look, too, and there, sprawled in the gutter, was Taylor, oblivious to the world. With little time to spare, we heaved the man into my car as he stirred from his stupor and I all but poured him onto the launch which would take passengers out to the boats not docking in Beira harbor. Taylor told me he was going to Australia "to shoot rabbits." He was more likely shooting the breeze that day as I watched the launch ease away from the quayside, Taylor sprawled across a seat.

Contentious stories had long made the rounds of his less-than-legal hunting habits upon occasion and of his falling foul of the authorities in Nyasaland and Mozambique. I remember hearing about his arriving back in Africa in a classic English sedan after a visit to his wealthy family in England, and of his having the first outboard motorboat on the Zambezi, as well as a top-of-the-range English motorbike. I always regarded Taylor's extravagant claims as to the number of elephant he said he had hunted successfully and on his own, as just that extravagant. In addition, the befuddled man I knew somehow did not tally with the author of subsequent books. I also took issue with some of what he wrote about Mozambique and the Portuguese. His Irishness notwithstanding, a little of the pukka Anglo arrogance had infected Taylor. That day at the Beira docks would not be the last of my links with that melancholy man.

In October 1953, I married Henriqueta, who had been born in Mozambique. We established our home in Beira, where our four children were born. We suffered the unspeakable tragedy of losing our first baby daughter at ten months of age. She is buried in Beira. My only son, Adelino Junior, known universally as Tim-Tim, was our firstborn. He grew up into a strapping young man and became a professional hunter who accompanied me to many locations in Africa. Something of a history buff on the Portuguese in Africa, and a collector of Africana, he is now ostrich farming in Spain. He and my daughters, Palucha, the mother of my two grandsons and my granddaughter, and Angela, an information-technology expert and an even more inveterate gypsy than I am, are my most valuable testimony to my life in Africa for they were all born in Mozambique.

The telephone rang late one evening in Beira, in March 1956, bringing alarming news. My father was desperately ill on our farm, with a suspected ruptured stomach ulcer. He was losing a lot of blood, and my mother urged her two daughters and three sons to return to the farm instantly. We left immediately, traveling in convoy as fast as we could over 260 miles of bad roads, and reached the farm at dawn.

With the nearest neighbor being the *chefe de posto* 25 miles away, and the nearest small town, Vila Gouveia, some 50 miles away, our farm was the only real activity in a vast area. In times of crisis, such as this, we faced daunting logistical problems. This hit home when I saw my father. A doctor had already managed to get there and was doing his best to stabilize him. Two other doctors eventually arrived, one from Tete, over 100 miles away and, later on, another doctor came in from Vila Pery, which was over 130 miles away. They set up a blood transfusion, but my father was losing more blood than he was receiving. We were told that he had to be evacuated to Beira, as that was the nearest place with the requisite medical facilities for an emergency operation. Otherwise my father would die. The shock was that we were told bluntly that he could under no circumstance be evacuated by road because of the time involved and the often terrible condition of the roads. If we could not organize air evacuation, he had no chance of surviving. The nearest airfield was over 50 miles away, at Vila Gouveia and, if I remember correctly, was not even operational at the time.

It is appropriate at this juncture to mention that, like everyone else, my father, a heavy smoker, an introvert, and a worrier by nature, had had to do battle with the system in Mozambique. I had become increasingly aware of this during my time in the bush, running the stores and helping work the farm. He was often very stressed out. The Lisbon oligarchy dictated our lives. There was no real free-market system to encourage and reward enterprising hard work. The Banco Nacional Ultramarino also exercised an absolute stranglehold over Mozambique. Several of the same superwealthy families of those days are still in control in Mozambique today, over a quarter of a century after independence from Portugal. After twenty-three years of often-Draconian hard work, my father was a wreck. He was dying.

By mid-afternoon, after final consultation with the three doctors present, I called the whole family together and made a decision. It was rather like preparing for a forthcoming battle. We summoned the entire able-bodied labor force of our farm, numbering some 150 men, and explained the situation and the need to carve out a landing strip with whatever implements we had at hand. Picks, hoes, shovels, rakes, and axes were gathered together and work parties organized. We chose the best available site down in the maize fields where there was a clear approach and safe takeoff area free of trees or hills.

The maize was already five feet high, and the height of summer was on the wane. It was around 6:00 that late summer twilight as we set to work to clear the field for a runway 1,300 feet long and about 25 feet wide when something very touching happened. A sizable crowd of tribal women, some already advanced in age, showed up carrying their *padzas*, the typical iron hoes of the Mozambican bush, and insisting that they, too, be allowed to help their men clear the field. The sense of solidarity that day was overwhelming. My father was extremely well known and had a lot of friends in the entire region, where he was respected for being a strict, but fair employer.

By nightfall, over three hundred people put their minds and muscles to the task, working nonstop for twelve solid hours by paraffin lamplight and vehicle headlights until the crude runway was as ready as it ever would be. We drove vehicles up and down in an effort to compact the soft earth while my mother, sisters, and staff members ferried coffee and snacks to the workforce throughout the night. The men sang and chanted to keep up everyone's spirits and to lend rhythm to the cutting, slashing, digging, and uprooting.

In the meantime, I used the old crank telephones of the day to get in touch with a good friend in Beira who was a highly experienced bush pilot. I first had to get hold of Vila Gouveia which, in turn, called Vila Pery and then Beira before I could finally speak with my pilot friend at 5:30 the next morning. Nobody in this age of fax, e-mail, the Internet, cell phones, and satellite technology can know what we had to face in those days. But there was a profound sense of solidarity, of community back then, which all our modern inventions appear to have dulled, to the detriment of meaningful human interaction. The Blacks manning the telephone exchanges at Vila Gouveia and at Vila Pery that fateful night played a direct role in saving my father's life.

Our pilot friend immediately contacted a good friend of my father who was a medical doctor in Beira, and the two men took off for our farm in a Piper Tripacer. This type of aircraft was ideal for our conditions because it could land and take off on short runways. We had rigged up a rough windsock with a large piece of cloth hoisted on a pole at one end of the runway. The anxiety-filled wait now began.

A murmur and then a sustained shout went up from the entire exhausted workforce, especially from the tribal women, when the aircraft became visible at around 7:30 that morning. No aircraft had ever landed in that area because, until that morning, there had never been any runway facilities. Not one of the women or children had ever seen an aircraft, so this was a captivating experience for them. I heard an older woman say that this was a great bird sent by *melungo,* the supernatural force. She seemed quite unperturbed at the sight of the Tripacer as it circled the runway once before making a very good landing. The old lady had already absorbed the event, internalizing it according to the value system of the world with which she was familiar. We could never have accomplished what we did that night had it not been for the goodwill and sustained effort of all those simple tribal people. Many of them, it is true, had been helped by our family, in times of sickness and distress of one or another sort, and now they were standing by us in our hour of need.

My father was lying on a mattress next to the runway. He was loaded into the aircraft, the pilot insisting that my mother accompany him. I was very concerned about the takeoff, but the pilot, displaying the typically nonchalant attitude of bush pilots, told me not to worry but, instead, to call together about six of us to hang onto the tail and to watch for a signal from the cockpit as to when to let go. We did just that and, after the tiny aircraft reached the very end of the runway, it gained height successfully and soon was out of sight. By mid-day, my father was on the operating table in Beira where the surgeons saved him, giving him years of life he had been on the point of losing that morning on our farm.

In early 1957, a curious thing happened. I was in Gorongosa, when I noticed two smart 4×4s. In chatting to the English-speaking visitors, I was startled when they told me that they were looking for John "Pondoro" Taylor who, they said, was back in Africa. I assured them that I had seen him onto a boat for Australia via Italy in 1953, and that there had not been one word of his returning to our part of the world. The visitors remained adamant. I subsequently learned that Taylor had ghosted back into Africa the previous year and had gone straight to his former gunbearer, Ali Ndemanga, at his village on Mangochi Plateau in Nyasaland. Deported in late 1957, Taylor spent twelve wretched years in London, dying there in March 1969. His ashes were flown back to Ali Ndemanga in Nyasaland. Whatever his failings, Taylor, Muslim/Rosicrucian misfit, ivory hunter, and poacher, Tete hellraiser, author, ballistics expert, and deportee, remains a legendary part of early Mozambique.

Life continues, and mine was again about to take a new turn. My intimate involvement in all aspects of the tourism industry and my long-standing and ongoing experience of the African bush and its wildlife resulted in my becoming increasingly aware in the late 1950s of the potential for hunting safaris in Mozambique. They were already an entrenched feature of Kenya, Uganda, and Tanganyika, with some hunting safaris going into Sudan. Teddy Roosevelt's historic 1909 safari in British East Africa heralded the golden age of big-game safaris in Africa, and much of the literature on African hunting concentrates on that region.

Mozambique had yet to reveal to the world what she could offer international sportsmen and I was well placed to show them. Until the late 1950s, most of the hunting in Mozambique was conducted by "meat hunters" who were contracted to supply game meat for the workforces on, for example, the vast Sena sugar estates in the Zambezi region. The heyday of the professional ivory hunters, as typified by "Pondoro" Taylor and Harry Manners, had vanished, although everyone recalls Harry's spectacular elephant. It was found on the border with Nyasaland in November 1953, its tusks weighing 185 and 183 pounds, respectively, listed fourth in Rowland Ward's *Records of Big Game*. In general, Mozambique had long since stopped producing big ivory and this could well have been because the gene pool had been affected by the indiscriminate hunting of bulls with big tusks in decades past.

There was a clutch of pioneer safari hunters in the late 1950s, such as a Swiss named Gustaf Guex and Alberto "One-shot" Araujo, an inspector for the TransZambezia railway line. They were among the very first in Mozambique to have paying clients on safari. The main areas for hunting incorporated four distinct types of terrain and an astounding variety of animals, from the famed Marromeu Flats north of Beira, flanking the Indian Ocean, with their teeming herds of buffalo and waterbuck, amongst other species, to the sweltering Zambezi valley in the northwest for superlative kudu, south to mountainous country, and slightly further inland to Guro and Macossa for the big five, and then to the savanna country east of Gorongosa for superb nyala. All this could be enjoyed in the space of a mere few hours' travel.

Our farm at Guro alone was at the heart of a concession of approximately 3,000 square miles, about the size of the state of Delaware. Quite apart from the big five, we had excellent game, such as greater kudu and sable, eland, Lichtenstein hartebeest, zebra, impala, bushbuck, duiker, warthog, and reedbuck, although the last-mentioned were never exceptional. The lions there were noted for their extravagant dark manes.

It was time to break out of our isolation and bring the attention of the world to the tourism and sport-hunting potential of Mozambique. We labored under the stigma of a not-too-benign dictatorship and, for the pukka British, horror of horrors, we spoke a different language. Despite their empire, the British of the day had remained an oddly inward-looking lot with a reticence—indeed, prejudice—toward all things non-British or non–British Empire. I was at ease in the English-speaking world and decided in 1959 to go to America and begin serious promotion of my country as a hunting-safari destination.

My education had just begun.

Accompanied by Francisco Salzone and Miguel Guerra, both of whom had been meat hunters for the sugar estates, we spent a month in Chicago in the winter of 1959, promoting Mozambique. This was my first visit to a country which would eventually become like a second home. The wind-chill factor in Chicago, the snow and ice, and the sheer lack of sun and blue skies were a shock to our subtropical systems. The second rude awakening was our inability at that stage to compete with the Kenya-based hunters who ruled the safari roost. They had had a head start of over half a century in attracting visiting sportsmen and I found that many Americans of the time were somewhat reluctant to go to places where English was not widely spoken. How strange this reads today when the American sport hunter thinks nothing of going to such exotic locations as Kazakhstan and Mongolia!

Disheartened, we left the United States. I decided to stop over in Spain on my way home. Fate again stepped in and that single decision altered my life forever and the course of the hunting-safari industry in Mozambique. In Madrid I met Max Borrell, the longstanding hunting and fishing companion of the Spanish head of state, General Francisco Franco. I never looked back.

Max was an unusual man. Although born in Cuba, he was of Spanish origin. He and his family became victims of Fidel Castro's communist policies and lost everything they owned before being forced out of Cuba, returning to Spain. There, Max eventually developed into a prominent safari-booking agent, accompanying General Franco on many hunting and fishing excursions in Spain. Quite naturally, he was extremely well connected with the ruling elite and with many of the prominent, often titled families of Spain, a country with a long hunting tradition. An open-minded and enterprising man, Max enthusiastically accepted my invitation to come out to Mozambique and see for himself.

Our safari season ran from April 1 to November 15. Max and a very famous Spanish hunter named Enrique Mayer arrived in Mozambique that season, where my associates and I hosted them on a thirty-day safari. A wonderful, custom-built camp on my family farm at Guro served as the headquarters for this crucially important experiment. Several species later, which included some of the big five, we accompanied our guests to the papyrus-and-palm paradise that was the Marromeu Flats on the Indian Ocean, where they were stunned at the seemingly endless herds of buffalo and waterbuck with clouds of egrets and oxpeckers skimming the swamps as they followed the buffalo. We flew up to the hard, hot world of the Zambezi Valley and the splendid kudu it contained, looping southward and heading for the blue magnificence of the mountains, before closing in on the hilly fringes of the Gorongosa Game Reserve, where a particularly handsome dark chocolate nyala bull completed this historic safari. It was all captured on a promotional film by Max and Enrique.

Anything they had been privileged to experience in places like Kenya and Tanganyika had been equaled and, in some instances, surpassed, they told me. They commented on the consistently good human relations with the tribal peoples they experienced in Mozambique, and they were at pains to point out how astounded they had been at the rich variety of terrain and abundance of species. The fine safari cuisine with its wines, venison, and game-bird dishes, and a relaxed, distinctly Latin way of life in a country with miles of broad, pristine beaches, lush lagoons, and outgoing people who welcomed strangers, rounded out the picture of a prime hunting country.

Max and Enrique returned to Spain, where Max became my agent to promote hunting safaris in Mozambique. The floodgates opened overnight, and my long, special relationship with Spain began. I picked up Spanish very quickly, indeed, and was soon hosting extremely distinguished clients. The word spread like a rogue bush fire in this word-of-mouth business, and soon I was receiving requests for information from many other countries. At last Mozambique was now becoming an increasingly popular destination for the foreign sport hunter, and the future was full of promise—not only for me, but for Mozambique.

A well-regulated hunting industry is the highest and best use of bush country where game flourishes and cattle and crops do not. It generates the funds to employ, train, and equip local inhabitants to help curb one of the scourges of Africa: poaching. Strictly enforced hunting quotas and ethical conduct in the field are potent conservation tools. Where hunting is banned, the poachers take over and the game vanishes. Kenya and the fate of its rhino, for example, and South Africa's hunting policy and flourishing rhino populations are but one example of this philosophy. If it pays, it stays. Conservation needs huge amounts of money, and a tightly regulated hunting industry is the prime generator of such funds. Mozambique had not yet suffered any serious losses through poaching because the AK-47 and the fever of African independence—*uhuru* in Swahili—had not yet arrived.

Under the auspices of Turismo, we formed a hunting-safari division which brought together some of the former meat hunters. These were early days, and the inevitable problems occurred. Some hunters found the transition difficult from commercial meat hunter to professional hunter and guide to sophisticated paying clients, where the emphasis was on trophy quality and not quantity. It takes years to cultivate the ability to judge trophy quality, and you need a special temperament to play several roles simultaneously in the bush as a professional hunter.

Quite apart from skill and experience with firearms, an intimate knowledge of the bush and wildlife as well as a very versatile, disciplined temperament, the professional hunter does even better if he is multilingual and has the ability to get on with all kinds of people under sometimes stressful conditions. He must be well informed, be able to converse, to entertain, and to lead. He must be able to handle crises, to control staff and to turn his hand to anything from a broken-down vehicle to first aid. Physical and mental stamina are prerequisites in the safari business.

Our farm at Guro became the focal point of Concession No. 9 as we geared up to enter the international hunting-safari industry. I never liked tented camps, preferring instead to get into the bush, select a scenic spot and, with my expert Sena team, build a comfortable thatched camp in ten days flat. Clients were seeking an African experience in an atmosphere in direct contrast to the concrete traps they called home, be they baronial palaces, high-rise apartments, or anonymous suburban houses, barking dogs and all. In those early days, safari meant campfires and paraffin lamps. It meant relaxing to sounds which did not exist in suburbia. It meant showering under the stars and enjoying a cuisine prepared very often in anthill ovens. It meant a journey into another world entirely, where life was different, where all the senses were revived into fresh awareness and where life was shared with the true citizens of the bush—the wild animals, the bird life and the often outrageously colored insects in the lung-jolting purity of the air. Why entomb the foreign hunter in a farmhouse? In my books, that was not what he was paying for. In fact, my finest promotional tool was the simplicity—yet comfort—of my bush camps. They were devoid of all the superfluous trappings of so-called civilization. My fly camps, for example, often afforded clients the chance to sleep under a baobab in a sleeping bag, next to a fire, surrounded by game, some of it dangerous.

My youngest brother, José Augusto, joined me at Guro as our reputation grew and we hosted an increasing number of truly memorable clients. He became a very accomplished hunter. My other brother, Jacinto, was also a valuable member of the team for a time. It was with him that we enjoyed a rather unusual experience with Dr. Necker Pinto, a medical doctor from Brazil. He was attached to the World Health Organization and traveled extensively. A tremendously keen hunter, Dr. Pinto was well into his eighties when I sent him on his last safari in Zambia in 1986 with Hunters Africa.

Dr. Pinto, who became a frequent visitor to Mozambique, was out with Jacinto during one of our early Guro-based safaris, hunting lion with his 30.06. A very respectable male came into his sights, and the good doctor took what appeared to be a perfect shot. While everybody was congratulating him, the supposedly dead lion suddenly got up and took off! That was it. They lost the lion, despite a tremendous tracking effort. There was almost no blood spoor.

Not two weeks later, I was out in a Land Rover with some Spanish hunters in the same area when, at 11:00 A.M., my tracker suggested we take a look at a particular waterhole. As we approached it, a lion suddenly manifested itself with a live, squirming warthog in its mouth! None of us had a camera! It had just caught the warthog when we appeared and it looked up at us, a few yards from the vehicle. The client eased out on the other side and took aim. The shot hit home and the lion spun, dropping the warthog which, in turn, took off, apparently uninjured. Just imagine the scene, the comic shock of it all! Speechless Spaniards, a flying warthog, and a dead lion.

We were far from camp and it was a hot day, so we decided to skin the lion on the spot. Just as we were gathering our wits after this strange event, my tracker came up, saying, "*Patrão*, this is Dr. Pinto's lion. Come and look." Apart from the bullet which the Spaniard had fired, the tracker found another which was a different caliber in the lion's shoulder. It was from Dr. Pinto's rifle, and it had only penetrated about two inches. The lion had not been injured seriously, which was why it had recovered suddenly and vanished that day. Feeling honor-bound, I wrote to Dr. Pinto to tell him that we had found his lion, but that it had since become another client's trophy.

We had a rather special way of "calling" lions in those days in order to attract them into an area. We would take a four-gallon paraffin can, insert a rough funnel-shaped object into the opening, filling the can one-quarter full with water before tying a string around it to make a vibration. The next step, which was not at all difficult, was to find someone who could imitate the roar of a lion and who would "talk" with the lion as it began answering, drawing it closer and closer to the sound and our blind.

"Calling" lions in Mozambique had its extremely humorous moments. In those early days, I remember two professional hunters, each with a client, conducting safaris in the same area. They each came across lion spoor, but it was the spoor of the same lion. Naturally, these hunters did not tell each other what was going on. Each went out with his funnel contraption, being separated from each other by some 6 miles. You can imagine what happened throughout that night. One hunter would "call" and the other would "reply," each hunter thinking that the reply was from a bona fide feline.

Back at camp, they would say, "You know something? I spent all night calling the lion and, funny thing, it kept replying, but it would not move!" Normally, when a lion replies, it moves away or toward you. As one of the hunters continued, "That damn thing kept answering from the same place all night." Then it dawned on both hunters as to what had actually happened. That story made the rounds for the entire season. How we laughed, the hunters not knowing whether to laugh, too, or to slink off sheepishly and hope the story would die a sudden death. It didn't.

When hunting lion under those circumstances, you usually stayed in your hunting car, which would be camouflaged by branches, the tracker calling the lion from outside the vehicle. It often happened that the lion would be called incessantly and then, like the infamous flash floods of Manica Sofala, there would be complete silence. Suddenly the lion caller would rocket back into the hunting vehicle with a lion right at his heels.

Those early years were filled to bursting with special people and often with even more memorable safaris, but it is here that I would like to share an experience which has remained unique in my experience as an example of selfless behavior. In early 1963, my father started showing serious signs of recurring ill health. He was finding it more difficult to lead his usual extremely energetic life on our sprawling farm at Guro and attend to his interests elsewhere. After consultation with our doctors in Beira, and after having taken my father to Rhodesia and to South Africa, I was told by specialists in Johannesburg that my father needed surgery for an abdominal aneurysm and that they had only recently started performing this type of cardiovascular surgery. Chances of survival were fifty-fifty.

The specialists went on to say that the only person known at that time who had the greatest chance of successfully operating on my father was Dr. Michael DeBakey, of subsequent heart-transplant fame. He was based in Houston and was already considered to be the world leader in this field. Not believing I would ever so much as receive a reply, I wrote to Dr. DeBakey, forwarding the medical reports and explaining our circumstances, especially that our family could in no way afford to pay him for the intricate surgery and post-operative care in Houston, in addition to flights, accommodation, medication, and the thousand-and-one often-mind-numbing expenses which arise in the face of serious ill health in a foreign country. Knowing that he was based in Texas, a great hunting state and one of my favorite places on earth, I offered Dr. DeBakey an all-inclusive free classic big-game safari in Mozambique if he would please help me save my father's life.

Dr. DeBakey replied. Not only that, he instructed us to fly out as soon as possible to Houston, giving me all the details, saying that he would operate free of charge at Methodist Hospital. My father would be hospitalized free of charge, all medication would be free, as well as any postoperative care in Houston. He explained that he was not a hunter himself, but that he would certainly like to visit Mozambique one day for a photographic safari.

Dr. DeBakey was as good as his word. We arrived in May 1963 in Houston and spent one month there. My father underwent successful surgery to replace his aorta. I shall never forget what Dr. DeBakey did for our entire family by giving my father an additional few years of a reasonable quality of life which he would otherwise not have had. As of this writing, Dr. DeBakey is still alive and consulting.

While in Houston, it was not all gloom and anxiety. In fact, my father made a fabulous recovery. Then I noticed a man in the same ward who was absolutely mute. He seemed in a state of deep shock, his face masklike in its motionlessness, his eyes blank. One of the nurses told me that the problem was nobody could communicate with him, as he was from Belgium and could not speak French.

My ears pricked up and I said, "I'll be able to talk with him."

The nurse retorted, "But you're from Mozambique and he does not speak Portuguese or English!"

"I know that," I replied and I walked over to the poor man and asked him how he was, speaking in Afrikaans, one of the official languages of South Africa which I had been taught at school in Rhodesia by "Jeeves" Hougaard. The Flemish language of Belgium is related to Dutch, which is the main root of Afrikaans. The two languages are largely mutually intelligible. When the man heard me, the effect was electrifying. His facial expression changed from that of a death mask to a man who had suddenly emerged from a coma. He and I were soon talking like a couple of long-standing buddies who had not seen each other in decades. The words came pouring out, and I tried to keep up in my rusty schoolboy Afrikaans. Not only that, the Belgian's whole recovery process from radical surgery was quite dramatic after that day. He no longer felt frozen and dangerously isolated in a foreign country. I helped him communicate with the nurses who, in turn, blossomed when they saw him smile and improve with each day. I was destined to return to Houston many times, and it remains one of my best-loved cities in the States.

My father and I had been back only a few weeks from Houston when fate again stepped in and introduced a Spanish family to whom I became very close and with whom I retain special ties to this day. I was still experimenting at Guro with big-game safaris for paying clients when an urgent call came in from the governor in Beira. He had a crisis on his hands. A Beira-based hunter/outfitter, who was supposed to host two very important couples from Madrid, guests of the Portuguese government no less, was unable to do so because his concession was not quite ready. The governor had a potential disaster on his hands and, in his near-panic, he turned to me and told me to expect the two couples on a special flight the next day.

With the drive and resilience of youth on my side, my staff, my family, and I were on hand to welcome Eduardo and Loli Aznar. She was the Marchioness de Lamiaco, and her husband was one of the most prominent entrepreneurs in Spain. Their companions were Carmen Franco, the only child of the Spanish head of state, General Franco, accompanied by her husband, the Marquis de Vilaverde. They were on a twenty-one-day safari which was conducted over several concessions. Both women were already extremely experienced hunters, as is often the case with the Spanish aristocracy.

It was an extraordinary time for all of us and a very successful safari. The hunter who was supposed to host our visitors from the outset eventually got his act together. He had not been successful in obtaining a leopard for Loli Aznar. On the last day of that landmark safari in my life, luck was with me and Loli obtained her leopard.

Eduardo Aznar, who became a great friend and frequent safari client right until his death in 1980, returned with José Ramon Mora Figueroa for another big-game safari with me the very next year. José was married to Carmen Domecq of the famous sherry family of Spain, which is still considered to be the number one sherry empire in the world. They were after lion, in particular.

I was already acquainted with the Figueroa family for rather traumatic reasons. José Ramon and his brother, Enrique, came out to hunt during that early Guro period. I didn't happen to be with them on that particular safari. On the first day out, the party returned to camp in the late afternoon and, after dinner, everybody turned in for a very early start the next day.

At dawn, Enrique did not appear. There was no answer when they called his name at his hut door. He had died in his sleep. The shock of that experience was acute, and it haunted me for a long time afterward. Apparently, Enrique was a diabetic, and his disease played a role in his sudden death. I had the terribly distressing task of month-long red tape involving the embalming of the body and then of accompanying it via Johannesburg back to Spain and down to Las Lomas, the family estate at Jerez de la Frontera. The Figueroa family was extremely gracious. They understood my distress at the tragedy, accorded me superb hospitality at their enchanting estate, and later introduced me to the culture of Spain.

My trepidation was understandable when Eduardo returned with José Ramon to hunt with me a short year after Enrique's death. I was spooked by the possibility of something untoward happening to José Ramon but, as merciful fate would have it, the Aznar/Figueroa safari turned out to be another very successful experience. It was highlighted by the lion hunt in the wild, rocky beauty of our concession at Guro.

Still a little jumpy at having another member of the world-famous Figueroa family back on safari after what had happened the previous year, I suggested that we take things very easy the first day or so, maybe taking a Lichtenstein hartebeest, whatever. Well, Mother Nature and weird luck dictated otherwise. Not one hour out of camp that afternoon, with the bark of baboons living on Guro Mountain intruding on the gentle sounds of the bush, we came across two fine male lions with very handsome manes, facing us brazenly at the side of the track. Not only were these felines beautiful, they were smart, streaking off like a high-velocity bullet before we could even get our thoughts together.

We successfully hunted a respectable Lichtenstein hartebeest, the tawny animal with its very distinctive S-shaped horns dropping instantly to Eduardo's shot. We selected a suitable tree to which we tied the carcass securely, to serve as bait for the lions we now knew were in the neighborhood. It was late afternoon, and we had begun "calling" the lions. They had begun "answering."

My experience in the bush had already warned me never to make rigid plans. In fact, I became known for my habit of refusing ever to say exactly when I would be returning to camp, as I never knew what would occur out there. I was always prepared with sleeping bags and enough food to stay out way past schedule.

We debated the situation and decided to stay out and watch the bait, rather than return to camp that night. We continued "calling" the lions for about an hour, but they stopped answering. We decided to stay in that area and see what would happen the following day. I remember that we were all spread out around the campfire in our sleeping bags not far from the bait tree, when we were awakened late that night by one lion roaring not 30 feet from us. It was obviously hungry. Just imagine the reaction in our group! Eduardo had one of those tip-off, claw-mounted scopes which, in his startled state, he had not seated properly on his rifle.

We could see the lion by the light of the campfire as it got nearer and nearer to us. No torch was necessary. There is no doubt in my mind that the lion was bent on making closer acquaintance with us, so Eduardo shot. But, as he did so, the scope flew off, causing a big cut on his nose which he sported for the rest of the safari. His shot went wide and the lion took off into the scrub. We did not manage to fall asleep after that.

The following morning, we picked up the spoor and could see that the lion was not hurt. We decided to stay in the same area. That same day, Eduardo shot "Dr. Pinto's lion," the one with the warthog in its mouth. With another lion license to go, we changed areas and went down to the papyrus and palm-graced paradise of the Marromeu Flats, flanking the Indian Ocean.

The vegetation was sparse, trees scattered here and there among the floating islands of marsh growth. Joaquim, the local tracker, whose eyesight was truly exceptional, whispered, *"Patrão, leão!"* The lion was up a tree, its luxuriant mane masked by the foliage. I could not recall ever having seen a lion up a tree before that day; but, according to the Marromeu locals, lions would climb trees in that flat country to spot game to hunt. I was not about to query the veracity of this as we left the vehicle and José Ramon approached the tree stealthily. Unfortunately, he gut-shot the lion, which plummeted from the tree and simply vanished into the very tall swamp grass. Here we go! A wounded lion in near-impossible terrain. It was becoming dangerous, and I was freshly spooked at the considerable risk facing another member of the Figueroa family.

We were using a right-hand-drive Land Rover with no doors. Amilcar Coelho, another professional hunter, was driving. Figueroa was sitting up front with him while Eduardo and I were at the back. We were driving clockwise around the island onto which the lion had fled in an attempt to flush the big cat into the open. Coelho stopped the vehicle and our tracker noted the grass moving. Before we could absorb this, there was a blur of movement and the lion erupted out of the long grass, coming right up to the exposed vehicle. Coelho had a revolver on his lap, and a shot rang out. I did not know if it was Eduardo, José Ramon, Coelho, or myself. The shot missed and the lion charged back into the impossible swamp grass and onto the island.

Oddly enough, it was very dry around that spot so we decided that the only way to flush the lion clear was to smoke him out by setting fire to the grass. Suddenly the lion charged without the remotest warning. This time, we were all ready. Shots were fired, but José Ramon was unable to get a shot off as he was sitting on the left of Coelho, the driver, and the lion was to Coelho's right, making it far too dangerous to shoot during a full-blown charge. The lion came to a literal dead stop just inches from the Land Rover. It was a splendid old male, with plenty of evidence of fights on its hide. The tousled, streaked mane was like a halo around the muzzle with its worn fangs. Above us, as if out of thin air, vultures were already beginning their ritual aerial ballet in anticipation of a feast at noon. Relief washed over us that day after that hard, particularly dangerous hunt for one of the prime trophies of African hunting. My addiction to the wild life was deepening. The hunt was now on.

THREE

THE HUNT IS ON

The thousands of animals, scattered over the arid plains, the flocks of wading, web-footed, and many other kinds of birds which fly over at sunrise to feed; the peaceful, solemn, yet imposing landscape, bounded on the blue horizon by the mountains of Gorongoza and Chiringoma; all these things will remain graven on my memory.

—William Vasse, *Three Years' Sport in Mozambique*

The armed struggle in Mozambique broke out on September 24, 1964, when guerrillas of the Marxist Mozambique Liberation Front, Frelimo, launched an attack on a Portuguese military base in the far north of the country in the district of Mueda, fairly close to the border with Tanzania. To give perspective here, in June 1960, a crowd had gathered to petition the local Portuguese administrator at Mueda about their grievances. This was met by rifle fire from Portuguese troops who killed many people that day, in an eerie echo of the Sharpville tragedy three months earlier in South Africa, where dozens died in a confrontation with the police. The smoldering, fractured resistance movements, which had been formed abroad by expatriate Mozambicans, eventually gelled into

Frelimo, in June 1962, in Tanzania which had gained its independence in December 1961. Frelimo and I were to become increasingly better acquainted.

All around Africa, the colonial powers were in retreat, the bloody civil war in the former Belgian Congo from 1960 until 1963 epitomizing the strife which endures to this day across most of Africa. It was inevitable that Portugal would eventually be challenged over her presence in Africa. Until the early 1960s, Mozambique had been very peaceful, and neither I nor any member of my family had ever experienced a single untoward incident of a racial or political nature concerning the Black population of Mozambique. Portugal, however, could not insulate her African possessions from events elsewhere in Africa. In fact, Portugal was shaken rigid on March 15, 1961 by the horrific, coordinated massacre of her citizens across a 500-mile-long front in northern Angola by Bakongo tribesmen from that region and from the central Congo. The rape, torture, and sheer carnage were beyond belief, and we in Mozambique took note.

Here I must let Robert Ruark speak. I knew Robert who, for all his sins and sad end, spoke the truth. In his foreword to Bernard Teixeira's book, *The Fabric of Terror,* he wrote:

> God knows the Portuguese were toughly dominant in their occupancy of the African territories they colonized. Perhaps they were not so cynical as the Americans, in their treatment of the Indians, or so stupidly arrogant as the British in their administration of the Raj. At least the Portuguese bedded with the natives and married with the natives, and never really discriminated racially against the natives.
>
> I have been four times to Mozambique in the last two years and I have walked, driven or flown over the entire country. I know Angola from one end to the other. . . . Certainly, in Mozambique the educational, health and other facilities in the towns and cities are superior to what so unproudly we hail in America. There is no problem of "integration" in Portuguese Africa. Interracially, it has always been integrated, and the lowli-

est bush native is a prince compared to a typical example of Harlem's ghettos.

The tragedy of the last outposts of what is called "colonialism" by the same people who gutted Hungary and Poland and the rest of the satellite states is that the so-called "freedom" movements are directed from outposts in Russia, China, Algeria, Tanganyika and the Congo. None of these states can manage its own business. The "freedom-fighters" never lived in the countries they are "freeing."

I am not a politician, and this is not a book for political scientists. No story, however, about Mozambique, spanning the period 1936–2000, can avoid core political issues. We, on the ground in the safari business, would experience increasingly the effects of the changing political climate in Mozambique and, up to the end, the ineptitude and, in some cases, the sheer cowardice among some of the officers of the Portuguese armed forces deployed in Mozambique, as well as the barbarity of the Frelimo guerrillas. The stress would increase, in tandem with the foreign-incubated contagion which eventually destroyed our lives in Mozambique and laid waste all we had developed. The hunt was now on; man increasingly becoming the prey.

During the early 1960s, I became aware of a pretty distasteful propaganda exercise in which the Portuguese Government was directly involved. Clearly, there was alarm at the growing number of African countries gaining independence. When Tanganyika became Tanzania in December 1961, and the principal haven and rear base for the Marxist guerrillas bent on the violent overthrow of Portuguese rule, the sociopolitical fabric of Mozambique began to unravel.

Large sections of the notoriously distressing film, *Africa Addio*, were filmed in Mozambique—more precisely on the Marromeu Flats, where cables were strung between vehicles and driven into herds of zebra, for example, breaking their legs. Further appalling incidents of cruelty involving elephant and other animals were also stage-managed in Mozambique, apparently in an effort to demonize the Black man in the eyes of the West, depicting him as barbaric, cruel, filled with blood lust, and worse, certainly not remotely capable of taking over the reins of government in humane, responsible fashion. All this occurred with the full support of the Portuguese authorities. As the tragic events of postindependence Africa are continuing to reveal in places like Angola, Burundi, the Democratic Republic of Congo, Eritrea, Ethiopia, Rwanda, Sierra Leone, Somalia, Sudan, and Zimbabwe, there was no need for a film such as *Africa Addio*. The reality continues to be bad enough.

Although the political climate was certainly changing in many places in Africa, we continued to enjoy a remarkably peaceful situation in Mozambique in the early 1960s. But, in 1965, the Banco Nacional Ultramarino amalgamated most of the hunting concessions being run by the former meat hunters and formed an organization called Safrique. One or two others and I were not invited into this cozy little Lisbon-run club and were left to fend for ourselves which caused increasing stress in my life alone.

The reasons were political. I had long since become a thorn in the side of the Lisbon bureaucrats because I would not accept their stupidities silently and, let it now be said, their sometimes unethical and dishonest practices—certainly, their exploitation and greed concerning Mozambique. One example was the leasing to foreigners of prime hunting concessions when these individuals did not even live in Mozambique. They owned nothing in the country, had no responsibilities there and, consequently, nothing to lose. They certainly had no incentive to improve Mozambique. These prizes were dished out to those who curried favor with the Salazar regime.

I already had the profile of a "separatist" and, as such, was at the bottom of the list when it came to receiving any kind of thoroughgoing assistance from the authorities. On the contrary, I once flew to Lisbon for the sole purpose of having a blazing confrontation with the Deputy Minister of Overseas Provinces concerning the handing over of concessions to foreigners to the detriment of we who lived in Mozambique and who intended on dying there. The minister himself was "busy." This was to be the first of many such clashes.

I was starting to make enemies as I became more convinced and more vocal that Mozambique needed greater autonomy all round in order to thrive. The country needed far greater latitude, for example, to be able to set its own prices and determine its own markets for its produce. The monopoly of state organizations, whose risible prices bore no relation to the expense and effort involved in cultivating that produce, would become one of the elements in the fomenting of growing antagonism to Lisbon. This was heresy in the ears of those in power. They used to burn heretics at the stake; but, as I discovered, there are other ways to destroy people.

In November 1965, Southern Rhodesia declared UDI—Unilateral Declaration of Independence—from Great Britain, an event which set in motion a whole chain of often tragic events, culminating in full-blown guerrilla warfare and worldwide sanctions. Fate saw my becoming a sanctions buster for a country I considered my second home and where, years down the line, I became a safari operator in a red-hot zone infested with guerrillas and land mines. For the most part, my fellow Mozambicans were politically apathetic, neutral, and not overly concerned with or interested in what was going on right next to them. They had the passive mindset of people in one-party states. Portugal had Salazar, who told them what not to do. Critical independent political thought and argument were not encouraged and, as most of the people were trapped in a unilingual Portuguese-speaking world, they were further shielded from realities. I could already read quite well what was beginning to appear on the wall of my intuition: eventual all-out war in Mozambique and bloody revolution. Some people thought I was a little touched or subversive when I began expressing concern about the region's problems.

But I had more pressing issues to attend to. My own company, Cotur, was established in 1965 in Beira. Until, 1969, when I left to join Safrique, I was able to expand my business and host an increasing number of significant hunters from Europe. Here, I remember with great clarity and pride, some of France's finest sportsmen: François Edmond-Blanc, the president of the Conseil International de la Chasse, the French-based international hunting organization, his wife, Martine, and their daughter, Elée, the Countess de la Rochefoucauld, who hunted as well. I recall Edmond-Blanc's successor, Bertrand des Clers, with his immaculate English and manners to match. George Nemes, the managing director of the Rothschild family's vineyards, was a another special client from France whose memory is particularly vivid.

My lawyer dropped by for lunch at our house in Beira not long after the Nemes safari. As my wife and I were not great wine drinkers, there was none on the table that day. Our lawyer requested some wine, and we recalled that several cases of wine had been sent out to us airfreight by George Nemes soon after his return to France. We opened one of the cases and brought the bottle to the table. Our lawyer, who was not only a wine drinker but a connoisseur, took one look at the Château Lafite label and at the vintage, sucked in his breath, and asked us if this was some kind of joke. I replied that no, the labels had not been pasted onto bottles of local plonk. This was the real thing, from my safari client and boss of the Rothschild family's Château Lafite vineyards in France. He took one taste and that was it.

The word raced around Beira that something truly extraordinary was happening at the Serras Pires residence. Long-lost "friends" and vague acquaintances with total strangers in tow presented themselves on our doorstep around lunchtime every day for the next couple of weeks or so, where prodigious quantities of the French nectar were enjoyed as bottle after bottle came onto the table in a seemingly unending stream. Several empty cases later, and with many members of the Beira populace in a state of Lafite-induced languor, the party ended. In retrospect, I should have kept a case or two, and retired on the proceeds.

French hunters like these eventually smoothed the way for the arrival in Mozambique of Valéry Giscard d'Estaing, then Minister of the Economy and Finance and eventual president of France. He hunted with me and elsewhere in Africa. His lovely wife, Anne-Aymone, came to my aid some years later when I found myself in dramatic circumstances in another African country.

The European market was becoming increasingly important in my business, and the Portuguese authorities started taking note. People of often enormous political and social clout elsewhere in the world came over to Mozambique to hunt with me. I never attached undue importance to this. It was the client who counted, and his or her ability to respect Africa's fauna and flora, to shoot straight and to appreciate just what a privilege it was to be in a wildlife paradise like Mozambique in the 1960s. Lisbon viewed this differently as, understandably, such contacts could be cultivated to support Portugal in the international political arena. I would see this more clearly later on. Countries cultivate access through people who already have it.

The safari business had a way of bringing one into contact with some memorable and extraordinarily accomplished people. This sometimes happened through sad circumstances, as demonstrated by my father's worsening health. His heart was acting up again, and he spent the greater part of 1965 and early 1966 with all of us in Beira, away from the farm at Guro. He was on oxygen and had to be close to a hospital.

An emergency developed, and I had to take my father down to Groote Schuur Hospital in Cape Town, where the cardiac team was his only hope of some alleviation. In Cape Town, Dr. Christiaan Barnard, a member of the cardiac team, spoke to me alone about my father. He told me that my father had anything from one month to about a year to live, and that I should take him home to the farm and let him do exactly as he pleased. I never forgot Dr. Barnard's words: "What your father needs is a new heart." I looked at him hard as he said, "We're not quite there yet." That was May 1966. In December 1967, Dr. Barnard made medical history with the first human heart transplant. I often pondered whether my father could have been that first recipient had he lived just a little longer.

A few weeks later, my father suffered a heart attack at the farm and died instantly. The entire labor force and friends for miles around attended the funeral on our farm. I hardly remember the Catholic priest's words at the service. What I do remember clearly were the words of an old Sena man who had worked for my father for many years: "Our father, too, has gone." That said it all of a man who, at sixty-six years of age, had spent exactly half of his life in Mozambique.

The profound sadness of that day lingered as my mother came to terms with what had happened. She elected to remain alone at the farm which she ran in conjunction with our dedicated workforce, a few of whom had been with my father since Tete, three decades earlier. For some days after the burial, the staff reported seeing our farm dogs lingering all day at the grave site, which was set amid gigantic eucalyptus trees in wild country. The dogs sensed our loss and our somber mood. We were all numb. The ritual of farewell would be repeating itself over and over from then on.

Although I had access to only one concession, No. 13 at Macossa, compared with the huge bank-backed Safrique operation, my client base was of the best and I was often extremely lucky with the quality of trophies and the way in which the hunts were conducted. Eventually that concession was auctioned off and, inevitably, Safrique acquired it. This was a poorly disguised attempt to clip my rebel wings.

But the wheel always turns. Safrique continued to experience a multiplicity of problems. A new administration was put in place and, irony of ironies, I was asked to join the team. I agreed.

If you cannot beat them, join them. *Then* beat them.

This heralded a grand period in my life and the heyday of hunting safaris in Mozambique, during which I enjoyed the trust and personal support of Dr. Castro Fernandes, the governor of the Banco Nacional Ultramarino and former Minister of the Economy and Finance under Salazar. We were now responsible for the day-to-day management of a company which covered seven enormous concessions embracing four different types of country and many species, stretching from the Zambezi River down to Gorongosa Game Reserve and east to the Indian Ocean—almost 12,000 square miles, making it the largest safari company in Africa between 1969 and 1974. It was a miniempire, and I had the authority, responsibilities, and worries to match.

We spearheaded a thorough shake-up of the whole Safrique organization, paying lightning visits to inspect the camps and oversee refurbishment of facilities and the upgrading of bush airstrips vital for our entire business. New staff and professional hunters were hired as this huge enterprise was freshly coordinated. Our seven concessions—

Nhamacala, Catulene, Guro, Marromeu, Inhaminga, Macossa and Bambu—with their sixteen camps and all amenities, were better organized in every way, quite frankly, than the Portuguese army ever was in the bush.

For starters, we hunters knew the terrain and we had that most important ingredient in the defense of a country—it was our permanent home. We had a territorial imperative to defend. The Israelis know all about this.

In the meantime, guerrilla activities by Frelimo, once confined to the far north of Mozambique, had moved farther and farther south. In fact, guerrilla attacks on isolated trading stores, on vehicles travelling along any of dozens of equally isolated bush roads, and cases of general intimidation of the local tribal people started occurring in Tete Province from 1968 onward. A message of racial hatred was being propagated, of driving the White man out and of taking by force what he left behind. This was very dangerous talk in the ears of impressionable tribal people. Memories of the horrors of the former Belgian Congo were still fresh.

My family and our safari organization had not been directly affected by these very worrying developments, but there was an increasing presence of Portuguese soldiers in Manica Sofala to try to contain the contagion. Our farm workforce would report to us the arrival of Mozambicans speaking languages they did not remotely understand. These would have been, among others, Makonde- and Macua-speaking people from the far north, who had infiltrated southward to spread terror.

These strangers would pay clandestine visits to villages, preaching the message of revolution, sometimes engaging in violent acts of intimidation to cow the villagers and to soften them up for the next visit by "comrades," and the next, and the one after that! Wasn't it Mao Tse-tung who spoke of guerrillas having to be like fish, swimming in the waters of a compliant or terrorized populace who would be obliged to feed, aid, and hide them? Vietnam is the perfect example of this philosophy. The Chinese communists, for one, were intimately involved in training and equipping guerrillas for Mozambique.

While it was my absolute responsibility to be aware of any shift in the wind, as it were, I had hardly had time to catch my breath since taking over operations for Safrique when I had one of the most unusual experiences of my life. It was already October when the governor-general of Mozambique contacted Safrique in a highly excited state. We were told to prepare to take on safari a prince of the royal house of Swaziland and that we had to satisfy his very particular hunting request. The Portuguese government itself was taking a direct interest in this safari. I was selected for this extraordinary exercise in international relations and it went something like this: "Your Royal Highness, welcome to Mozambique. I'm Adelino Serras Pires, and I'll have the honor of being your professional hunter during your stay in my country."

The Prince, scion of the royal house of Swaziland, a minute lush kingdom bordering Mozambique in the far south, had just arrived by air in Beira on a furnace-hot day in October 1969. The prince—in the *mahiya,* the bright red togalike traditional dress of the Swazis, his feet bare, red and white beads around his neck, a stunning red feather from the showgirl plumage of the touraco in his hair, designating his royal status—shook my hand and said, "I say, awfully kind of you to arrange this safari at such short notice. The heat's a bit of a bother, what! Daresay, we'll feel somewhat better towards evening."

I thought I was hallucinating. The man's Oxford English was remarkable, reminding me of my favorite teachers in Rhodesia. I knew I was going to get along just fine with the Prince. His personal bodyguard, drawn from the ranks of the Swazi queen mother's guards, accompanied by a member of PIDE, the Portuguese State Security Police, flanked us as we wove our way through the colonial government dignitaries and press who had gathered to greet the prince upon his arrival.

The air was heavy with the smell of aviation fuel as we walked across the apron to board our light aircraft, ready for the hourlong flight north to Concession No. 6 in the savanna country and Nhamacala ("The Place of Game") Camp. As we banked over the brilliant Indian Ocean, heading inland and away from the humid coast, my mind thrummed with a last-minute check list of what had to be in place for this unusual safari client whose trip had been coordinated between the highest levels of the Swazi and Portuguese governments. The sole objective? A leopard fit for a king-in-waiting.

Since being briefed for this safari, I had taken a crash course in Swazi tradition and politics. Now, the noise of the Piper Apache aircraft made ordinary conversation impossible, so I sat back and reviewed the essentials. No professional hunter worthy of the title can ever be complacent about clients, especially if governments and the press are watching every move.

The prince's father, King Sobhuza II, had been installed in 1921 and was the longest-reigning monarch in the world. He had numerous wives and even more sons. Swazi tradition is incredibly complicated, there being no clear law of succession. Any one of dozens of sons could be the next monarch, and my client was rumored to be among the favored sons for eventual accession to the throne. The queen mother, the *Ndhlovukati*, the "*Great She Elephant*," plays a central role in the whole process, which remains totally secret and inaccessible to outsiders.

As the Piper Apache started its descent into Nhamacala Camp—we had two aircraft to cope with the additional baggage and extra personnel—I glanced again at the prince. He was a striking man in his late twenties and I could tell by his expression that he was tense. So was I! It had been made very clear to me that this leopard safari was no mere holiday for the prince. It was a critical rite of passage. In order to be considered for possible accession to the throne, his royal male ancestors had all been expected to kill either a lion or a leopard with a spear! The very title of the Swazi king is *Ngwenyama* (lion).

With Swaziland's wildlife depleted and much of its hilly habitat overrun by humans, the traditional hunts of the prince's ancestors were no longer possible there. At that time, the logical place for a leopard was next door, in Mozambique. Times and methods for hunting leopard change—we were not about to go into the savanna country of Sofala Province, armed only with spears and a prayer! Heavens, no! This was serious business in which the Portuguese government was taking a direct, daily interest. Modern rifles, scopes, and four-wheel-drive vehicles would be central to the success of the safari. Royal ritual had to be adhered to, a tradition fulfilled, for the prince's future status depended on our bagging a fine leopard.

The dozen or so traditional circular thatched rondavels of the camp with their pretty miniature gardens, nestled among mature acacia trees on the banks of a then-dry river, came into sharp focus as our pilot throttled back and lined up with the bush runway right next to the camp. The aircraft gently bumped into contact with the parched earth of the flat country which had been scorched by the customary winter fires and the relentless African sun. The welcoming oasis of the camp against this backdrop of sun-scarred savanna was a refuge from the harsh realities outside it.

My chief tracker, Radio, a member of the local Sena tribe, was immediately on hand with my driver, Bito, and the Toyota Land Cruiser, to ferry the baggage and take a look at the new arrivals. As the prince alighted from the aircraft, followed closely by his equally traditionally dressed bodyguard and the secret service man, Radio and Bito exchanged glances. You could read the silent questions: "*What* is going on? Who *are* these people?" After all, as bush Africans who had spent their whole lives in remote areas of Mozambique, and whose experience with safari clients was confined all but exclusively to white Americans and Europeans, this was something different. How different we were all soon to find out.

With due ceremony, the guests were installed in their rondavels, and the dining hut was readied for the first dinner of the safari: smoked-salmon appetizers, buffalo-tail stew, and chilled fruit in brandy sauce, washed down with superior Portuguese wines and liqueurs. I had changed into fresh khakis and was settled into a chair to await our guests. I thought I suspected the beginnings of a malarial attack when down the pathway came the security man in an ill-fitting tuxedo, like something out of a 1930s Mafia movie. The jacket was too short, his stomach strained at the waistcoat buttons, and his plump neck bulged above the collar of the shirt like a badly tied *chouriço*, the Portuguese smoked sausage.

I blinked again and decided this was not malaria but reality. Catching my obviously amazed look, he explained, "We dress for dinner when with His Royal Highness." Clearly, I had better put on something a bit more formal and send out the message to the American couple and a prominent member from the British "establishment" still in camp and set to join us for dinner. What followed was heartwarmingly hilarious. I still smile at the memory.

I found a jacket, of sorts, to put over my khakis, but I had no tie. The British gentleman turned up in a tweedy shooting jacket that must have been murder in the heat which was still in the nineties at nightfall. The American couple outdid us all, the lady floating in on a cloud of deep blue silk to the ground with a train and a sequined neckline that was vastly more interesting than anything I could spot in the vicinity at the time. Now, what that evening gown was doing in her luggage is anyone's guess, but I suppose this delightful television personality from the West Coast took to heart the saying, "BE PREPARED! FOR ANYTHING!" Finally, accompanied by his minder, in came the prince, who had added an emerald feather to his hair, the vivid green flirting with the crimson feather as they sat side by side on his head.

I knew we were in for a memorable evening. The generator had kicked in and lights softly punctuated the blackness as the tree frogs and assorted night birds tuned up the bushveld orchestra. Our waiters, resplendent in their white tunics and ruby fezzes, respectfully took up their positions. I introduced the prince and savored the looks as his honeyed English accent warmed the evening with anecdotes of his years in England. He and the Englishman compared notes on wine as they enjoyed the Portuguese *vinho verde,* the plump security man cozying up to the American lady, who showed gracious tolerance of his shaky English.

When the talk turned inevitably to rifles and game, I quickly discovered that His Royal Highness had never handled a firearm of any sort in his life, and had never hunted. Here we were, on the brink of the rainy season, with precisely seven days to bag a respectable leopard when sometimes highly experienced clients of mine never even so much as saw spoor on a twenty-one-day classic safari. Such was the nature of leopard hunting in Mozambique—a vast, open, unfenced country offering countless opportunities to a creature as wily and cunning as a leopard to ghost in and out of an area, unseen.

Compounding the lack of time and experience was the tinder-dry countryside, which had been stripped of the lush cover typical of April through to early June, when we preferred to hunt leopard. With the cover gone, it was more difficult to conceal oneself from the ever-watchful gaze of the leopard and to attract them to bait. They, in turn, found it much easier to spot, stalk, and kill their own prey in these conditions. They did not succumb easily to man's trickery at the best of times, let alone now.

What was the best and most immediate course of action? Target practice!

At dawn the next morning, I organized some targets just beyond the camp perimeter to give the prince some basic instruction with my .300 Winchester Magnum. So, after a breakfast of fresh impala liver and eggs, off we rode, the prince still in his *mahiya*, but minus the bright green feather. The only concession he made was a pair of robust shoes.

"Squeeze gently, Your Highness. Please don't jerk the trigger."

"This is a touch more difficult than one would imagine," came his reply as the shot flew high or waltzed way off the paper target.

We went through a worrying amount of ammo until I called it a day and suggested we return to camp and freshen up for a game drive later. In the meantime, I had organized the hanging of several leopard baits at carefully selected spots in riverbeds and other prime places which I knew as intimately well as I did my favorite pair of hunting boots.

The other clients' safaris had ended, and they had left. The prince's old retainer was becoming better acquainted with the delights of our *pombe,* a fermented sorghum brew, and *sura,* the local palm wine, leaving the prince and me to accomplish the task in hand. We set off and soon came upon antelope. From the prince's reactions, he was obviously not familiar with the bush. He seemed unaware of many species on the concession, even the fine nyala, and he had difficulty in spotting a small herd of buffalo that came into view. I heard Radio muttering, *"Fungula masso!"*—chiSena for "Open your eyes!" To him, the African bush was an open book which he read with total fluency, and he was able to track such as no other man I have met before or since, including the fabled Bushmen. Radio had difficulty in accepting that a fellow African could not do likewise.

By the fourth day, the reedbuck leopard baits had still not been hit. We had gone through the exercise of sitting in blinds to the point where the prince could not endure the necessary motionlessness, silence, and endless patience. I was becoming edgy. Each morning the radio back at the camp would crackle out the same question: "Has His Royal Highness got his leopard yet?" The town-bound Beira types were starting to get on my nerves. They understood little of the realities of a hunting safari, especially when the client has no interest whatsoever in hunting, but was there only owing to a traditional necessity. The Portuguese government was out to cultivate all the countries it could, particularly a neighboring country, as the clouds of guerrilla warfare began to thicken and darken over Mozambique.

Comic relief came the morning we visited a remote village. The prince came across a particularly fine-looking young girl and promptly wanted me to negotiate a bride price with the father and take her home to Swaziland at the end of the safari. Thinking quickly, I respectfully suggested to the prince that before making such a weighty decision, he should at least attend a *batuque,* the local tribal dancing, in which men, women, and children participated.

The word went out and, that night, Nhamacala Camp throbbed to the rhythms of the drums and marimbas, as a huge crowd of people sang and chanted in the hot night air, their glistening bodies highlighted by the huge campfire. Young, bare-breasted beauties swayed and clapped to the distinctive resonance of the marimbas. Before the night was over, my distinguished client had discarded princely protocol and was strutting with the best of them, his feathered headdress barely visible in the throng of tribesmen and their womenfolk.

An interesting change was coming over the prince. With the camp to ourselves now, he relaxed visibly, started calling me by my first name, and expressed the desire to drink the local brew instead of the European wines and spirits, and to have a change in menu. Soon he was regaling himself at the dinner table, eating *cima,* the local staple maize dish, with his hands, as is tribal custom. The camp staff smiled with approval as they discovered that the prince, after all, was indeed one of them.

Day six dawned. No leopard. No sign of any of the baits having been hit. It was time to take a long, hard look at the situation and to chat with the prince. I knew he could not return to Swaziland without a leopard; the people would question his very manhood. His tribal traditions were weighing heavily on my mind as I sat down with him in the cool of the dining hut that dawn.

The prince confirmed my fears. I asked him if he would accept the skin of a leopard already honorably hunted. "My good fellow, what a question? But of course! A leopard is a leopard, is it not? Can't change its spots, what?" he said, chuckling at his humor. I began to see a fairly bright light at the end of this safari's tunnel.

The salted skin of a fine old tom was available. It had the typically light coloring of leopards found in that region, unlike the darker cats of the Marromeu area in the southeast. The skin was prepared carefully for the return trip the next day. When the radio communication from the office in Beira crackled into the camp's ether with the increasingly anxious question about the prince and his leopard, jubilation sailed over the static when we announced that indeed, we had secured a leopard at sundown the previous day. Unfortunately, I continued, by the time we had recovered it, Africa's inky blackness had descended; most regretfully, no photographs had been possible and, of course, the leopard had had to be skinned immediately.

The relief was immense. I had made a pragmatic decision for this was no ordinary safari. Honor was at stake, and the dictates of age-old traditions had to be accommodated. That last night, as we heard the excited muffled chatterings of hyenas on a kill in the murk, the prince made me consular agent for Swaziland in Beira.

The final episode of that amazing week occurred at Beira Airport. Turning to thank me in the presence of a mob of dignitaries, the prince admired the new shirt I was wearing to such a degree that I felt obliged to take it off right then and there and hand it to him. Someone murmured something about a "brotherhood bonding" as I made my way, barechested out into the mirage-glazed streets. This was an amazing start to my Safrique years. They were to become more so.

I did not hear from the prince again. I was in Houston when his father, King Sobhuza, died in July 1982, thirteen years after that unique safari, a year after his diamond jubilee on the Swazi throne. I scanned the papers to see if "my" prince was the successor, but a youngster was chosen, eventually becoming King Mswati III. As this manuscript goes into production, he is about to take his eighth wife.

If the prince ever reads this story or gets to hear of it, I should like him to know that I have never forgotten him, that I never regretted the decision we made together almost thirty years ago, and that I hope, when he wears his leopard-skin regalia at royal Swazi events, he recalls the time we spent in the Mozambican bush and how hard we tried.

I am in my seventy-first year as I write this. My head lies easy on the pillow at night. In over forty years of African hunting, I still believe I made the right decision in finding a cat fit for a king.

At this juncture, my life took another exceedingly lucky turn when I met Bert Klineburger of Seattle, Washington. He had come out to have a look at Mozambique's potential in the latter part of 1969, soon after I had joined Safrique. We met and formed an immediate and enduring friendship as I introduced Bert to my country. The Klineburgers ran a flourishing safari booking agency and taxidermy business and were directly instrumental in augmenting my contacts to market Mozambique throughout the States, Canada, Mexico, and elsewhere. We attended the Mzuri Safari Club meeting at exquisite Lake Tahoe in Nevada. This was a full three years before the formation of Safari Club International, today the premier hunting/conservation organization in the world whose founding convention I attended in 1972.

The Klineburgers took me under their collective wing and I accompanied Bert on a promotional tour to end all promotional tours. We went over to Victoria in British Columbia and down to several locations in Mexico, where I eventually had to say in Guadalajara, "Bert, *basta!* No more bookings. We are bursting at the safari seams now. We cannot accommodate any more clients from the Americas for the coming season." It was phenomenal.

Bert was destined to become one of the truly remarkable people I have met in my life. A hunter and booking agent of worldwide, often pioneering experience as well as a published author, it is no accident that he wrote the foreword to this book because we came to know each other very well and to trust each other completely. I never once signed contracts with any of my safari clients. Even when vast sums of money in hard currencies were involved, safaris were booked and deals clinched with a handshake. This is a risk no safari operator or client can take today. Dare I say that times have changed, for the worse.

After a quick Christmas at home in Mozambique where the news spread of the forthcoming boom year for Safrique, I shot off to Spain, France, and Italy to sign up my quota of European hunters. I always tried to keep a balance and maintain my excellent European safari client base. Being of Latin origin, I was able to communicate on several levels with the Europeans, especially with the Spaniards.

Safrique roared into new life in that season of 1970. Rather like the fire-engine-red Land Rover used for the technical inspections of our camps. It was usually driven by Pierre Maia, one of the last old-time ivory hunters in Mozambique, whom we employed as our roving inspector to keep our camps up to scratch, sort out technical and mechanical problems on the spot, and ensure that camp staff were on their collective toes. We had tractors and Caterpillars at our disposal and helped open up and maintain roads on our concessions. We were given whatever we felt we needed to run this first-class operation. The bank never second-guessed us.

Our largest camp was Nhamacala in the savanna, Concession No. 6, where we had luxury accommodation for twenty-two people. We tended to reserve the camp for emergencies and, especially, for VIP guests of the Portuguese government, or of the bank which owned the company. Just such an emergency developed when three bank guests suddenly had to be accommodated on a hunting safari, and we had no suitable vehicles left. Pierre Maia's red Land Rover was the only option we had.

I called Pierre over the radio and had him come over to Nhamacala for a couple of days as the bank guests wanted to hunt a few antelope. While Pierre was on his way, these gentlemen, all city boys from down south in the soft world of the capital, Lourenço Marques, kept telling me how hard they had found the hunting there. This was in a region bordering the famous Kruger National Park of South Africa at a place called Chicualacuala. I was told that they had to remove all objects such as wristwatches because of reflections which could disturb a stalk, and that they frequently had to crawl and crawl to get close enough to the skittish game. Imagine these guests' faces when Pierre drove into camp in his bright red 4×4. They thought they were dealing with a bunch of amateurs. A red hunting vehicle! Had the world gone mad? I loved it. I love nothing more than a challenge.

I took out our south-of-the–Save River softies with their preconceived notions. Now, I knew that the game might be a bit wary in some places where they would take off as soon as they heard a vehicle approaching. The very first animals we came across, a herd of zebra, froze as if hypnotized. It was amazing. The majority of the animals we saw that day reacted identically—even the nyala. I tell you, it was quite a show. The brief safari was successful, guests being able to get fairly close to their quarry before getting out for the mandatory stalk.

I have mentioned this story often because it is not typical. Back at camp, with three very satisfied guests around the fire while we waited for the dinner drum, we discussed this situation at length and wondered if the animals were color-blind to red. Most safari hunting vehicles are dark green or khaki, and I wondered what would have been the result had we decided to have a fleet of red vehicles instead. I know Selous and several of the classic African hunting authors dealt with this aspect of protective coloration in the bush. Maybe the red was so different that the animals did not associate it with humans and potential danger.

Talking of danger and fiery colors, I was exceptionally lucky in not ever having suffered serious injury while hunting, but there were some very dangerous moments. In the early 1960s, a veterinary surgeon from the States grazed my scalp with an accidental discharge from his rifle. I took him back to camp and had another hunter accompany him for the rest of his safari. There is such a thing as tempting fate! Then there was the time when I was out hunting elephant, also with a client from the States. I was carrying a .458 Winchester Magnum, my favorite rifle for years before I got to know the Weatherby rifles. We were resting up in the heat of the day, on the spoor of a fine old bull. I had my back to a baobab tree, my rifle leaning against the trunk of a smaller tree nearby. There was a bush fire a mile away which did not pose any hazard for us. We had had some water and were chatting quietly when we heard an odd noise from the direction of the bush fire. There, through the haze of the smoke and bush came a young bull elephant. It was running straight at us, but I was not alarmed, as it was not charging us as such. It seemed to be escaping the fire and heat behind it.

In a flash, everything changed. Suddenly the elephant sped up and bore down on us with petrifying speed. I looked for my assistant. He had already vanished! And my rifle was about twenty feet from me, against that tree which seemed impossibly far away as my thundering heart nearly choked my breath off from my lungs. With adrenaline-induced velocity, I managed to grab my rifle and, with a crazed young bull just a few yards away, I had to fire. A brain shot. A very lucky shot. The young male collapsed and died at my feet. The client was up a tree, my assistant hunter nowhere to be seen, and my two trackers up another tree.

The results of my 1969 promotional trip to the States and elsewhere, in close cooperation with Bert Klineburger, were beginning to flow in by early 1970. That year saw Safrique host significant hunters, some of whom I was privileged to accompany. One such person was General Jimmy Doolittle who entered the history books for his bombing raid over Tokyo in April, 1942.

General Doolittle had a grand sense of humor, frequently cracking us up in the middle of the bush. His hunting companions, Dick Farr and Wayne Ewing, helped make the Doolittle safari one of the most enjoyable I can recall. The general was a fine shot, not surprising when one thinks of the job he once performed. The holder of many records and prestigious positions, Doolittle remained unaffected by it all. Quite a number of military men are hunters, which flows from their familiarity with weapons and the need to face challenges. I hit it off with such hunters every time.

Our clients were not always young. Here, I recall Dr. Charles Hendricks of Pennsylvania who was a gun collector of note and a superb shot. Already in his eighties, Dr. Hendricks had the vigor and spirit of a man half his age. A certain baron also comes to mind when thinking about older clients. I was a guest on the Aznars' vast hunting estate in Spain at one stage where I met the baron. He and I were quickly on first-name terms, the baron expressing his eagerness to come out to Mozambique to hunt. I was invited to come to Paris as soon as possible to discuss this.

Not long afterward, I flew to Paris and was ushered up to the baron's sumptuous office suite with its bank of telephones on his desk. When I walked in, I greeted the baron by his first name, extending my hand. He remained seated and reminded me to address him by his title and family name!

Not missing a beat, I explained immediately that I had called in person to regretfully inform him that our next couple of seasons were fully booked and that he could not be accommodated. With that, I took my leave of the baron. My safari seasons were always "fully booked" thereafter. The same held true for the number-one legal man in France, a *Maître* (attorney), retained by the rich and famous. He was already hunting with Safrique when I took over the field management. Word reached me that unethical practices were taking place at the good *Maître*'s camp.

I paid a surprise flying visit when I knew for a fact that he and his professional hunter were in the field and I ascertained that the reports were correct. Female animals had been shot, and the quota for the good *Maître* had been exceeded. I fired the hunter that day and blackballed the *Maître* forever after from Safrique's concessions. My colleagues wrung their hands and tried to impress upon me what an important man he was and so forth. He remained blackballed, the hunter remained fired, and I remain satisfied to this day that that is the only way to deal with unacceptable behavior in any business.

Mozambique was taking off as a superb, refreshingly new destination for the international big-game hunter. What launched us in absolutely spectacular fashion was the arrival of several astronauts between August, 1971 and July, 1973. The Bank, with Bert Klineburger masterminding the operation from the outset, hosted as their special guests in Mozambique in August 1971 astronauts James Lovell, commander of the *Apollo 13* mission to the moon, and Stuart Roosa, commander of the *Apollo 14* mission.

This was a unique time for us all and a very strong vote of confidence in Mozambique's still poorly known potential as an international hunting and tourism destination. We all met up in Lisbon and, amid much official protocol-laden pomp, we accompanied the astronauts and their wives on the aircraft out to Mozambique and tremendous publicity and excitement. The welcome reserved was heartfelt and, when I think back on those wonderful days over thirty years ago, there was a genuineness of hospitality and warmth which made one feel hopeful for the future.

Of course, Lisbon was set to make political capital out of this high-profile visit, which was perfectly legitimate. Countries do this all the time. We, on the ground, simply wanted our safari business to take deep and responsible roots, not only for our personal futures, but for the overall good of Mozambique. Anything which enhanced sound international relations increased the chances of improved economic prospects. This was good for the wildlife because of a consistent and responsible presence over a vast region where poaching could be contained. The conservation of our wilderness areas and the fauna and flora cost money, and controlled hunting was starting to generate greater and greater income for Mozambique. Whether it always went where it should have gone is another matter entirely. Sound principles were in place, however, and we were starting to host the sort of people who could spread the word and help us in Mozambique to progress.

We celebrated Stu Roosa's thirty-eighth birthday at the hugely atmospheric Pompue Camp on the Pompue River, southeast of our family farm. With its comfortable wooden chalets and dining hut, ensconced among giant trees at the very heart of big-five country, the camp was a refuge after tough hunting. Stu was presented with a gigantic elephant-turd "birthday cake" with a candle stuck into it, the brainchild of Bert Klineburger's wife, Brigitte! Of course, we had a special cake baked with lunar motifs to decorate it as we went all out to celebrate his birthday in a way we knew would probably not be celebrated again in his life. I was greatly saddened to learn, subsequently, that Roosa died very young.

My chief tracker, Radio, when introduced to the astronauts and told of their landing on the moon, looked at me quizzically for a moment, stared up at the moon that night, and then asked, "*Patrão* we cannot always see the moon. Didn't they get lost going there?"

James Lovell returned the following year, 1972, with his son and with fellow astronaut, Donald "Deke" Slayton, the chief instructor for the Apollo missions. We were fortunate to have had such successful safaris with the astronauts that a special honor came my way in the form of an invitation to attend the official launch of *Apollo 17* in December that year in Florida, preceded by a special party attended by the who's who in the astronaut business. It was a great time to be alive, and this level of personal recommendation for hunting safaris in Mozambique was of incalculable value.

In the early days of Safrique, through Bert Klineburger, I was fortunate to meet and hunt with Roy Weatherby of Weatherby rifle fame. We hit it off immediately. One truly memorable day, when Roy lost a wounded kudu at twilight and we could no longer track it after dark, he turned to me and said, "Adelino, when are we going to manufacture a rifle to stop these damn things?" He was shooting a .300 Weatherby Magnum!

Now, I do not purport to be a ballistics expert, but I have always liked the Weatherby rifles, having owned several of them, personal gifts from Roy. In fact, at the time, I had Alejandro, the eleven-year-old son, and Rocio, the sixteen-year-old daughter, of Eduardo and Loli Aznar, hunt lion, buffalo, and the whole range of plains game with two .240 Weatherby Magnums which are still in perfect condition and in use to this day in Spain. It was the fashion at one stage to knock Weatherbys. This was often the case with the English, prima donna East African crowd. I have always suspected it had little to do with ballistics and a lot more to do with a deep-seated complex about Americans and their entrepreneurial skills.

Through Roy, I was honored on several occasions to attend the Weatherby banquet in the States where a very prestigious award was made to international big-game hunters. I am not much for the chest-thumping aspects of hunting, as it can encourage an unhealthy level of aggression and competitiveness which has nothing to do with hunting and everything to do with ego. Roy's banquets, however, were different. He had style, taste, and humor. His death was a particular loss because he was my friend, a kind and generous man whom everyone respected.

June 1972 saw a veritable invasion from the States when a sixty-strong group of an elite, VIP-packed club called the African First Shotters arrived in Mozambique to hunt. Safrique's impressive facilities were put to the test, and we had to juggle the logistics to have everybody well accommodated and spread about our "empire." That party attracted a fresh blaze of magnificent publicity, thanks to the groundwork and follow-through, once again, of Bert Klineburger.

From this sustained upsurge in business flowed further promotional activities in the States, starting with the Game COIN conferences in San Antonio, Texas from 1971 onward. There, I met great characters such as Harry Tennison and Stan Studer and developed a liking for Texas and the Texans. Our safari bookings were filling up nicely. We hosted Alaskan outfitters, who offered to return the favor if I would accept their offer for an Alaskan hunt. After some thought, I could not see myself hunting in those subzero temperatures. I had spent all but the first eight years of my life in temperatures which often exceeded 100°F. The heat and dryness of the Zambezi Valley, and the steaming wetness of our coastal concessions alone had permanently programmed me away from snow and bears. And this brings to mind something special. . . .

The American oil prospecting industry played a direct role in providing me and all at Safrique with a genuinely unique vehicle for our Concession No. 10 in the humid, swampy paradise of the Marromeu Flats, on the Indian Ocean. Monster swamp buggies. Manufactured in Lafayette, Louisiana, they had been brought out to Mozambique by Mozambique Gulf Oil under the general management of Dave Dawson, himself a keen hunter. We acquired thirteen of these amphibious vehicles with gigantic tires seven feet high, introducing a fantastic dimension to our Marromeu safaris.

We could move in among herds of literally thousands of buffalo and waterbuck, coming so close that we could almost touch the animals. Clouds of egrets would rise before us as these four-cylinder Ford-engine buggies plowed through the papyrus, reeds, and muddy mangrove flats, past palm-fringed islets and on under endless blue skies. The big-bodied buff would routinely stand, transfixed and staring, their malevolent eyes not quite believing what they were seeing, we humans high above them with ringside seats at one of Africa's great natural spectacles. Although the Marromeu buffalo horns rarely went over 40 inch spreads—the best buffalo in Mozambique being found high up in the mountainous regions—the No. 10 experience never failed to enrapture even the most experienced of hunters and international travelers.

Other much-smaller gadgets had a way of rendering unforgettable a hunting safari with Safrique. Take, for example, the American client with a state-of-the-art tape-recording device secured to his chest with a microphone on his shirtfront. During an elephant hunt, the client was charged, the elephant actually falling onto him as it collapsed from a perfectly positioned brain shot by the professional hunter, Luiz Santos. The entire drama was captured on tape from the staccato breathing during the stalk to the warning cries, yells and general uproar of the charge and fatal shot. The florid-language "soundtrack" was an experience in itself. As for the client, most of his body turned crimson-purple from very severe bruising. He was lucky not to have broken any bones or to have been killed. Had that episode been filmed, we would have had a winner.

On the political front, the presence of Portuguese soldiers in Mozambique had swelled to more than 35,000 by August 1970. In May of that year, the massive "Gordian Knot" offensive was launched under the Commander of Land Forces in Mozambique, General Kaulza de Arriaga, with whom I would eventually lock horns. The objective was to regain the Frelimo-controlled areas in the far north of the country. By September 1970, almost the whole of Cabo Delgado and some of neighboring Niassa Province had been swept clean of Frelimo guerrillas. The Portuguese embarked on an ambitious plan to construct a network of roads linking new settlements to be built from the coast inland, close to the Tanzanian border, and a series of new landing strips.

Meanwhile, some 250,000 tribal people had already been resettled in about 150 fortified villages, *aldeamentos*, in Cabo Delgado, bordering on Tanzania. This was part of a strategy to deny local support to the Frelimo guerrillas infiltrating from their bases in Tanzania and also to curb intimidation of the local people, many of whom had no idea what was afoot, just that their usually predictable, rural lives were being overwhelmed by forces and ideas quite alien to anything they had known.

A low-intensity guerrilla war was now under way. Frelimo had been stunned at the scale and results of the "Gordian Knot" offensive, taking a decision which was to be the beginning of the end of Mozambique as we all knew it, certainly of my life and that of my family in Mozambique. Rather than attempt to fight back in the north, Frelimo moved its guerrillas in 1970 through Malawi, with President-for-Life Hastings Banda turning a blind eye at the time, and activated operations in the Tete district, north of the Zambezi River. This forced De Arriaga to switch his attention from the north to the Zambezi region, spreading the Portuguese forces more thinly on the ground, and placing increasing strain on the war budget back in Portugal. The guerrillas then started a campaign of unsuccessful attacks on the massive Cabora Bassa Dam, but these attacks on the dam were the direct reason why the South African and the Rhodesian military were drawn into active service in Tete district. Attacks were now being launched on the crucially important Salisbury-Blantyre road, linking Rhodesia and Malawi, through Tete.

Mozambique's towns remained remarkably quiet and safe throughout, these guerrilla attacks often occurring in wild, isolated country. This was not widely known or their occurrence was duly censored by the military authorities. The general public was never given the whole picture immediately. Had they known what was now afoot, alarm and despondency would have set in overnight.

We in the safari business spent our lives in the wilds and in close contact with the local tribal people, from whom our trackers, skinners, cooks, drivers, and general camp staff were drawn. We spoke their languages; we knew their villages; sometimes we had spent years closely associated with one another. Often two or more generations of the same family would be in our employ. A relationship of strong, broad-based trust developed with some of these people and they would talk to us of changes in the air, of danger.

In early July 1972, Safrique's safari calendar jam-packed for the entire season, I was out hunting with two executives from Morgan Guaranty Trust Bank in the States not far from the family farm in Guro. My chief tracker, Radio, came to me one night, while we were out fly camping, and said: "*Patrão*, there is trouble coming. We must be strong because lions do not talk to hyenas." He did not elaborate, and I did not push him. He was warning me, and it could only have referred to Frelimo. Not one week later, I discovered in a few terrible hours just what Radio had meant.

FOUR

LIONS DO NOT TALK TO HYENAS

Africa is burning because it is being set on fire from outside.

—Antonio de Oliveira Salazar

Inhasalala Camp calling. Inhasalala Camp calling. Pompue Camp has been burned to the ground! Everything is destroyed! Pompue staff is here, safe. Get Adelino! Urgent! Repeat, urgent!"

Gabbling with shock on July 26, 1972, Armindo Vieira's voice came over the radio in static bursts as Safrique headquarters in Beira received the news. Frelimo guerrillas had now penetrated the huge hunting concessions for the first time in Manica Sofala Province, many hundreds of miles south of their original bases over the Rovuma River in Tanzania. Once distant, the war was now a reality which would engulf our homes and our lives, Black and White alike, sweeping away an entire way of life in hatred and madness whose effects are still being felt decades later.

I had just flown into Beira the previous day from the Pompue area to prepare for the imminent arrival of Valéry Giscard d'Estaing, then Minister of Finance of France and eventually president of that country. He was a very keen and experienced big-game hunter. I had a potential catastrophe on my hands. The minister's visit was being kept completely out of the press, at his strict request. All we needed now was sudden attention by the media on a region where he was scheduled to hunt. Worse, the implications for his safety were now dire. I got on an aircraft that same day and flew over the still smoking, blackened site of Pompue Camp before heading straight for our family farm at Guro, which was just southwest of there. My mother was alone at the farm, except for the staff, and I now feared for her safety. In guerrilla terminology, she was a soft target.

As we leveled for touchdown on the landing strip I helped scrape that desperate night sixteen years previous for the emergency medical evacuation of my father to Beira, I felt my throat go dry and the rage start to surge. Below me was an oasis in arid, tough country, home to several hundred people with whom we had lived on good terms for decades, where game flourished and life had a purpose. Nobody ever starved. No sick person was ever ignored. Now everything we knew and treasured was being threatened by faceless guerrillas who moved at night, struck at will, and left traumatized people in their revolutionary wake.

The human hyenas had arrived.

I was not entirely surprised. Not eight days earlier, on July 18, to be precise, I had called at the farm in the middle of a safari to wish my mother a happy birthday, accompanied by the two executives from the Morgan Guaranty Trust Bank, mentioned at the close of the previous chapter, who were hunting with me.

My mother immediately told me that our staff had warned her a couple of days beforehand that Frelimo guerrillas had been spotted in the area and that I was to exercise particular caution from then on. When I expressed my concern for her safety, she replied, "Nothing will happen to me, son." Our family could have been annihilated at will as we lived very openly, but we survived. There was a reason for this, which was given to me later on by Frelimo guerrilla commanders to my face.

The smell of danger was now everywhere. Our farmhouse and entire huge property had no keys in any door locks, no barred windows, no electrified perimeter fencing, and no alarm systems of any sort. What desperate irony as I write these words on the eve of the new millennium and realize that all such security precautions are an everyday feature throughout neighboring South Africa, where crime levels are unprecedented in every possible category, and where farmers are being slaughtered left and right in numbers which make a mockery of anything the Angolans, Kenyans, Mozambicans, or Rhodesians had to endure in their years of guerrilla warfare.

The Frelimo guerrillas had arrived in the murk of the previous night, like a pack of slavering jackals looking for easy pickings. They had rounded up the staff at Pompue Camp and threatened them with instant death at the receiving end of their AK-47 assault rifles if they did not get the hell out of there while they stole all our food supplies, medical kits, a two-way radio, and blankets before torching the camp which was reduced to a burned-out skeleton and smoldering ash by daybreak. Vehicles, all accommodation, all furnishings, generators, and equipment of every imaginable kind at that camp were destroyed in a few hours, the careful, sustained investment of years wiped out with a few matches, some gasoline and limitless hatred.

The guerrillas were not from Manica Sofala. According to the Pompue staff, they belonged to other tribes from the far north and spoke a different language. As the guerrillas started sloshing gasoline about the place, the members of the camp staff fled on foot, heading for Inhasalala Camp about thirty-five miles away over rough terrain where predators lurked.

The staff arrived at dawn and alerted Armindo Vieira, whom everyone knew by his nickname, "Marabu," the African stork. He got hold of the Beira office by radio before fleeing with all the staff, overcome with panic. Life had taken an inalterable turn for the worse that day. Nobody would escape the effects of this bitter bush war. It pitted guerrillas against metropolitan Portuguese forces, and Mozambicans against one another. It divided families, sowing fear, distrust, and suffering in a country which had been remarkably integrated and peaceful, despite its undoubted problems and deep-seated injustices.

The sustained publicity in the Mozambican and Portuguese press concerning Safrique's elite clientele, people with clout in their home countries who were becoming eloquent ambassadors for Mozambique, was a major factor in encouraging the eventual attacks on our concessions. The publicity had become a two-edged sword. The Pompue attack that chilly July night in 1972 signaled a new and increasing threat to a significant part of the Mozambican population and further attacks, such as a car ambush a mere five miles from Guro the day before the Pompue outrage, and the blowing up of a section of the Beira-Tete railway line that same year, had a profoundly damaging psychological effect on many people.

With Frelimo's entry into the Manica region, the unraveling of the colonial fabric started accelerating and I was caught up in the very heart of it all from day one. My own mother was eventually ambushed near the farm as she was on her way to Tete. An AK-toting teenager in scraps of camouflage flagged her down, motioning her and the driver to get out of the vehicle. My mother, a very direct and fearless woman, berated the youngster for not addressing her correctly and politely, saying that she was on her way to Tete on business and would he kindly step out of the way. She and the driver remained seated in the vehicle. The kid recognized my mother instantly and said: "Sorry, Dona Maria. You may pass." And she did, not being harassed again.

I then took a decision to fly to Guro, go on to Pompue, and enter the war in my own way. We had radios, landing strips, food supplies, serviceable vehicles, intimate knowledge of the terrain, the ability to track human and animal spoor, and knowledge of local languages and customs. More importantly, we had the trust of significant sections of the local population, some of whom were our right-hand men in the bush and had been so for years. We belonged. The deployed soldiers from Portugal did not and never would. We had a territorial imperative to defend our homes. They were there under military orders given by some officers who were the core of the problem from the outset. The "captains"—these left-leaning so-called intellectuals—had their hearts and minds firmly anchored back in Portugal and socialist rhetoric. They had no motivation to imbue the troops with fight, with purpose, with vision—because they had none themselves. I knew in a flash we were alone.

Some hours after my arrival at our farm, a light aircraft buzzed the farmhouse and came in to land. I went down to the airstrip in one of our vehicles and got there just as a friend of mine was getting out of the aircraft. It was Colonel Zigfredo Costa Campos, the officer commanding the *Grupos Especiais Paraquedistas,* the GEPs. These were mostly Black Mozambican crack commandos who had been trained up very late in the day in an effort to contain the spreading guerrilla contagion. The colonel and I were destined to become deeply involved in really clandestine aspects of the war. We frequently flew to the various GEP camps in the region in his self-piloted Auster aircraft, a solid bond of mutual trust already forged between us.

Costa Campos quickly drew me aside as I noticed a second person alighting. It was Jorge Jardim, a Salazar confidant until the latter's death in 1970. He was a greatly complex man who would eventually enjoy more power in Mozambique than the often-dreaded PIDE. We were never friends, despite the mendacious rubbish published about me years later by Frelimo hacks. As far back as 1953, I had become known for my attitude to those who siphoned off the economic lifeblood of Mozambique and who carefully stored their wealth elsewhere. The Jardim clan knew my attitudes. They did not remotely share them. I was a "separatist," a White Mozambican who wanted autonomy for Mozambique and an end to its economic rape by that cozy cartel of Portuguese families. I was never part of the Portugal clique.

"Adelino, be careful! Jardim and the authorities suspect you are with Frelimo and that you are behind these attacks."

The colonel's words stunned me. Had we not all been in such a threatening situation, I would have convulsed with laughter. Now I really was on my guard because I realized I was dealing with political paranoia of the first order, with people who immediately regarded one as an enemy because their views, instead of being accepted cravenly, were questioned and challenged.

In the meantime, fellow professional hunter Carlos Costa Neves and I drove over to Guro Camp, which was about twenty miles from the farmhouse, to collect the hunting rifles, the radio, and other essential equipment which we had always left in total safety in the camp, between safaris, even if nobody was there. Overnight, times had changed forever. Back at the farmhouse, I radioed another great friend, Steve Liversedge, and asked him to drive over to what remained of Pompue Camp where we could meet the next morning. He was working for us and was at Nhamacala Camp, some way off.

Costa Campos and I were joined by another good friend and fellow hunter, Pierre Maia of red Land Rover fame. I left certain instructions with the farm staff concerning my mother, who was remarkably calm and determined to stay right where she was in the world she had helped build from bush at great personal sacrifice. We then headed for the settlement of Macossa to step up protection for the chefe de posto, who was now a major target of the guerrillas, as the symbol of Portuguese authority in the bush. We did not speak much as we drove over a road I had traveled countless times and through bush where I had felt so safe and free for so long. Being winter, the light was starting to fade quite fast as we drove into Macossa. With nightfall came the hugely increased risk of an ambush.

At first light the next day, we drove over to the remains of Pompue Camp, where Steve was already waiting for us. We were quickly joined by a platoon of *"pisteiros,"* trackers of the so-called elite Portuguese army unit from Portugal who were based at Vila Gouveia, over 90 miles away. I had my trackers with me, men of vast local experience who read the ground like a newspaper. This was going to be interesting.

"Let's go!" I said, ready to track the guerrillas in belated hot pursuit with Steve and our group. One of the *pisteiros* then spoke on behalf of his men, declining because they could not find the tracks for the confusion of spoor around the burned-out camp. In any case, I was told, the men had not brought rations with them and would therefore have to return to their camp at Vila Gouveia. Their mothers would have been proud of them. This was the flower of the Portuguese army! God help Mozambique, I thought.

I snapped, telling the lot to get the hell out as all they were now doing was adding to the confusion and that we had no time to babysit a bunch of incompetents. With Steve, our own trackers, and Jardim and his group in tow, we took off. Literally, within five minutes, we had found the right spoor. We set a murderous pace and managed to follow the tracks of the group of guerrillas up a mountainside and into a cache of supplies which had been taken the previous night from the Pompue Camp—blankets and beer, for the most part.

We chased the guerrillas for the whole of the next day, losing and then finding their tracks again as they bombshelled and backtracked across dry riverbeds. We suffered from the heat and the tension, but we pushed on, Jardim developing very painful blisters in the process. I like to think I had something to do with that. I realized that the guerrillas had been in the immediate region for the entire week I had been close by, hunting with the Morgan Guaranty Trust bankers right under their noses and probably in their sights. The guerrillas were an advance guard. Their tracks eventually bombshelled definitively and we were obliged to give up before Jardim radioed for a military helicopter which picked us up and returned us to our vehicles amid the ashes of Pompue Camp.

Giscard d'Estaing was about to arrive in Mozambique, and we had to make urgent changes to his itinerary in order to keep him as safe as possible and to prevent the Pompue attack from leaking before he arrived. It was damage control of the first magnitude. All we needed was a murdered French cabinet minister, and we could close shop forever.

"Adelino, to prove to you that hunting is more important than politics, I have yet to report to the president!"

Giscard d'Estaing had just arrived from Iran and had come straight to his Ministry of Finance offices in Paris from the airport. Apparently, President Pompidou could indeed wait while we fine-tuned D'Estaing's forthcoming safari to Mozambique. He and I had been in touch and I had been asked to come to Paris to finalize details.

With the Pompue Camp fiasco barely behind us, the D'Estaing party arrived in Beira, where they were met on the apron and immediately whisked away by air taxi straight into Nhamacala Camp in the savanna, south of Pompue Camp, two PIDE agents accompanying them throughout for security reasons.

D'Estaing was accompanied by his delightful wife, Anne-Aymone, two sons, two daughters, and fellow Frenchman and hunter/companion, Maurice Patry, who had spent decades in Gabon as a hunter/outfitter. I never elaborated on the Pompue tragedy, saying that there had been a slight change of itinerary because the Pompue area was suffering from drought. We hunted in three of our concessions before the party flew out, spending that last day at my home in Beira rather than at a hotel, where D'Estaing may have attracted undue attention. We did not discuss politics at all. D'Estaing was a true hunter, as opposed to a plain collector/killer. He took only record-class animals, preferring to pass up a mediocre animal than to simply fill out his safari quota. He was a fair chase, disciplined man in the bush, representing the apex of the French market I had been fortunate to cultivate. As future developments will indicate, we remained on very good terms.

The D'Estaing party had not been in camp for more than a couple of days when I received a call from General Kaulza de Arriaga, requesting to see D'Estaing. He duly arrived with Jorge Jardim, and the two spent some time in earnest talk with the French minister. I have no doubt they were conferring with D'Estaing as to the deteriorating security situation in Mozambique. I kept my distance.

The whiff of unrest in Manica Sofala was now turning into the stench of impending revolution, so much so that the Costa Campos GEPs set up their base on our farm at Guro because of the availability of water and all other basic amenities. I got to know Costa Campos much better, taking him hunting in increasingly "hot" areas. He would pilot us in his Auster to visit GEP camps which had been installed in places where Safrique had had to terminate safaris because of escalating guerrilla activities. Costa Campos could see how motivated I was not to be hounded out of the only place on earth I shall ever consider as my real home—Mozambique, especially the bush.

It is now safe to speak openly for the first time of a remarkable Black soldier from the then Portuguese Guinea-Bissau, a sergeant José Ribeiro, code-named Carnaval, and of a totally clandestine group he headed and with whom I worked very closely between 1972 and 1973. I never met his equal in the entire Portuguese army. If I carry only one valiant memory of the Mozambican bush war, it will be of Carnaval. I was best man at his wedding in Beira, an honor I treasure.

Carnaval and Costa Campos had fought together in Guinea-Bissau before Costa Campos was posted to Mozambique, bringing the sergeant with him. Within the GEPs was a twenty-five-man-strong entity called the Mandiocas, headed by Carnaval. They were ex-Frelimo or *turned* guerrillas whom Costa Campos allowed me to use in a series of very successful operations for almost two years. They were brought into Safrique disguised as employees. In their operations they mostly carried AK-47 rifles, also with the drum magazines, which had been taken off Frelimo guerrillas.

The Mandiocas would go into villages in Manica Sofala, disguised as Frelimo fighters, to gauge the political sympathies of the chiefs and the tribesmen. They were usually very well received but, sometimes, they would be rejected at a village. The information gathered was passed on, this group proving to be more effective than most of the Portuguese army during that period. You cannot fight any war without fresh and accurate intelligence assessments. This was to be one of the fatal weaknesses of the Portuguese forces in Mozambique.

I was able to talk to General de Arriaga around that time and tell him very plainly how I felt about the whole situation. He did not like what he heard from me. Neither did his two companions, both very senior PIDE men, who no doubt promptly filled out more reports for my already-fat file at PIDE headquarters in Lisbon. I warned them that they could never win an unconventional war by using largely conventional methods. Such was my insistence that day, that De Arriaga authorized me to receive twenty-four G-3 rifles for distribution to the professional hunters working for Safrique. The rifles used 7.62 NATO ammunition. De Arriaga had hunted with me previously and I had exchanged a Weatherby .22 LR rifle with him for an AK-47 which I now carried with me at all times. Special canvas covers were made for the G-3 rifles so as not to alarm our safari clients.

I gave repeated and severe warnings to our professional hunters. They had to become increasingly vigilant because we were going to be hit sooner or later. They largely ignored my warnings.

Then it happened.

On July 1, 1973, at 9:10 A.M., as a safari party of five was descending from a brand-new Aero-Commander at our base camp at Nhamacala 125 miles north of Beira, Frelimo guerrillas struck in a massive machine-gun attack from the long grass, 80 yards from the airstrip, peppering the tanks, killing one member and injuring two more before vanishing. It was all over in seconds, the flabbergasted professional hunters waiting at the strip with not a firearm in sight.

The dead man had been shot straight through his heart. He was Dr. Angel Garazaibal, an eminent Spanish surgeon and personal physician to General Franco, who remained head of state in Spain until his death in 1975. Consequently, the repercussions of this attack were felt at that level in Spain. The injured man was none other than the scion of the Osborne sherry empire, Enrique Macpherson Osborne. His wife, Macha, had been hit in a toe. The other two persons who escaped death and injury that day were the Spanish couple, Ricardo Cayo Garcia Montes and his wife, Isabel Iguiguren. They were back on their second safari in Mozambique, accompanied by Carlos Costa Neves.

One of the hunters at the rondavel near the airstrip grabbed a G-3 and started shooting on full automatic at where he thought the terrorists had been lying in wait in the grass, but it was already hopelessly too late. The group was long gone. Now, I thought, maybe someone would start listening to my repeated warnings that the guerrillas would be stepping up their activities in our hunting concessions.

I was supposed to have been on that flight but, once again, a change in plans probably saved my life. Panic gripped the Safrique office in Beira when the news came through and I was on the next possible flight out to Nhamacala where, once again, I was faced with the trauma of initiating arrangements for the removal of a body and the medical evacuation of injured people, thankfully not seriously so. A Portuguese convoy not more than three miles away refused to assist us in going in pursuit of the guerrillas. The officer in charge of the convoy replied that he first had to obtain permission from his officer commanding in Maringué, about thirty miles away.

The OC shot back his decision: "No! Your duty is to escort trucks, not chase guerrillas!"

The nervous voices of the Beira office crackled over the radio again. General de Arriaga was demanding to see me at once in Beira. I shot back in pretty strong language: "Tell General de Arriaga the action is here, not in Beira. If he wants to see me, tell him to fly down here. We still have whiskey, beer, and a nice camp. He knows the camp because he has hunted with me. He will not have to go without hot and cold water because I'm still here. I'm not quitting!"

Let it be said now that Isabel Iguiguren and her husband had more courage than most of the so-called men that day. They were not about to let anybody ruin their safari, least of all faceless revolutionaries. In my experience, the Spanish women who came on safari tended to be rather special people, with few peers. Isabel wrote a book in which she described that traumatic day and the safari that followed.

We were all obliged to return to Beira briefly where the injured were hospitalized. The Safrique office took care of the distressing formalities to repatriate the body of Dr. Garazaibal. It was inevitable that the press would get hold of the story, which made headlines in Mozambique and in Europe. We quickly reformulated plans in order to continue the safari on Concessions No. 10 and 12 on the Marromeu Flats, bordering the Indian Ocean. They were now the only guerrilla-free hunting areas we still had.

While we were back in Beira, the Banco Nacional Ultramarino, the owners of Safrique, held a high-level meeting about the Nhamacala tragedy and decided that it was time to withdraw. Naturally, I was at the meeting, and I refused to abandon the camps. Withdrawing was not even for discussion with me. I can remember shouting at the bank crowd and at the other Safrique directors that day: "Lisbon and Lourenço Marques are not in charge anymore! You may be so in the cities up as far as Dondo (twenty miles north of Beira), but from then on it is the man with the machine gun who is in charge. I have a machine gun. I'm in charge now. So to hell with the lot of you, and that's the end of this conversation!"

Then I left the room.

With three other camps in that area where we could no longer take clients because of the guerrillas, I needed professional hunter volunteers to help me consolidate Nhamacala. This was where I was in for a third profound shock after the attack and the gutless display by the toy soldiers in their convoy. Some of my professional hunters at Safrique had been born in Mozambique, but the majority evaded helping me out. In shameful contrast to these individuals was Carnaval, the Black Guinea-Bissau paratrooper, whom I trusted completely. He never left my side; he never sidestepped danger of any sort, neither did his men. Greater is the shame that he was to die an inglorious death fighting for the South Africans, as I shall explain later.

A tiny group eventually came forward to assist me and Carnaval's Mandiocas in regrouping whatever we could possibly save and move from the other camps. The Safrique office said it did not matter if all was lost. I rejected this with a contempt I still feel. We refused to cancel a single safari to the very end of the season of 1973. I was accused of trying to be another Mike "Congo" Hoare, but I paid no attention. I have always marched to my own drum, sometimes with negative consequences, it is true. That tragic day at the Nhamacala airstrip galvanized me into action for my own private war, Carnaval and his men at my side throughout. I had the complete support of Carnaval's commanding officer. No safari clients were aware that these men in camp were anything but safari staff.

With our hunting areas now very much reduced, we only had our two concessions in the Marromeu area, bordering the Indian Ocean, which were still free of guerrillas. I had to ask Cayo and Isabel if they would mind sharing camp facilities on the Marromeu for a few days with Charles Duke of *Apollo 16* fame and with his wife, Dotty. With characteristic graciousness, they agreed, Isabel being very excited at the prospect of being able to meet someone who had actually walked on the moon. Details of the Duke safari can now be revealed for the first time. Steve Liversedge was part of the Duke safari, as was Carlos Costa Neves.

Charlie Duke had already successfully hunted several species such as leopard, bushbuck, waterbuck, reedbuck, sable, Lichtenstein hartebeest, and buffalo. We all became involved in a lion hunt to end them all. Cayo had come across a splendidly maned animal in the swamps, on the edge of dense mangrove vegetation. Well and good, but unfortunately he hit it in the paw. Before he could take aim and place the shot where it should have gone, the lion bounded into the mangroves.

Now, anyone who has ever seen a mangrove swamp up close will tell you that it is treacherously difficult to negotiate. There is no open, clear, firm ground on which to walk. It is a twisted mass of roots where you can break an ankle or a leg before you have taken two steps. Cayo and his professional hunter, Carlos Costa Neves, were big men and this would have made the going even tougher in that dangerous terrain where a lightly wounded and still very mobile lion had all the advantages.

When Charlie had had a chance to digest the implications of this situation, he looked at me and said, "Adelino. If you go in, I'll go in." I quickly thought about the press if an astronaut was killed by a lion. But, backed by my chief tracker, Radio, who had the most phenomenal eyesight and hearing, and his assistant, I decided it was a calculated risk and that we would go in after Cayo's lion.

No sooner had we started the painfully slow maneuvers inside the mangroves when even hunters with nerve-damaged hearing would have picked up the low, liquid rumbling sound of the lion. Then silence, broken only by the occasional cries of marsh birds above and, let it be said, my heart thudding in my ears. Maybe this had not been such a good idea after all.

There was little warning—an urgent sign from Radio, and then shots shattering the oppressive tension. Charlie shot true, and the lion, superbly camouflaged in a devilish morass of roots, dank foliage and mud, fell dead, not more than a handful of yards from our party. Such was the impenetrability of the terrain that we knew we would never be able to take out the lion for skinning back at our camp. It had to be done on the spot, the head and skin being removed with immense effort. We had honored the code and not left a wounded animal. It was a bit of a letdown for Cayo that he had not been able to be in on the kill, but it was his lion as he had fired the first shot which had wounded it. The animal had been taken honorably on terrain where humans were at a dangerous disadvantage.

With most species on license in the Marromeu area now taken, we were ready to leave. Isabel and Cayo flew back to Beira and, in theory, that is what the Dukes and I should have done. It was then that I made a decision which could have gone fatally wrong for us all. My instinct, however, told me to proceed. I drew Charlie aside and explained that because of escalating guerrilla activities, our other concessions were now officially off-limits. That meant that Charlie could not get his nyala or kudu, amongst other species, and that his safari had to be cut short. I remember saying, "Charlie, I don't want to influence you at all. Your safari is nearly over. You've got your leopard, your buffalo and whatever else you could take in this area. You can go home now, and I'll go back to my war."

Duke asked, "Where are you going now?"

I replied, "Back to Nhamacala, where Franco's doctor was killed the other week."

He replied, "Well, if you're going back there, we're coming, too. I trust you, Adelino. Make your plans. Dotty and I are going with you."

I then spoke to Carnaval and explained our real intentions and that nobody at all in the camp was to know about them. I put out the story that we were now off to Gorongosa Game Reserve for some really special photographs. Mr. Duke wanted to go up to elephants and so on with his rifle, but just to have pictures taken. I explained that we would have to pack up the entire camp and move over to Gorongosa in two vehicles. The staff seemed quite happy with the idea, many coming from that area and now having a chance to visit their home villages again. My chief tracker, Radio, was especially happy at the idea, as his village was southeast of the towering Gorongosa Mountain.

Off we went the next day, effectively entering Gorongosa where we spent the night at Chitengo Rest Camp. I had an odd sensation upon seeing Chitengo again. It had been my "baby" a solid twenty years previously. I knew that life as we had known it in this wild Eden of over 2,000 square miles, larger than the state of Delaware and the average size of some of our hunting concessions, had altered forever. The more I realized this, the more determined I was to defend what I loved and to fight to the end, however it came, whenever it came.

And it was coming.

At 3:00 A.M. the next morning, I got the essential crew up and out of camp with Carnaval by my side and Radio, already clearly aware that something was up. We headed for Concession No. 1 and the Kanga N'thole Camp region. As if presaging good fortune, our vehicles at dawn flushed flocks of crested guinea fowl, after which the camp had been named. There they were, at the sides of the tracks and ahead of us, their alarmed calls bringing alive the morning as the impudent chatterings of troops of vervet monkeys scampered before them.

Instead of taking pictures, we hunted with great success that whole day in a very game-rich area. I radioed ahead to the staff at Nhamacala Camp to prepare for our arrival. Come nightfall, we drove into camp and spent a peaceful bush winter night under skies awash with ice-white stars. I remember thinking that the moon somehow looked "different" that night, with Charles Duke at the campfire. It had been an extraordinary day, perhaps because of the element of heightened risk now.

The next day, we were back in the bush at dawn where we hunted hard, managing to complete Charles Duke's entire safari quota, enjoying the rugged countryside and the sense of achievement. At no stage were we aware of anything untoward. In fact, I took every subsequent safari client that season into the "hot" areas, right to the end and expressly against official decisions. I was always careful to explain to them what the risks were but not one client backed away. There is no doubt our presence was known to Frelimo the moment we entered the concession, but I knew there were no land mines there as yet and my instinct told me to proceed. I never felt any fear.

That afternoon, in a show of thinly veiled bravado, I must now admit, I radioed Beira and asked for an aircraft to pick up the Dukes. The office asked, "Where? At Gorongosa?" "No," I replied. "I'm at Nhamacala. Send the aircraft to Nhamacala, please."

"You're where? Adelino, are you totally out of your mind? We can't send aircraft there!"

"Oh, yes, you will," I shot back. "We've had a great safari. We're here, enjoying our drinks and waiting for the plane. It's peaceful and we've hunted what we wished to hunt. And I tell you, I'm going to come back here. Now please send that aircraft down to get the astronaut and his wife out."

The aircraft duly arrived, but not without some coaxing of the pilot, who did not want to fly into Nhamacala for understandable reasons. Charlie and Dotty had had a grand safari, and a treasured possession reminding me of the Dukes is an enlarged photograph of Charles Duke standing on the moon's surface, saluting, a miniature American flag next to his photograph. The flag had been taken to the moon on *Apollo 16*. No money would buy that memento now.

Before my last safari that season with the Aznar family of Spain, I had several sobering experiences which underscored the worsening situation in Mozambique. My chief tracker, Radio, and a group of fellow Sena tribesmen asked me to accompany them to Radio's village just southeast of Gorongosa Mountain as there was serious trouble there. Apparently, a Portuguese army patrol had paid a rather aggressive visit to Radio's village, warning the inhabitants that they were going to be given just twenty-four hours to get ready to abandon their village and be transported to a fortified village, known as an *aldeamento*. This was said to be imminent, hence the urgency of Radio's request.

We arrived very early the next morning, but the people did not come forward readily to meet us. There was a shiver of fear and suspicion in the air now, so unlike the spontaneous, free exchange I had known nearly a quarter of a century previous, when I was involved in the trading store business and was able to approach any village with complete confidence of a cordial reception at any time of the day and, indeed, night. Suspicion hung heavily in the air before the villagers were assured that it was not the Portuguese army patrol, back to carry out its threat to burn down the village and remove the people forcibly.

As soon as Radio had identified us, his mother, the matriarch of the village and a fierce old lady, came into the village clearing, alive with gaunt, yapping village curs, tiny children, chickens, and the ever-present goats. She launched into a chiSena tongue-lashing, expressing all the fear and anger of her people. Her near-toothless mouth spat out the words as she gesticulated, flailing her arms about at the huddle of huts, the communal cooking area, and other primitive structures, saying over and over that they could not leave their ancestral burial grounds to strangers; they could not abandon the only place they had ever truly known all their lives, where almost all of those present had been born. They were not leaving, ever. They could not understand why the people were now fighting. There had been peace. Why were the people fighting? The village did not want to fight anyone.

Apparently, the same Portuguese army patrol had called at that particular village several times in recent weeks. The soldiers, profoundly ignorant and arrogant, had threatened the villagers, broken cooking pots, and generally behaved very badly indeed as they warned the people that they would be forced to abandon their village and move into an *aldeamento* some distance away. This policy aimed at insulating the population from Frelimo and at denying Frelimo support bases. The entire village was refusing to leave, even though the patrol had threatened to burn down their village in an effort to force them to relocate away from what was now a "hot" area. This bullying behavior probably won more recruits in that village for Frelimo than we shall ever know about.

Tempers were fraying. I told Radio to let the people settle down and discuss if they would accept my offer to move the entire village, together with their possessions and their livestock, to a tented facility we would erect next to Nhamacala, only about thirty miles away, where they would have water. There would be enough tents, as we had already consolidated several camps at Nhamacala. I told Radio to assure his people that I would see to it that nobody interfered with them there.

With that, I took my coffee flask, withdrew from the crowd, and walked to the edge of the village, where I sat up against a baobab tree and waited. I waited from well before noon until 4:00 P.M. that afternoon. I was used to waiting. Africa teaches you very quickly to be patient, especially rural Africa. Undue haste can be interpreted as lack of courtesy. As for punctuality such as First-Worlders understand it, it is simply ignored. As I waited, I felt an increasing sensation of uneasiness. My AK lay on the ground, right next to me, but the feeling did not abate. At one stage, I felt my neck hairs prickle, and I turned to stare into the fairly thick bush to the rear of the baobab and the rickety village enclosure. I felt I was being watched. I remained seated for another hour or two, thinking that I was not ready to die quite yet, such was my sensation of alarm. After all, the village was in a guerrilla-infested area.

The sun was now starting to slide lower and lower. We had to make a decision and get going. Radio returned and said that the whole village would agree to move over to Nhamacala but only because they knew me and because the matriarch's son, Radio, had been with me for years. Our trucks and tractor with trailer were piled high with mostly elderly folk, children, chickens, goats, pots, pans, blankets, some food knotted in sacking, and other possessions. We set off, the whole crowd oddly silent as we creaked out of the village and headed for Nhamacala. As we left, I noticed a boy of about fifteen standing at the entrance, who obviously had refused to come with us. He was one of Radio's sons, which gave me an odd sensation because the look of hatred on that boy's face as our eyes met has remained with me. Clearly, he had been "got at" by outside forces and was projecting his infected thoughts onto me, obviously rejecting his father's loyalty to me.

By the next day, the little tented settlement was functioning and the villagers seemed more calm. They remained at Nhamacala for the rest of the time I was there, the Portuguese army not setting foot on the place or harassing them. Radio kept me briefed, and it appeared that the people felt safer for the time being.

Not more than a few days after this drama, I was at Nhamacala, when the military radio we had, in addition to the Safrique radio, crackled out a full-blown emergency at Chitengo Camp inside

Gorongosa Game Reserve. I was asked to race over as fast as I could. It was the 18th of July, my mother's birthday.

Carnaval and I jumped into the Toyota Land Cruiser and took off, driving into Chitengo later that night to be confronted by an alarming development. A group of Frelimo guerrillas had entered the game reserve entirely undetected and had shot up Chitengo, the main camp, around dinnertime. Miraculously, nobody was hit, but the sound of AKs letting loose was terrifying to visitors. Among them was Charles Williams, a member of the National Parks and Wildlife of Rhodesia, who subsequently became general manager of Safari South, the noted Botswana company. What was even more alarming was the sight of sixty Portuguese paratroopers who had been deployed at Gorongosa to protect the place, lounging around in civilian clothes and drinking beer at the time of the attack, all their weapons in a rondavel over 200 yards away. Any comment from me now is superfluous. This detail merely emphasized what we in Mozambique had long since discovered about the Portuguese military in Mozambique.

I asked for men to join me in tracking the guerrillas at first light. No takers. That left Carnaval and me to go it alone, which we did. We pushed ahead as far and as hard as we could at dawn the next day, but eventually had to admit defeat in the face of excellent countertracking skills. Let nobody believe for a moment that Frelimo did not have some highly trained forces. More importantly, they were consistently highly motivated.

Guerrilla attacks of all kinds were now escalating throughout our region. Road and rail links in Manica Sofala and Tete provinces were sabotaged, as were the road and rail links between Beira and Rhodesia. I lost a cousin in an ambush on the tarred Beira-Save/Lourenço Marques road. In the so-called "open" hunting areas not far from Nhamacala, José Simões's entire camp was burned to the ground, whereas Miguel Guerra's camp, very close by, was left untouched. Carnaval and I were the first on the scene to remove Miguel's guns from his camp as a precaution. After this attack, Simões decided to leave for Angola. People now had to travel in military convoys. I refused to do so for the simple reason that military convoys were increasingly being ambushed, and I felt I had a better chance of survival by traveling alone, my AK next to me.

Eduardo Aznar, accompanied by his daughter, Rocio, sixteen, and his son, Alejandro, eleven, came out as my last hunters for the 1973 season. We had a glorious swan-song safari on the Marromeu flats before moving into the "hot" areas around Nhamacala. Eduardo was fully alerted beforehand as to the risks involved, but would not be intimidated and dictated to by faceless foes. The Aznars hunted lion, leopard, buffalo, elephant, and a full bag of all available plains game on license.

An astute man who did not shy away from risks, Eduardo knew exactly what was going on and wanted to buy out the bank on the spot and have us take over Safrique immediately. I refused to even contemplate the idea. I knew Lisbon was going to jettison Mozambique, like so much excess political baggage, and I was not about to have my closest, most trusted friends in Spain trapped, as they surely would have been. The bank would have been delighted to take Eduardo's money and be rid of one more headache as the revolutionary clouds thickened, darkened, and got ready to burst. I remember that night at Nhamacala as I told Eduardo, "It's too late. It's too late, Eduardo."

Between Beira and Lourenço Marques and their liaison with the bank in Lisbon, it was confidently concluded that I was some kind of madman, a loose cannon. As soon as I was back in Beira, I headed straight for Safrique's offices from the airport and got hold of the subdirector, his two seniors being conveniently "out." They knew I had not come in peace. I let the subdirector have it. Harsh words were traded as I laced into that bunch, giving vent to all that my crew and I had had to endure in the preceding months, during which we had had no support or encouragement, just vicious comment and constant criticism, exactly like a relationship gone sour. I could no longer stomach the cowardice. My conscience was clear: I had organized the consolidation of the camps and had left a special group in place to protect Safrique's property. I slapped my written resignation on the table and walked out, straight into another adventure—taking over the entire field management of a company called Safarilandia from the controversial Werner von Alvensleben, the "Baron" who never was.

Mario and Jorge de Abreu, wealthy businessmen of Lourenço Marques whom I knew, I having been associated with Jorge in business in the mid-1950s, owned Safarilandia, which had hunting concessions south and north of the Save River, where many notable people hunted from the late 1950s through to the end of 1974. Robert Ruark had a camp on the banks of the Save River named after him, and Juan Carlos, the future king of Spain, had also been a high-profile guest. It was one of the great hunting companies of the day. The late, inimitable Wally Johnson worked for the company and hosted many prominent people in the big-game-hunting world, chief among them being Ruark. Safarilandia had long become a destination for the international sport hunter.

The Abreu brothers sent a colleague to see me in Beira with their proposal for me to take over the field management, as Werner von Alvensleben was leaving Mozambique for good. German-born Von Alvensleben, who died in Portugal in 1998, arrived in Mozambique under highly dramatic circumstances at the outbreak of the Second World War. He married a Portuguese girl from Lourenço Marques and spent well over three decades involved in every aspect of the safari industry. He had spent some of the most memorable years of his life with Safarilandia, but he saw no point in trying to continue in the face of the revolutionary storm. He and his wife had decided to go to South Africa. I flew down to Alves Lima Camp, near the Save River, to see Werner and discuss finer details of the handover. It was a very melancholy day for him.

In January 1974, Mario Abreu and I flew to Las Vegas to attend the Safari Club International convention, where I helped Mario meet the main people in the international hunting-safari industry. The keynote speaker was Senator Barry Goldwater. His address made a tremendous impression on us because the senator spelled out what American policy and strategy should be in defending Western interests against communism in the Indian Ocean by using the island of Diego Garcia and bases on the East African coast. He spoke of the geopolitical significance of the Suez Canal and of Mozambique. Mario and I were fortunate to spend some time with Senator Goldwater, who wished us well and expressed the hope that Mozambique would weather the storm. He was surprisingly well informed, but, unfortunately, his was a voice in the political wilderness.

The growing fires of revolution came uncomfortably close a few weeks after our return from the very successful trip to Las Vegas. My son, Tim-Tim, escaped death by a whisker near our farm at Guro. He had completed his education in Rhodesia in 1972 and was back at the farm in 1973, where he was actively engaged in growing cotton and in helping his grandmother run the farm, hunting for the pot in between. He had with him Eric Stockenstroom, a South African, who was working with us on the farm.

Tim-Tim, Eric, a Portuguese signals specialist named Folques, and two of our Sena employees, Kalima and Romão, were hunting for rations in Concession No. 9, bordering our farm, when their Toyota Land Cruiser got stuck. As they were laboring to free the vehicle, an RPG7 rocket came screaming at them, mercifully missing them and hitting the treetops behind them. Tim-Tim immediately returned fire with his AK, Eric and Folques joining in with their firearms. Folques also lobbed a hand grenade in the general direction of the RPG7 launching area. It was quickly apparent that they were outgunned and outnumbered, so they broke into the bush and escaped the ambush, firing as they moved. I still do not understand how they were not even so much as grazed by a stray round, let alone not killed. Twenty miles later, my son and his group arrived back at the farm. At dawn the next day, Eric and some commandos based on our farm returned to the scene to recover the vehicle, only to find it burned out. Less than a month later, on April 25, there was a coup d'état in Portugal. It had been a long time coming.

The coup had been orchestrated and led by leftist officers belonging to the Movimento das Forças Armadas (MFA), the Armed Forces Movement. They overthrew the government of Marcello Caetano, and General António de Spínola became the new president. Portugal's African wars had politicized Portugal in unprecedented fashion, down to the lowliest conscripted country boy. A leftist rot had set in among the young officer class of the Portuguese army and this affected fighting morale. Soldiers found themselves thousands of miles from home in an environment they could not understand, where the climate was often intolerable for a European, and where they faced increasing danger of being killed by a faceless enemy in a country where they had no ties at all except for an accident of history which made certain countries in Africa Portuguese-speaking. When the maimed and the dead started returning to Portugal from the African wars in increasing numbers, the mothers and fathers of Portugal started asking what their children had been doing there in the first place. Portugal's Vietnam was under way, fanning the flames of guerrilla warfare, in Mozambique, which had already started destroying the very viability of the safari industry. A huge swath of the world media aided and abetted the process, demonizing White Mozambicans and deifying Frelimo. The truth is never on one side alone in any human event.

Confusion and chaos ensued in Mozambique immediately after the April 25 coup. Military units were refusing to fight, and there were many instances of their fraternizing openly with Frelimo. This did not stop Frelimo from continuing the guerrilla war, refusing to grant a cease-fire, targeting Whites and Portuguese property, in particular, for attack. All sorts of political groupings started appearing, representing the interests of conservative Whites, radical Whites who backed Frelimo, and Blacks who did not support Frelimo. The jails freed their political prisoners, the state security police was disbanded, and the entire country began to disintegrate. The army and the civil government in Mozambique were at a loss as to who was in charge, adding to the chaos. Portugal was disengaging from Africa at any price. We, the "settlers," and vast numbers of Black Mozambicans would be handed the bill and, in many instances, would pay with our lives.

Safrique never took off for the 1974 season. On the very first day of the first safari, the party was ambushed, spelling the end of that company. In order to avoid a chaotic situation and panic in our overseas markets, I made a deal with Safrique for all their clients to be sent down to me at the Safarilandia concessions, which were now under my control. I had not given up the areas in the north and had the use of Kanga N'thole Camp in particular because that area had never really belonged to Safrique. It was known as Concession No. 1 and I used it as one of my base camps in 1972–73. Anyway, it had been abandoned by Safrique.

Just before my first clients were scheduled to arrive for their safari down south, I was given a handwritten letter in perfect Portuguese, delivered to me by one of my trackers on behalf of Frelimo, asking me to meet them. This was a mere few days after the April coup in Portugal. Clearly, they were in contact with our staff. In any case, Frelimo was all over the place, in the villages, in the countryside, and now in the cities as well. The smell of a supine handover by a prostrate Portugal was in their collective nostrils, and Whites began leaving Mozambique in droves as the signs became more and more ominous that the Marxist-Leninist Frelimo had it in for them in a big way as, indeed, it did.

The letter started with the standard communist salutation: "Comrade Adelino, we would like to see you. . . ."

Was this a trap? Was I being set up to be killed at point-blank range?

I decided to speak to Radio, my chief tracker, whom I trusted implicitly to tell me the truth. He said that Frelimo wanted to talk to me because they admired what I had tried to do to help the people, that there were good words about me throughout the region, that I was a just man. At the risk of sounding self-serving because only I know the details of this story, I discovered that I was not really afraid. Nevertheless, I waited a full eight days before I sent word back to Frelimo that I would meet them. Back came another letter from Frelimo, specifying a day and place.

Accompanied by all my men, I went unarmed to the specified meeting place. We passed a Portuguese army checkpoint, where I was stopped and quizzed as to where I was going. After all that had gone on before, I snapped back, "It's none of your business! I'm hunting around here." They stepped out of the way and let us pass.

Dolores Sainz Piñera, the Marquesa de Lamiaco, with her leopard in Mozambique in 1963.

The Marquesa de Lamiaco, known to her friends as Loli, in 1970.

Tete on the right bank of the Zambezi in the 1930s.

The pontoon on the Zambezi at Tete.

The gunboat docked at Tete in the 1940s.

A *highway* in Tete Province in the 1930s.

A wooden bridge in Tete Province in the 1930s.

José Serras Pires in 1937 at Benga with a man-eating lioness.

The indomitable *Dona Maria*, the author's mother, at the family farm at Guro.

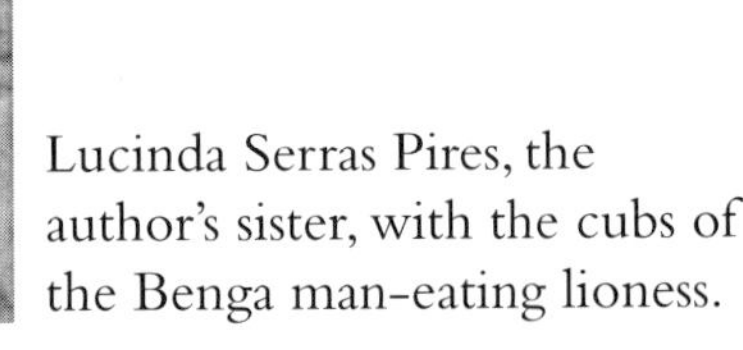

Lucinda Serras Pires, the author's sister, with the cubs of the Benga man-eating lioness.

The Serras Pires family's farm at Guro in the 1950s.

General Jimmy Doolittle and the author with a kudu in 1971.

James Lovell, Commander of *Apollo 13*, and the author with a nyala in 1971.

Left to right: The author, Dottie Duke, *Carnaval*, and Charlie Duke, Commander of *Apollo 16*, with his buffalo in 1973. *Below*: Stu Roosa, Commander of *Apollo 14*, and the author with a sable in 1971.

Angolan lion hunt.

Left to right: A *Frelimo* guerrilla, Luis Santos, *Radio*, the author and another *Frelimo* guerrilla in 1974.

Abandoning Angola.

The author on Masuko Island, Lake Kariba, Chete Hunting Concession in 1976.

Left to right: The author, President and Mrs. Giscard d'Estaing of France at the Chambord hunting estate in France in 1976.

Kenyan president Daniel Arap Moi, second from the left, his entourage, the author second from the right, and the hotel manager, Clive Walker, on the extreme, right in Kenya in 1977.

The author's son, Tim-Tim, with a Bohor Reedbuck, Sudan, 1978.

Dr. John H. Brandt and Cisco Urrea after having survived an air crash in Central African Republic in 1979.

Bert Klineburger and his Nubian ibex in the Red Sea Hills, Sudan, 1981.

John Shumway of Houston, Texas, with his one-hundred-pounder, taken in February 1980 in the Central African Republic, the last elephant to be hunted on license before elephant hunting was shut down overnight in that country.

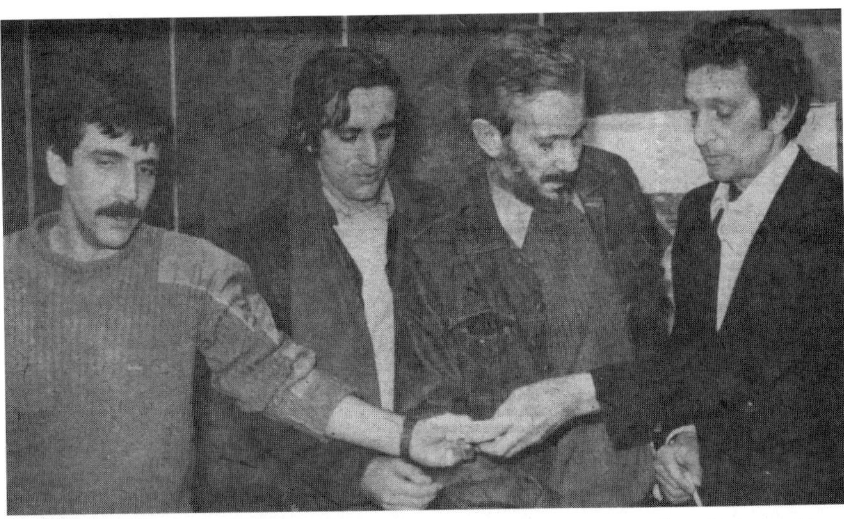

Left to right: Caju, Tim-Tim, Rui, and the author, on arrival at Lisbon Airport, January 1985, after the Tanzanian/Mozambican ordeal.

The author with *Renamo* personnel on the landing strip inside Mozambique in 1991.

Female *Renamo* guerrillas, December 1991.

Safari Club International Convention—Reno, Nevada, February 2000. Valéry Giscard d'Estaing, formerly President of France, and Adelino Serras Pires.

Looking ahead: The author with his granddaughter, Margarida, in 1998.

We reached a burned-out village which appeared deserted. I got out of the car and looked around. Then, one by one, cautiously at first, a group of about fourteen Frelimo soldiers dressed in the camouflage of the Tanzanian armed forces, began emerging from behind the shells of huts and from the surrounding bush. They were all armed with AKs and were mostly young men.

"I am Adelino Serras Pires," I called out.

The obvious leader of the group answered, "We know. I am Luis Cunha." We shook hands and then the fun started. Suddenly, a youngster with a huge smile came up to me and said, "*O senhor Adelino! Como està?* How are you? My father worked for you at the farm." As it then turned out, most of the group there that day in the burned-out village had been connected with me through our farm, our family, or the safari business. That broke the ice as we found one another through such links, establishing a cordial, totally unthreatening atmosphere.

Luis Cunha was from Zambezia Province on the Indian Ocean. I immediately discovered that he was quite educated, as he began explaining to me that his commander wanted to meet me. He said, "We admire you. We need men like you in this country. You've got a very good name here, and we want you to become part of the new Mozambique. Would you be willing to meet our commander, Cara Alegre?"

I knew instinctively that Cunha was on the level with me. His commander's nom de guerre meant "happy face" and was used by a man named Tembe, who later became a colonel in the new armed forces. I agreed and was asked to be at a certain spot at the base of Gorongosa Mountain two weeks later. My men and I took our leave and moved off. I was not quite sure what to make of this extraordinary meeting, set against a backdrop of years of violence and suffering on both sides.

My life had long taken on a schizophrenic quality. On one hand, I was a fierce defendant of the legitimate, hard-earned interests of my fellow Whites in Mozambique, roundly condemning the communist-infected, imported plague which was destroying Mozambique. On the other hand, I never hesitated to castigate Portugal for its ignorant, rapacious, exploitative administration and the consequent abuse suffered by Black Mozambicans as well. I stood for a vigorous, autonomous Mozambique able to steer a course independent of Lisbon's whims and greed, a country in which all could live in peace.

With these thoughts uppermost, two weeks later, I kept my date with destiny at the base of Gorongosa Mountain. I was unarmed and unafraid as I entered a village where a jovial young man in camouflage strode toward me, hand outstretched, saying, "Adelino! Finally we meet! I'm Cara Alegre. I hope the name fits."

Indeed it did. We hit it off from the outset and I was to spend two highly charged and memorable days in the Gorongosa bush with this Frelimo commander, who was responsible for the whole Gorongosa area. He told me that he had been on the point of killing me the previous year, when I was at Radio's village helping rescue his people and move them to Nhamacala, ahead of the Portuguese army's threat to move in and burn down their village to force them to relocate to an *aldeamento*.

"I had you in my sights that day, Adelino, as you sat leaning against that baobab tree. But I decided I could not kill you because you were helping the people. We all know that you are a friend of Mozambique. We all know your family at Guro. That is why we want to talk to you. We need you in Mozambique. You must stay here and help us reconstruct the country."

In a flash, I recalled the sensation of creeping anxiety I had experienced that afternoon as I waited for Radio's people to decide what to do, my neck hairs bristling. Cara Alegre and I spoke in great detail and with total frankness about our respective hopes and fears for the future of Mozambique. We struck a deal whereby I could return to Kanga N'thole Camp, rebuild it, and bring in a male nurse, medicine, and supplies to help the local people. In exchange, I could hunt there with my foreign clients in total safety and build up our safari business. As Frelimo commander of the entire area, Cara Alegre had the authority. He put out the word to his troops and was as good as his word. I had struck a deal with the "enemy," as it were, but I never regarded Black Mozambicans as my enemies in those dramatic and dangerous days, especially the rural Blacks, with whom I had already spent almost four decades. I regarded them as fellow Mozambicans. We needed each other in order to make a success of our country. Neither could wish the other away. There had to be a decent compromise.

As forthcoming bitter experiences would teach me, it was one thing dealing with the local Frelimo members who belonged in the region and who, in many cases, had known me and my large family for decades, as they had known many other White families rooted in Mozambique with the will to remain and contribute. It was quite another dealing with those individuals who had spent years in exile in places such as France, the Soviet Union, China, North Vietnam, Algeria, Cuba, and Eastern Bloc countries like East Germany. They returned to Mozambique with a demonic agenda of summary arrest, imprisonment without trial, "purges," confiscation of privately owned property, sweeping nationalization, torture, reeducation or "mental decolonization" camps, murder, prohibition of religious education and baptism, and the wholesale Marxist-Leninization of Mozambique, reducing it to an economic one-party shambles and the status of the poorest country on earth by the early 1990s, while the West sat and sometimes watched. Naturally, the Portuguese were blamed for everything.

For all its sins, dictator-driven Portugal and certain psychopathic elements in the security forces had never wreaked the sustained havoc that Frelimo did in less than two decades, rebel movement and civil war notwithstanding. Mozambique is now a South African economic satellite state, being recolonized with foreign checkbooks, the Marxist-Leninist insanity shelved. As will be explained, this came too late for me, for my family, for my generation, and for numberless Black Mozambicans.

As instant proof of the empathy among fellow Mozambicans in those last days, Cara Alegre entrusted his aged father to me for the trip by road back to Beira, where I was to deliver the old man to another son, who was living in Beira. I did better than that. I had him stay in my house in Beira for a day or two before handing him over, safe and sound, to his son. This caused a major scandal when the news got out. Adelino Pires was labeled a pro-Frelimo subversive. I paid absolutely no attention. I had been a controversial figure for the past twenty years, anyway. I had work to do with my son, Tim-Tim, and others as we hastened to reconstruct Kanga N'thole Camp and keep our side of the bargain with Cara Alegre.

Down in the Safarilandia concessions, we were confronted by poaching on a massive scale. Time out of mind, we would come across trapped, severely injured animals which were still alive. The cruelty was stomach-churning. Throughout his years on those concessions, Werner von Alvensleben had conducted his own private war against the poachers. The trouble was that the bush stores would readily stock steel cables, wire, and actual traps which they would sell to the locals. This was where the scourge had to be dealt with, not down the line, on the ground alone. In Safrique, I found that the most effective way to deal with poachers was to include them by letting them have regular supplies of meat. This resulted in an immediate and sustained scaling back of their activities to negligible incidents of poaching. It was a question of approach, of attitude to a reality of life in the Mozambican bush. Once again, a compromise had to be struck.

We conducted several successful safaris down south, although the concessions were somewhat flat and not remotely as scenic or as challenging as were the Safrique areas. Our American clients would get a kick, however, out of staying in Camp Ruark, where Bob once hammered away at articles on his typewriter, safari staff then making a mad dash for the border with Rhodesia at dawn the next day to send the material to Ruark's editors in America. Electronic mail and satellite technology have their undoubted advantages, but something of the magic, the challenges, and the old-time romance of those days, such as Bob Ruark knew in Mozambique, have been snuffed out forever. Today, it is not unusual for safari operators to be requested to have fax and other electronic amenities installed in camp for certain clients, who are cursed with never being able to shake free of the office.

We had our share of scares while south of the Save River. Once, Carlos Castellanos, a Mexican client of ours, wounded a lion, which turned on professional hunter Candido Veiga, mauling his right leg so badly that he spent months in a hospital in Lourenço Marques. In 1999, after many years, Candido and I met again. The deep scars of that lion safari were still clearly visible.

We returned north to prepare for the arrival of three prominent Americans from Houston, all well-known members of the big-game-hunting fraternity. Ray Schriver, Ray Petty, and Jerry Henderson were supposed to have hunted down south, but it had been over-hunted by then, so I decided to take them to Concession No. 1 and to trust Cara Alegre to keep order. I told the party that I was taking them into a "hot" area but that they were to relax. A special agreement had been struck, and they would be safe. We all enjoyed a classic safari, during which lion, leopard, elephant, sable, kudu, nyala, and other species were hunted successfully. There was no trouble of any sort. It was a splendid experience for all of us, and I was beginning to have hope that we in Mozambique would be able to ride out the independence storm and stay on to rebuild and make plans for a fresh future.

Beira and the Portuguese military authorities blew their collective tops when the news made the rounds that Pires had taken clients into a "hot" area, but that he had come to no harm. The uproar was quite something, and the ensuing jealousies to boot. Everyone wanted to know how it was that I could have gone into a guerrilla stronghold when nobody else would have dared do so. Things deteriorated to such an extent that Cara Alegre sent me a note, urging me to pack up and leave Kanga N'thole forthwith. It was a clear warning. It could only have meant one thing: Cara Alegre no longer had overall control of the area. Someone else in the Frelimo hierarchy was calling the shots now.

This turned out to be the final safari I conducted in Mozambique. Just a few weeks before that, I had had perhaps the most distressing experience to date. I had hoped so fervently that the arrangement overseen by Cara Alegre would hold. I now knew Portugal was pulling out at any cost, and that our futures hung by the thinnest of threads.

The pressures of internal military jealousies were taking their toll on Costa Campos as Mozambique slid into chaos. One night, just before the Kanga N'thole safari, he told me he had put in a formal request to be placed on the reserve and to be sent back to Portugal. His request had been granted. I was devastated.

He broke down, clearly overcome with stress and remorse. But it was too late for tears. I had a taste of ashes in my soul that night as I contemplated the immediate future. Revenge was in the air as very hostile Frelimo elements had already installed themselves in the cities, including Beira. They were outsiders who clearly overruled the local Frelimo. They had no idea who we were and could have cared less, anyway. We were White; we were "settlers"; we had to go. Any Blacks who had worked with us were traitors and would be dealt with accordingly. That was the bottom line. The point of no return was reached on September 7, 1974.

The first negotiations between Frelimo and the Portuguese government took place in June 1974. The government wanted a cease-fire, but Frelimo refused. In fact, they continued with their guerrilla war until September, resulting in the disintegration of what remained of law and order in the country. A series of secret meetings between Frelimo and the Portuguese coup officers then took place in Tanzania, resulting in the signing of the Lusaka Accord on September 7, 1974 in Lusaka, Zambia, another Frelimo haven. This accord, a prostitution of any attempt at consultation and agreement, paved the rocky way for rapid and unconditional transfer of power to Frelimo, with no prior elections. There were no checks or balances as the Portuguese government caved in to every one of Frelimo's demands. The obscene joke of a so-called "transitional government" lasted nine months. Frelimo appointed the prime minister and two-thirds of the nine ministers making up this "government," whose task it was to prepare for independence. There was no referendum to determine the future of Mozambique.

On September 7, 1974, I was with Frelimo, at their invitation, in their camp at Dondo, just twenty miles north of Beira, where I had been called in to assist them and the Portuguese military with erecting a tented camp. My presence and the cordial reception accorded me all flowed from my relationship with Cara Alegre. I was determined to stay in Mozambique and make a go of things.

On September 7, there was a White uprising in Lourenço Marques and Beira. The radio station was seized, and messages were broadcast throughout the country, urging the Whites to revolt. This resulted in tremendous loss of life and the spectacle of the Portuguese military opening fire under orders to crush the rebellion by the Whites. It was chaos as indiscriminate firing mowed down hundreds of people, Black and White. I could not believe the stupidity of those townsfolk. They had, for the most part, spent all those anguished years shielded and sheltered in their towns while we faced the terror. They were always the ones to criticize and now, as they stared into the face of reality for the first time, they thought they could hang onto their cozy little lives by revolting. The Soviet Union and the world media were behind Frelimo and this pathetic, panicked reaction merely underlined how detached from reality these people had become. Frelimo has never forgotten or forgiven that day. It did incalculable harm.

Clearly, with no guarantees as to assets, no decisions about compensation, no financial or commercial accords to protect and retain skills, and in the light of Portugal's total unilateral abdication of all responsibility, despair set in and Whites started flooding out of Mozambique. My two sisters relocated to Salisbury before independence, my wife and children following, as life became dangerous and absolutely untenable, even in Beira. My aged mother could no longer risk living alone at the farm as the military was about to pull out and she would be at the mercy of whoever decided to take over her property—by force, if necessary. Like thousands of others, she had to abandon a lifetime and leave, too, joining the family in Rhodesia. She left behind her my father's grave, almost forty years of hard work and memories, a working farm, a huge staff, many of whom had been with the family for decades, and the farmhouse and all its contents, except for her clothes and some family memorabilia she could hand-carry. Like so many other anonymous, elderly people, Black and White, who were bundled out of Mozambique or who were displaced internally, she did not recover from the trauma. Lives were ruined in a flash. Nobody cared.

The safari industry in Mozambique was finished. I sat down with Cara Alegre at Dondo, and we spoke. My brothers and I had decided not to leave Mozambique. The dangers were great, but this was our home, and we would ride out the madness and try to reestablish family life once some calm and order had returned. I could not sit around in Mozambique, however, waiting for more stable times so I decided to join a group of fellow Mozambicans who had been in Angola for a year or so and who were hunting in the southeast.

A deal had been made with Angola Safaris, and I already knew that excellent trophies were being taken and that there was considerable interest in the international hunting fraternity to come to Angola. At the back of my mind, I hoped to be able to work in Angola and wait out the situation in Mozambique. I had no trouble at all in signing up clients in Europe and in the States to try Angola. Cara Alegre then assured me that I was to be his personal guest at the independence celebrations the following year, on June 25, 1975, and that I should return anyway to start afresh with my family.

Carnaval was spirited out of Mozambique well before independence and was absorbed by the South Africans to fight their war on the border between South-West Africa and Angola. It was the scene of a war against the South-West African People's Organization (SWAPO) who were bent on driving the South Africans out of South-West Africa. Carnaval went on many missions deep inside Angola to fight the communist-backed and -indoctrinated SWAPO guerrillas.

Thousands of South African troops had already been deployed inside South-West Africa, which was administered by South Africa under a 1919 League of Nations mandate. Conflict had been going on since 1966 and would last twenty-three years, eventually involving Cubans, Russians, and other Eastern Bloc countries in a combined bloody guerrilla and conventional war. There was an uneasy calm on the ground when I arrived in Angola but, like it or not, I would become directly involved in the looming revolution.

FIVE

REVOLUTION—ANGOLA

Oil and diamonds: poor, poor Angola!

—Adelino Serras Pires

There it lay below our aircraft: the sweep of the bay and the palm-lined promenade of Luanda, capital city of Angola. Distant boyhood memories surfaced: of our trip down the west coast of Africa and of the first time I had set foot on African soil almost 40 years previously and fully 400 years since the Portuguese first settled there. At over 480,000 square miles, Angola is a vast country, roughly four times the size of Arizona. It borders the former Zaire, Zambia, and the former South-West Africa, flanking the Atlantic Ocean on the west. Angola derives its name from the word *ngola*, denoting one of the rulers in the early 1500s of a region situated due east of Luanda.

By the time I arrived in Angola, the country had been embroiled in guerrilla warfare since the 1961 massacre of Portuguese in the far north, along the border with what is now the Democratic Republic of Congo. There were three main guerrilla groups, all of them eventually present in the southeastern hunting concession, or *coutada,* at

Mucusso, where I was to become active. I knew I was going into a very uncertain situation.

In transit through a rather tatty Luanda Airport, I noticed the heavy presence of Portuguese soldiers and of Portuguese military aircraft. I also noticed a palpable air of resignation, of detachment on the faces of the young soldiers. I sniffed trouble as I boarded the aircraft for the flight southwards to the town of Sá da Bandeira, where I would fly by charter aircraft eastwards to our hunting concession at Mucusso. Bob Lee, the noted American big-game hunter and entrepreneur whom I had met, wrote evocatively of that very region as he once knew it in the glory days of hunting safaris in Angola. His words are worth quoting, especially now:

> I can state without reservation that the south-east concession known as "Mucusso" is one of the very finest general game areas in all of Africa. The game is so thick in this area that only two or three camp moves of perhaps 60 miles each, during a twenty-one to thirty day safari are sufficient to collect an excellent selection of trophies. . . . I saw literally dozens of rhino. . . .
>
> (*Safari Today*, 1st edn., Harrisburg, Pennsylvania: The Stackpole Company, 1960. p. 200)

Lee meant black rhino. When I arrived in that area in early 1975, there were still reasonable numbers of them, although they were not on license.

The Mucusso concession was situated in the district of Cuando-Cubango in the semiarid Kalahari region. Days were often extremely hot and the nights icy. Vast, flat, sandy, four-wheel-drive thorn bush and *mopane* savanna country surrounded our base camp on the Quito River at a place called Mpupa. In areas above our camp, there were fine, white sandy stretches by the river, a veritable paradise for antelope and aquatic birds of all kinds. Duck, geese, water hen, and white-plumed jabirú wading birds could be seen in great numbers, interspersed between the crocs and the aquatic plant life. From west to east, the Cubango, Cuito, Luina, and Cuando rivers rise, flowing southeast into the Okavango, Chobe, and Zambezi rivers, the sandy sides of some riverbanks being home to thousands of birds.

The entire region was devoid of any village life. A mere decade or so previously, the characteristic cone-shaped thatched roofs of the villages could be seen on the fringes of the hunting concessions. The spreading guerrilla contagion, however, had already destroyed traditional life in this part of the Angolan bush as the villagers were forced to seek protection in the larger settlements.

It is the same in Angola today—worse, in fact, as millions of despairing people have bloated and burst out of the pathetically few facilities of even Luanda, the capital city. The only people we saw living and roaming at will in the Mucusso area were tiny bands of Bushmen.

On the other side of the river was a deserted Portuguese military base with a long landing strip. Officially, Portugal was scheduled to hand over power to Angola only in November 1975, but the mute testimony of that deserted base revealed that Portugal had already largely abdicated. Today, a full twenty-five years afterwards, as I write this, that once-magnificent country is racked by unprecedented civil war, famine, and despair, with absolutely no end in sight. Vast oil and diamond wealth, manipulated by major foreign powers, is fueling the civil war as never before. Angola is the most heavily mined country in the world, and what remains of the wildlife is severely endangered. Classic hunting safaris in Angola are finished forever because, apart from the demise of the game, there is no way the country can ever be cleared of land mines. Fresh land mines have been planted where the few have been lifted, at enormous expense, in the last handful of years. The number of permanently injured victims—many of them children—continues to rise.

The tragic symbol of this turmoil is the all-but-certain extinction by now of the royal or giant sable antelope *(Hippotragus niger variani),* unique to Angola and found in the north-central region. Photographs of this jet black beauty with its sweeping scimitar horns remain just that, photographs. And as for the giant sable emblem on the tail fin of the Angolan national carrier, it is a mockery of what once was. Nobody has been able to show me an authenticated, recent photograph of even one giant sable, let alone a breeding herd. Until I see such evidence, I am forced to conclude that this spectacular creature is already extinct.

When I arrived at our base camp at Mpupa, there was a large South African military base about 30 miles southwest of us, at Rundu, on the Okavango River in South-West Africa, where we became very friendly with the base commander, Major Erasmus. The South African military had been actively engaged against the guerrillas of the South-West African Peoples Organization (SWAPO) since the first guerrilla attack on the border between South-West Africa and Angola in 1966.

We obtained all our supplies from Rundu, which would soon become our lifeline as Angola began collapsing into preindependence chaos. In 1974 and early 1975, Angola was a pretty hair-raising place to be in and safaris there took on a different dimension because of this growing political turmoil. Guerrilla groups, all at one another's throats, eventually infested the hunting concession.

I brought over my core staff of nine Mozambican Blacks, headed by Radio, my chief tracker, when it became clear that we would not be able to recruit enough appropriately experienced local people for our operation. The exception was the Bushmen, or San, the legendary trackers and the original hunter-gatherers of Africa, several of whom we employed immediately. The origins of these slender, light-skinned people who differ markedly from the southern African Negroid people, is still shrouded in conjecture. A particular hell lay ahead for those who served with the South African forces in the war against SWAPO. There was tremendous, historic antipathy anyway between the Bushmen and the Blacks, the latter having enslaved the Bushmen through the ages.

As we reconnoitered our new area, I gained first-hand insight into the astounding endurance of the Bushmen. One late afternoon, around sixty of them, including women and children, arrived at our camp with a very sick old woman on a crude stretcher. The Bushmen had come to us for help.

I took one look at her wizened face and emaciated body and concluded that she was dying of sheer old age. I found it difficult to gauge the age of Bushmen because the harsh sun aged people in a flash. Maybe the old lady was only forty years old. Maybe she was much older. What was certain was that she was seriously ill.

Not knowing quite what to do, I gave the old lady a broad-spectrum antibiotic with some fluid, which she managed to swallow. The band was invited to stay in the vicinity of the camp until daylight so that we could see how the patient was doing.

Very early the next morning, as we were preparing to go out, I asked Radio how the old lady was, *"Patrão,* they have all gone. They left the stretcher. The old lady has gone with them. I saw her walking, like the rest of them."

I could not believe what I was hearing. Two days later, in the late afternoon, as we were hunting towards the northeast side of the concession, approximately 50 miles from our camp, Radio called out to me that he had spotted several Bushmen on the horizon who were running towards us.

When the group came up to us, I recognized the man who had been the spokesman for the little band when they called on our camp. He was all smiles and, through gesticulation and, using the characteristic click sounds of his language, which resembled firecrackers going off in his mouth, he conveyed that the old lady had recovered and that she was with them. The spokesman clapped his hands, smiled at us, and was gone.

The point is this: The old lady, who arrived in a debilitated state, unable to walk, had not only stood up from the stretcher, she and the rest of the group had promptly traveled such a distance on foot in two days. I was astounded. I would not have believed this story had I not experienced it myself.

Apart from the vast Mucusso concession, where clients hunted up to the Cuando River on the Zambian border, we also hunted in the southwestern area of the Moçâmedes Desert. This lay on the Atlantic coast, west of the town of Sá da Bandeira, now called Lubango. Clients would fly in there from Luanda, hunt the desert concession, and later connect by air for the Mucusso concession. The desert region with its thorn scrub, sand, and rock amid the spectacular Chela Mountains, was very tough hunting country. It was home to a particularly small leopard and to numbers of giant oryx, springbok, and mountain zebra. Here and there, amid the rocks, burning sands, and cactus would be one of the rarest plants in the world, the *Welwitschia mirabilis,* with its weird long leaves draped over the sands. This was a hauntingly different world in every way.

After a promotional trip to Europe and the States, I returned to Angola in February 1975 with the late Frank Green. An old friend from 1963 and a major safari-booking agent from Houston, Frank wanted first-hand information on conditions in the concessions. My son, a qualified pilot, was with us and was invited to share in the flying. He was at the controls when we left Sá da Bandeira aboard a push-pull light aircraft. Not long afterwards, one of the engines started acting up, and we limped into our refueling stop at Serpa Pinto—now called Menongué perched at almost 5,000 feet. Precious daylight hours were hemorrhaging away as emergency repairs were made. The pilot took over, and it soon became apparent to all of us that he seemed to be struggling to get his bearings. The painfully slow aircraft droned on and on as the sun slid lower and lower in the western sky. The Quito River and our camp seemed no closer after what seemed like an increasingly dangerous amount of time in the air.

Finally, feeling my gut go into spasms of anxiety, and being aboard a barely airworthy aircraft, I told the pilot he had better look for any reasonably clear space in the sandy savanna below to land because we would soon be out of fuel and out of daylight. We were going to crash. Then it appeared: In the deepening gloom of twilight, we picked out the undulations of the narrow but deep Quito River and the weak lights of our camp set back from its northern bank. As the wheels made contact with the runway at the abandoned military base, the last scrap of light in the skies was extinguished. We had made it with no time at all to spare. The fuel tanks were as good as dry. Death had passed me over, for the umpteenth time in my life. Staff from the camp were waiting for us in vehicles and we crossed the Quito River by pontoon in inky blackness, all of us somewhat shaken by how close we had all come to dying that day.

Frank wanted assurances as to the basic stability and predictability of our operation in Angola. While there was never any lack of clients who were even more eager to hunt in "hot" zones because of the greater risks involved, certain facts had to be faced. Angola was at the mercy of three major guerrilla groups: the Popular Movement for the Liberation of Angola (MPLA), the National Front for the Liberation of Angola (FNLA) and, finally, the National Union for the Total Independence of Angola (UNITA), each wanting a share of the postindependence cake.

The FNLA was backed by the Chinese and the North Koreans, whereas the MPLA was backed by the Soviet Union. Tensions between these two guerrilla movements were high. The last Portuguese governor-general in Angola was Admiral Rosa Coutinho, known as the "Red Admiral" because of his close relationship with the Portuguese Communist Party. He turned a blind eye to the weapons flooding in from the Soviet Union for the MPLA. Angola would be the last battleground in Africa between the superpowers.

Meanwhile, UNITA, which had long been attacked by the two other movements, tribalism and personal animosities being at the core of the hatreds, managed to broker a deal in which there would be a period of transition, with all three movements cooperating closely with Portugal. A timetable for independence was worked out, scheduled for November 11, 1975. The accord called for a joint Angolan defense force. On January 31, 1975, a transitional government was installed in Luanda and Angolans across the spectrum were very hopeful of a peaceful transition. We, in the safari industry, took particular note of all this as our livelihoods and immediate future depended on basic calm.

As the world now knows, there was no peace and no smooth electoral transfer to independence. On the contrary, Cuban soldiers started arriving in Angola as early as January 1975. The toxic combination of Russian ruthlessness to get hold of potentially one of the richest countries on earth, also of great strategic importance because of its Atlantic ports, its runways able to take heavy aircraft, and its oil and diamond wealth, for starters, and Western complacency and trauma in the wake of Vietnam, guaranteed the bloody birth of so-called "independent" Angola in November 1975.

The MPLA and FNLA escalated attacks against each another from about March 1975 onwards, mostly in eastern and northern Angola, far from our hunting concessions. UNITA was then attacked by MPLA elements, and the seeds of civil war were sown in the fertile soil of tribal animosities, greed, and international interests. This civil war has persisted into the new millennium, almost a quarter of a century after the shameful abdication by Portugal.

The South Africans in South-West Africa were inevitably drawn into the war in order to defend their territorial interests. Our safari operation was eventually affected directly by the South African military involvement in Angola, which came *well after* Soviet and Cuban forces started arriving in that country, and not before, as apologists of the left proclaimed to an often alarmingly ignorant West.

The foregoing is a necessary thumbnail sketch of the general situation in which we found ourselves in early 1975. An artificial calm prevailed in our hunting concession, but it was becoming increasingly difficult to obtain aviation fuel and, soon, even the simplest of supplies. The ominous presence of guerrillas in our hunting concession at Mucusso was a clear sign of serious danger ahead. Although we never came across any guerrillas while out hunting with our clients, we did see sickening quantities of badly wounded game, riddled with AK rounds and still alive: dead black rhino with their horns chopped off, and elephant with their tusks hacked out—even very young bulls with toothpick ivory. As Angola began its descent into a preindependence Armageddon, the smuggling picked up as despair mounted. The wildlife bore the brunt.

As we hunted and managed to conduct safe and successful safaris which produced some excellent trophies for our foreign clients, we never saw so much as a single Portuguese army detachment in the Mucusso concession. Not far off, there was a concentration of UNITA guerrillas in Calai, opposite the South African military base at Rundu. Calai also hosted a fair-sized crowd of MPLA guerrillas.

Both formations were increasingly hostile to each other as they jockeyed for position as overall leader in the eons-old African tradition of one-party rule. In fact, at one stage, UNITA managed to deal a tremendous blow to the MPLA, chasing them out of the district. It was inevitable that we would be caught in the midst of these deteriorating political tensions. In my case, it involved American safari clients and a standoff with the FNLA.

The client and I were scheduled to hunt buffalo, leaving his wife behind to relax, read, and get some sun. We anticipated a tough hunt in that sand and under a baking sun. Luck was with us, however, when we came across a respectable bull not far from camp. As the day was still young, I suggested that we return with the buffalo to camp, where we could have a brief break before setting out again to hunt until sunset.

As we neared our camp, the trackers signaled for us to stop. They pointed to a multiplicity of fresh tire marks in the sand, indicating that several vehicles had driven towards our camp after we had left at dawn to hunt buffalo. This was an alarming sign: There were no other hunting operations for miles around us, and we were certainly not expecting vehicle traffic of any sort. Something was up. I did not let the client see my anxiety, but I was clearly worried as all hell about his wife who was alone, except for the core camp staff.

The moment we entered the camp, the client's wife came out in a terribly distressed state. She was overcome with fear and was sobbing as she told us that about eight vehicles had roared into the camp soon after we had left, disgorging a ragtag bunch of mostly Blacks and a couple of Whites in tatty camouflage uniforms, brandishing machine guns. The apparent leader of the group was extremely aggressive as he ordered her to get to her feet and remain standing, his machine gun pointed at her stomach. He barked at her in fractured English, demanding to know where we were, saying that the group was looking for us. We had to answer some questions. When it became clear that we were not in camp and that there were no vehicles there, the group eventually left, threatening the poor woman that they would be back to "get" us. The poor woman was so traumatized, she wanted to leave for the States right there and then.

The immediate reaction of the Spanish professional hunter with me and the two Portuguese hunters was to pack up that day and leave Angola, saying that matters were now becoming truly chaotic, even life-threatening. I decided to cross the Quito River immediately with our pontoon and drive over to the former Portuguese military base. I had a strong feeling that I would find these political freebooters there. If anybody wished to come with me, they could.

One hunter, Victor Cabral, accompanied me. We reached the pontoon and crossed the Quito River, driving into the base on the other side. I was right. The once-abandoned base was now apparent home to some thirty or so guerrillas, most of them Black with a sprinkling of Whites. We were kept waiting a full hour as we observed the comings and goings at the ramshackle buildings. Nobody took the slightest notice of us, so I strode up to an individual and asked to be taken immediately to their leader. He turned out to be a most aggressive Black from Zaire, glorying in the name of Odinga Odinga, a name which would crop up again in the annals of Angolan guerrilla warfare. He was flanked by his deputy, a ratty-looking White, named Chisto. The Black spoke neither Portuguese nor English. I spoke no French then. Quickly establishing that they were FNLA, I went onto the attack and addressed the scruffy little White man: "I believe you're looking for us. Who gave you the authority to invade our camp this morning and intimidate our guests from America?"

Then followed a seesaw "conversation" in which the deputy backed down rather quickly when he realized that we had not come in peace, we had come to confront. I clearly remember saying, "We're from Mozambique. We have no interest in your politics here, but do not think you can intimidate us with your guns. We have guns, too. You should be ashamed of yourselves for behaving so badly in front of our lady guest from America. What do you think they will say about you when they go home? You owe her an apology."

Chisto then mumbled something about coming to apologize "soon." I barked back that this was unacceptable; he would come back with us now, and apologize to our guest. He then asked me if we had whiskey in camp.

"Yes," I replied, "but you will not help yourself to it. We shall invite you to take a drink. It is our camp, and *we* decide who touches our whiskey and who doesn't."

Chisto and four other equally disreputable-looking Whites followed us back to camp in their vehicle. Very often, the best defense is an attack. I knew that had we not confronted this crowd and shown them we were fearless, they would have returned to attack the camp. Right from the beginning, I knew they were not regular soldiers, but a bunch of mercenaries.

Lured no doubt by the promise of a little Scottish firewater, they apologized to the safari client's wife and then settled back for the next few hours, getting sloshed on our whiskey. They were real lowlifes, typical of the White flotsam of Angola.

In his drunken state, Chisto finally answered my repeated question as to why he had barged into our camp "looking" for us. Apparently, he had stopped off at the hunting camp of an ex-Mozambican, situated north of us, who told him a lurid tale about our close ties with the MPLA, enemies of the FNLA. This man obviously wanted us out of the concession by smearing our name and, quite frankly, endangering our lives in the process. All the worse for wear, the group left. Chisto and I parted on good terms. We had no further trouble from that crowd for the rest of the time we were in Angola. We subsequently learned that one of that bunch fell off the pontoon one night, landing in crocodile-infested waters, never to be seen again.

It was already early June 1975. While my colleagues held the fort, I flew back to Mozambique as the June 25 day of independence was approaching and I had been invited to attend as Cara Alegre's personal guest. It was a chance for me to gauge the mood of the people and the possibility for us all to return to Mozambique as soon as possible. I was hoping against all odds that the independence would proceed in relative calm and that we could then get down to reconstructing the country together. If I am honest with myself, however, I already sensed that immense and bloody trouble lay ahead.

Beira airport had assumed a nasty look. Brazen-looking Frelimo soldiers were everywhere, clearly in charge, making a mockery of the

Portuguese flag which was still flying. I had been met by Miguel Guerra and had just started unwinding at his house when, on June 10, late at night, a Land Rover, overloaded with Frelimo soldiers brandishing AK-47s, screeched to a halt outside and a loud banging at the door told us we already had trouble. Short and sweet. "Are you Adelino Serras Pires?" When I answered yes, the arrogant leader of the pack then asked, "Are you the man who was always going to the United States of America?"

"Of course. That's where I signed up clients for the hunting safaris here. I've been doing it for years. You know that. I'm very well known. America was our main market. I didn't go to Russia because they have no money. The people are not allowed out of the country, anyway. What's your problem?"

The leader of the pack gestured to the Land Rover outside, snarling, "Get in! You're under arrest." "For what?" I shouted. "I'm here to attend the independence celebrations as the personal guest of Cara Alegre! What the hell are you talking about? I've just come in from Angola! Mozambique is my home. What's this 'arrest' nonsense?"

"Get in! *We're* in charge here!"

There was no arguing with a man, carelessly holding a Kalashnikov, now pointed at me, a faint whiff of booze on his breath. I climbed into the Land Rover while the other Frelimos leered at me. Miguel stood, transfixed, no doubt wondering when his turn would come. It was a chilling moment nobody can understand who has not been summarily rounded up by tipsy guerrillas with revenge on their minds. The name Cara Alegre seemed to mean nothing to this lot, who jabbered away in some language I did not understand as the Jeep careened through the streets to the central jail. Clearly, they were not locals. And that was a bad sign. The witch-hunt had already started.

I was roughly bundled through the main entrance of the jail, down some steps, and into a poorly lit cell. No registration formalities were observed at all. The cell, which had about twelve bunk beds, was empty, but not for long. By the next morning, about twenty Whites, a few mulattos, and some Indians were shoved into the cell, all of them dazed and shocked, none of them having been formally charged with any actual "crime." The motive was definitely racially based, but I was worried that my clandestine activities with Carnaval and his Mandioca group were the reason why I had been rounded up.

We were crammed into the filthy cell. The toilet facilities down the passage were a fetid disgrace, human excrement on the floor, around a hole in the ground. There was no toilet paper, and the shower and basin did not work properly. This kind of squalor breaks morale very quickly. Worse followed when we found a radio in the cell in perfect working order. It started blaring out the voice of Samora Machel, the leader of Frelimo, who had just crossed the Tanzanian border into Mozambique. In a speech laced with racial hatred, he singled out White Mozambicans for a megadose of loathing. Straight after this harangue, the cell door burst open and one of the guards pointed his AK right at us, saying, "If anything happens to Comrade Machel when he gets to Beira, you are all going to be shot dead right here!"

Beira had always been a reactionary city. Ironically, it still is today. The bulk of anti-Frelimo supporters are from the Beira region—certainly, north of the Save River. They were of different tribes from the southerners. Let nobody be so naïve or misinformed to even remotely imagine that tribalism, in all its permutations, is not alive, well, and being used as a weapon in Africa today. Clearly, the local Frelimo were nervous that, indeed, someone would attempt to assassinate their leader in Beira; hence the roundup of certain well-known people.

In the cell was a former member of the commandos. He and I got together and told the rest of the group how we should react if the cell door flew open and the guard started firing at us. The commando and I had worked out where we would position ourselves to at least attack the guard and attempt to wrest his AK away from him and fire back as we broke out. Somehow, the fact that the cell now had a plan and a rudimentary leadership, however desperate and lunatic it sounded, gave us all fresh hope.

We had been cooped up together for five days when the cell door opened and my name was called. What now? A firing squad? I was taken into the office of the jail's superintendent, a pleasant mulatto, who told me a mistake had been made, that there was nothing against me, and that I was free to go. As I digested this piece of news, he asked me to stay on in Mozambique. My sort were needed to reconstruct the country, and so forth. I had heard this speech before.

To this day, I do not know if Cara Alegre had had anything at all to do with my release. All I do know is that I no longer had the slightest faith at all in the moderating influence of the local Frelimo, especially not after Machel's racial diatribe to a population already worked up into a dangerous frenzy of expectation at what they thought was going to fall into their laps after independence. I was not contacted at all by Cara Alegre or by any deputy of his, asking me to attend the independence celebrations as his personal guest, as had been promised. They certainly knew I was there. I decided not to press my luck any longer in a city which was becoming visibly more unstable, hostile, and dangerous the closer we came to June 25. I decided to return to Angola and wait it out from there.

At Beira Airport on June 19, 1975, I was rudely processed by gun-toting, hostile Frelimos, who now ran all the customs/passport facilities. My suitcase was forced open in front of me, and I was told that nobody needed so many clothes. The case and all its contents were confiscated. The large carton of cigarettes given to me by my brother was also taken; I was left with one pack. I was searched for money or any other valuables and was allowed to depart with 500 escudos, the equivalent of a few American dollars, the clothes I was wearing, and my passport.

As I flew out to Angola, full of rage and shock, I had no way of knowing that I would not see Beira again for two solid decades. When I was arrested, the Portuguese flag was still flying, and I shall always hold the Portuguese government responsible for what happened to us. They were still formally in charge of Mozambique, although they had already abdicated. To this day, over twenty-five years later, there has been no attempt at all to compensate any of us, Black or White, for what was stolen from us and destroyed. This trauma was the direct cause of my mother's totally unexpected death, as will be revealed. There were many more like her.

I landed back at our camp on the Quito River and into an increasingly tricky situation. All flights from Sá da Bandeira to our camp had been stopped because there was no more aviation fuel for such frivolities. Under the South Africans, Rundu became our lifeline. All our clients were now arriving at camp via Windhoek, the capital of the then South-West Africa. We were also linked by radio to the military base in Rundu. With hunting parties booked back to back, we were tremendously busy keeping the logistics under control and ensuring that our clients were treated with as much care as possible.

The general situation was clearly deteriorating. In August 1975, I received information that the political climate in Angola was taking a dramatic turn for the worse. Chisto and most of that FNLA rabble across the river at the former Portuguese military base had received orders to move out and head north to Quito and to Serpa Pinto, and west to Sá da Bandeira. A major offensive was in the offing, and only a small group of Black FNLA members would be left behind at the base when the others deployed northwards.

A Bushman reported that the approximately thirty Blacks in the FNLA group who would be remaining at the Mpupa military camp had spoken of their intention of coming across the Quito River with their machine guns to raid our camp and steal whatever they could. Our camp was extremely well stocked with food, medicines, vehicles, tools, spares, other equipment, and fuel. We were a perfect target.

I knew I could trust the Bushman's raw intelligence report, although I had to keep in mind the age-old hatred between Bushman and Black which could have skewed the information. We discussed our options before contacting the South Africans in Rundu. They sent someone I knew across to see us, a former professional hunter who had a Botswana passport. He told us plainly that the South Africans would have to come in sooner or later, as it was clear that a confrontation was close. Our Rundu liaison man said that our camp would have to be occupied by the South Africans before long because it was clear that the Portuguese were going to simply hand over everything to whoever managed to grab control in Luanda.

There was now the distinct possibility that the FNLA crowd were planning to raid our camp. I was told that if we elected to stay, we would have to move out in a month or so, anyway. With clients' lives now definitely at risk, we decided to pull out that very night, before the FNLA came across with their machine guns and their blood up.

How provident that it was a Saturday because, after crossing the Quito River by pontoon, we would have to drive by the FNLA camp. They were usually plastered out of their collective minds during weekends and, we hoped, would not react to the sound of vehicles. We always kept the pontoon chained on our side of the river for security reasons. The FNLA would use dugout canoes to cross.

At dusk, we packed up our rifles, personal belongings, and all possible equipment. With every vehicle refueled to capacity, piled high and ready, we drove out late that night and made for the pontoon. It was a tremendously risky undertaking. Even the scavengers of the African night had gone oddly silent. Within a space of just over two months, I found myself being forced to leave yet again. It was a numbing experience.

Having ghosted past the FNLA base where raucous, inebriated voices masked our passage, we drove as fast as we could over the sand tracks to Calai, on the banks of the Okavango River and more or less opposite Rundu. The dark savanna scrub crept past our zebra-striped vehicles, the icy night air of this dry country scything through our clothing. At 4:00 A.M. we reached Calai; Rundu had been alerted. Dawn broke as we drove onto the pontoon and crossed into South-West Africa and safety.

We had several hunting groups and their clients still in the Moçamedes Desert concession and we had to wait in Rundu for one anxiety-filled month before they managed to get out of Angola. They had tried previously and had been caught and pushed back by very aggressive MPLA elements who did not want them to leave with anything at all. Eventually, our colleagues got out with their vehicles and basic possessions, joining us in Rundu. In the meantime, we had been accorded magnificent hospitality by the South Africans who gave us the exclusive use of the official guest house. We were treated like VIPs, not refugees.

All my Mozambican staff were treated very well, too. They had been given a decent campsite with facilities nearby. I was responsible for their safe return to Mozambique, but I feared what would happen to them once they returned home. The military medics were also available to assist us as Rundu started overflowing with refugees from Angola, the frail elderly and newborn babies being among the waves of human misery pouring into South-West Africa and an uncertain future.

Rundu was filling to capacity with truck- and carloads of severely shocked and desperate Angolans fleeing the fighting and the threat of worse to come. They were leaving behind a lifetime, as we had been forced to do. The scenes were a prelude to a new kind of purgatory. It is unfortunate how some humans prey on the despair of other humans. In Rundu, the Portuguese refugees were selling their cars, trucks, jewelry, and anything else of value, however paltry, just to survive and get out. They were paid derisory amounts by mostly South Africans, but I also know of several fellow Portuguese who picked up vehicles for practically nothing, gloating over their bargains.

We were in limbo in Rundu, keeping contact with our group in the Moçamedes Desert until they were able to penetrate MPLA lines and get to Calai and cross the Okavango to join us. Their stories were of a total breakdown of any semblance of law and order, of chaos at Sá da Bandeira, where that once-very-beautiful university town was succumbing to the MPLA hordes, of scenes of panic and chaos at the airport as people fought to board aircraft in order to flee Angola, of roadblocks and threats, random shootings and intimidation.

This was a solid three months before the November 11 independence date yet Portugal had clearly washed her hands of any responsibility, leaving her legal citizens at the mercy of mobs. All talk of transitional government and tripartite partnership with the Portuguese was forgotten. There was going to be a simple handover to the Marxist MPLA. Scapegoats had already been identified. By early August, in fact, the uneasy coexistence between the MPLA and UNITA collapsed into open warfare, which has continued until today.

While in Rundu, I saw the base commander, Major Erasmus, almost every day. He took a personal interest in our group. Our camp at Mpupa was immediately occupied by South African forces, who were preparing for a major operation into Angola. Twenty-four years later, I had the singular privilege of meeting Colonel Jan Breytenbach, South Africa's most highly decorated soldier and the founder of that country's special forces and of the redoubtable 32 Battalion, which distinguished itself in Angola. He and his men who took over our camp. He and I relived those tense days in Rundu, and he told me how much he had valued Carnaval with whom he had worked very closely. There is no higher praise than that.

Carnaval lost his life in a road accident in the border area between Angola and South-West Africa. A vehicle which was part of an oncoming convoy had tried to overtake in poor visibility, resulting in a head-on smash and instant death. Carnaval was buried in an unmarked grave in total secrecy at a military cemetery in Pretoria. His widow, a lady from Mozambique, took me to the grave. I had a chance to meet Carnaval's daughter and tell her how much her father had meant to us all, of what a truly extraordinary man he had been, and that he had fought against tyranny, whatever anyone may tell her in the future. Sometimes, the only thing left to pass on is the valiant memory of another human being and I like to think I did that for Carnaval's child.

Colonel Breytenbach has written several riveting books on his wartime experiences and he confirmed what I had suspected. Elements in the South African military had been heavily involved in the wholesale poaching of ivory and of rhino horn—from the Mucusso hunting concession, in particular.

In those anxious days, as we prepared to leave South-West Africa, the Americans and the CIA, with the behind-the-scenes approval of West European democracies, were busy encouraging South Africa to intervene in Angola. American aircraft were already coming into Angola in that year to deliver armament to anti-MPLA forces. South African troops watched Americans unload the weapons, which the South Africans then helped distribute. Senator Barry Goldwater confirmed in 1983, when quoted in the book *Angola in the Front Line* by Michael Wolfers and Jane Bergerol (Zed Books, London): "There is no question but that the CIA told the South Africans to move into Angola and that we would help them with military equipment."

On October 23, 1975, the South Africans invaded Angola in a desperate attempt to prevent a totalitarian takeover of Angola by the

MPLA, but it was too late. Large contingents of Cubans and other Soviet-bloc personnel had long since arrived in Angola and the South Africans were abandoned by the Americans who, through the Clark Amendment of December 19, 1975, severed the sending of all supplies of American weapons to Angola. The South Africans' arsenal was no match at that stage against the latest Russian hardware, forcing the South Africans to retreat. The rest is a bloody history which falls outside the scope of this book, but these basic details are necessary here for a clearer understanding of the rot which had set in. Angola is now a wasteland, the wildlife mowed down and reduced to a mere shadow of its former richness and diversity.

That September, we left Rundu and the increasingly intense military buildup for the South African invasion the next month, driving down to Windhoek on superlative roads, built by the South Africans. We had with us all the equipment we had managed to take out of Angola. Naturally, our Mozambican staff came with us. The others in my group decided to go on to Sudan, which did not appeal to me at all. In any case, I still had to assist my Mozambican staff in returning home.

This meant a long drive in two vehicles over the border, into South Africa and the town of Upington in the far northern Cape Province. My overriding memory of the trip to Upington was the indescribably vicious cold weather we experienced. It got so bad when night fell that we made for the first lights we could see in the distance, pulling in at a very isolated farmhouse. The Afrikaans couple opened their doors and their hearts as they welcomed in this large crowd of total strangers, Black and White, making us hot coffee and food and giving us what support they could. This was nearly two decades before the dismantling of the apartheid state, but that Afrikaans couple showed us nothing but heartfelt hospitality. I have never forgotten them.

We left a while later and drove straight into a police roadblock, where we were pulled over, the police no doubt curious as to the Angolan license plates. I was sure we would all simply freeze to death as we stood outside, explaining to the police who we were. After a call to Rundu, where none other than Major Erasmus assured the police of our legitimacy, we were allowed to pass. Not only that, but the police provided a two-man escort for the Mozambicans when they boarded the train in Upington for the long ride home. The escort stayed with them until they had entered Mozambique safely. It was an emotional moment when Radio and his men pulled out of the station. Somehow, we all knew we would not see one another again.

It was the end.

My colleague and I then drove back during daylight to Windhoek and a new parting of ways. I packed my few clothes and headed for the airport and a flight out to Johannesburg, South Africa. I had decided to go to Rhodesia where several members of my family had sought refuge after Mozambique. It was a country I knew well, considering it always as my second home ever since my now distant schooldays. It had outstanding wilderness areas and an established hunting industry. Perhaps I could catch my breath there.

I was soon flirting with fire.

SIX

FLIRTING WITH FIRE

We simply happened to be living in Rhodesia at this point in history, when we were challenged by the forces of evil. We decided to close our ranks and make a stand for those ideals of Western Christian civilization on which our country had been built. It was a time when it was a privilege to be able to say: "I am a Rhodesian."

—Ian Smith (former prime minister of Rhodesia), *The Great Betrayal*

The light aircraft circled several times, clearly trying to alert us. Our safari camp was situated on miniscule Masuko Island, just off the Chete Parks and Wildlife Reserve in the remote Zambezi Valley of Rhodesia. A small container was dropped, landing on the edge of the clearing where the dining hut was situated. It was a message from the Rhodesian army, asking us to be on the lookout for a soldier who was making his way over from the Zambian side of Lake Kariba, the largest man-made lake in the world, a veritable inland sea. We were to go out and assist him in picking up the rest of his stick, as the soldiers were called, from a place he would indicate and we were to give food and shelter to the men for the night.

In the early morning of that day in May 1976, as the mosquitoes rested after their nightly attack, we went out onto the lake in our outboard boat. Our tiny island faced onto the infinitely larger Chete Island, a Zambian possession infested with guerrillas fighting Ian Smith's Rhodesia. The gorge separating us from Chete Island was narrow, deep, and treacherous, and the lake was home to countless crocodiles which made the scene that greeted us all the more astonishing. There, straddling what looked like a large log, was a typical "Rhodie" combat soldier, paddling as best he could towards us, his deeply tanned legs in camouflage shorts immersed in the potentially lethal waters. Each stroke brought him nearer until we came alongside and he clambered in, grinning no doubt with relief at not having been shot at or grabbed by a dozen crocs. He then directed us back to the Zambian side of the lake, where his mates were waiting to be picked up from enemy terrain.

The stick had been on an operation into Zambia where huge numbers of guerrillas were based in transit and training camps and from where many raids were planned and launched into Rhodesia. The men were mute with fatigue as we headed back to relative safety.

By the time I arrived from Angola, the bush war in Rhodesia was gathering momentum. The jigsaw pieces of the guerrilla war in Southern Africa were slotting into place—the March 1961 attack in the far north of Angola, the September 1964 attack in the far north of Mozambique, the launching of guerrilla warfare on the border between Angola and South-West Africa in 1966 involving the South Africans and Angolan-based SWAPO guerrillas, and the infiltration that same year by guerrillas into Southern Rhodesia. The Black-on-Black political gangsterism of the early 1960s had fermented into full-blown guerrilla warfare in most of Rhodesia, the *chimurenga*. Our hunting concession was already "hot"—so hot that when the concession came up for tender almost nobody wanted it. Not even several battle-toughened Rhodesian hunters.

I was oddly energized by the prospect of fresh adventure, new challenges, and the chance of seeing my family again. Salisbury had that familiar, comfortable feel about it, like a seasoned relationship, as I attended to the red tape involved in obtaining permits and bidding for a concession.

Something in the country had changed, perhaps imperceptibly for most visitors. Conversations now included guerrilla activities in the more remote areas of a country covering nearly 151,000 square miles. Radio news bulletins had assumed a different kind of importance for ordinary people as the realization began to filter through the national psyche that all was not well, that life was becoming more tense as reports of attacks and intimidation increased. When the name of a well-known farmer was announced as the latest victim of guerrilla efforts to drive the established communities out, somehow it affected total strangers.

Subdued and hardly recognized at first, unease at growing instability became more pervasive in a country where it would not be long before there was hardly a household in the land not involved in the bush war, be it on the side of Prime Minister Ian Smith's forces or on the side of the two main guerrilla formations: the Zimbabwe African People's Union (ZAPU) and the Zimbabwe African National Union (ZANU), both communist-inspired, indoctrinated, and trained organizations, each with its own armed wing. The masses in the tribal trustlands were increasingly caught between two fires. Weapons were pouring into guerrilla bases in Zambia, Mozambique, and Tanzania, courtesy of places like China, Russia, and the East European satellite states. Rhodesia went onto a war footing, pressured by sanctions imposed by the United Nations. I entered a country which was going into the final straight of the race for its survival. Morale was high, but so were the stakes.

I linked up with my family and was lucky to meet an old friend, Sidney Sawyer, an attorney. We had known each other since our school days in Salisbury. A generous-spirited man, he introduced me to Ian Smith, the prime minister of Rhodesia, and to other prominent people, among whom was Barry Ball of the National Parks and Wildlife of Rhodesia. He was the key person to see concerning hunting concessions. After my own experiences in Mozambique and Angola, I felt no trepidation at entering the Rhodesian "hot" zones to hunt. I felt inured to threats to my personal safety, as long as I had the reasonable certainty that there were no land mines in the area to be hunted. Barry soon told me that the Chete concession in the

Zambezi valley, on the shores of Lake Kariba, would be available, but that it was in a "hot" zone and that nobody wanted it because of the definite danger posed by Zambia-based guerrillas.

I wanted it.

I put in my bid and was successful. Before leaving for Europe to canvass for clients, I was fortunate in being able to meet the hunting fraternity in Rhodesia through my old school friend and fellow hunter, Brian Marsh, who put in a good word for me where it counted. Nobody needed to feel threatened by an outsider. I have always valued what Brian did for me in those difficult days when life seemed to be an endless series of problems and uncertainties. No American could hunt in Rhodesia at the time because of political pressure and the impossibility of exporting hunting trophies, so Europe assumed an even greater importance. This was where I came into my own with the Spanish and French markets. The Rhodesians appreciated the role I could play and gave me their full backing. Anyway, they had reason to remember the Serras Pires family.

This is an appropriate place to mention for the first time the sanctions-busting activities by the Serras Pires family concerning Rhodesia's agricultural products. We already had a company established in Guro called José Serras Pires e Filhos (José Serras Pires and Sons), referring to my brother Jacinto and me. A branch of this company was established in Tete soon after the Unilateral Declaration of Independence (UDI) by Ian Smith's government in November 1965. The prime purpose was to help circumvent sanctions by exporting Rhodesian products from Mozambique.

For the next ten years, we were able to market Rhodesian maize, cotton, and tobacco elsewhere in the world. Heart-stopping moments aside, of which there were a few in the tricky world of sanctions busting, we were extremely successful. I never felt a twinge of conscience at what I managed to accomplish for the Rhodesians because I deplored the way that country was being treated and I abhor to this day the cowardice and double-dealing of the British and the South Africans which eventually resulted in the economic and administrative shambles of modern-day Zimbabwe, where the ordinary people are suffering hardships as never before. An inflation rate of 60 percent, an unemployment rate of 50 percent, chronic fuel shortages, all but nonexistent foreign exchange, illegal and violent invasions of commercial farms by so-called war veterans, and widespread intimidation, assault, and even killing of anyone suspected of opposing the ruling political party indicate that country's perilous situation in the early months of the new millennium. I had a very limited quota of animals for the season, in line with strict game management. I left for Europe and was soon completely booked with clients who did not hesitate to try something new. We had quotas of lion, leopard, buffalo, and elephant, as well as kudu and other antelope. We also had access to other concessions south of the Victoria Falls for species such as waterbuck and sable.

The Chete hunting area inland from the Zambezi was hot, rocky, tough country, but possessed its own arid beauty. The marula tree's richly scented yellow fruit was an eternal favorite among game and humans, while the flame acacia's bright red pods provided bursts of color among the dark rocks and the flat-topped umbrella thorn trees. Here and there was my favorite tree, the baobab, a tree surrounded by legends and superstitions. I have long lost count of the number of times I have slept out under baobabs, often with clients for whom this was a total departure from anything they had done in their lives before.

Clients would fly to Salisbury and then on to Kariba in the far northeast of the country where they would then travel with Kariba Ferries on Lake Kariba to our concession in the west. The stunning bird and animal life along the shores, the unpolluted magnificence of the winter climate, and the sunsets which set the skies on fire with their brilliance made for a very special safari atmosphere. When the moon was full, our tiny island was a magical place, silhouetted against the lake waters which reflected the pale magnificence of the light. Kariba Ferries was my vital link with the outside. Clients would also often charter right into camp from Salisbury and, sometimes, from Victoria Falls. It was a time away from this world.

Before flying back to Rhodesia for the season, I had another family crisis on my hands. My brother Jacinto had elected to stay behind in Mozambique after independence. It was a near-fatal mistake because he, like many others, was arrested summarily and thrown into the Beira jail for no reason at all. My brother was never formally charged with any crime. He found himself in the company of others, many of whom had been arrested on mere rumor or suspicion of "collaboration" with the previous government. That was all it took to have someone arrested or, worse, taken off to "reeducation camps" which many inmates did not survive.

The situation in Mozambique in 1976 was bad—and it was deteriorating. Revenge was in the air. It was no place in which to be jailed. In Lisbon, I accompanied my mother to the relevant ministry to see what could be done from that end to have my brother released. She had tried by herself and had met with nothing but deaf ears and stomach-churning hypocritical promises to assist her. As a parent myself, I understood my mother's anguish. There she was, back in Portugal, a country none of us could remotely call home, faced by a leftist bureaucracy with no desire at all to help her. I started boiling as we entered a typical Lisbon building from a faded era and confronted a secretary of some ministry who had seen my mother previously concerning my brother's ordeal. He was an air force officer whom we knew from our Mozambique days.

After it became clear that he could not help engineer my brother's release, I leaned over his desk and said, "I've just returned from France, where I was a guest of President Giscard d'Estaing at the Chambord hunting estate. How long do you think it will take me to discover and stake out the favorite nightspots of the Frelimo hierarchy, who often go to Paris to shop? Do you get my drift? Pass it on to your superiors. Come on, Mother. We're leaving." With that, we left, my mother in tears and I in a black rage seeing her distress and our seeming helplessness after all we had endured in recent years.

Very soon after that morning in Lisbon, a member of the Portuguese consulate in Beira called in Jacinto's wife, Melita, who had stayed behind, too, and who had suffered a great deal when my brother was jailed. He confided to her that Jacinto was to be smuggled out of the Beira jail on the pretext of severe stomach cramps and the need for X-rays. He would be hospitalized and then, with his wife, be smuggled aboard the Portuguese cargo vessel, the *Amarante*, which would take them back to Portugal. Melita was to be ready to leave at a moment's notice, and Jacinto was to start growing a beard. A timetable was discussed, and Melita had to convey the plan to Jacinto during her next visit.

My brother "took ill," beard fuzz and all, and was hospitalized. A few days afterward, he and his wife were spirited onto the cargo vessel and, after a departure delay, which caused tremendous fear, as can be imagined, the vessel sailed out of Mozambican territorial waters and to safety. The jail thought my brother was in the hospital, and the hospital thought he was going back to jail because he was "feeling better," the X-rays having come up normal. By the time the authorities discovered what had happened, it was too late.

None of this would have happened without orders from the highest level in Lisbon, and that would not have occurred had the Lisbon bureaucrats not been confronted that morning. I have often been asked if I would have followed through with my threat. I certainly would not have left my brother in a Mozambican jail. I would not have allowed my mother to be shunted around by people who knew nothing of what we had experienced in Mozambique and who cared even less. The language of menace with the promise of follow-through was the only one they reacted to.

Jacinto and Melita arrived back in Portugal. Jacinto eventually paid a brief visit to my Chete concession later that year. He then returned to Portugal, convinced that he had no future in Africa. He died of cardiac problems at the age of fifty-six, not having been able to adapt to life in Europe. After Mozambique, he simply was unable to be happy again. There are many people like my brother in various parts of the world today—eternal refugees who cannot settle and who cannot forget. Or forgive. Life forces us to go on, however, and I was soon totally concentrated on the Chete operation. My son was now part of the British South Africa Police in Rhodesia, and the rest of the family was safe, if not exactly happy.

Our camp was situated on tiny Masuko Island off the mainland and just east of the Chete Gorge for one very simple reason: the guerrilla war. By having our camp facilities on an island, we were a little safer from attack than would have been the case had we been based on the mainland. Two hunting colleagues, Fred Rademeyer and

Rob Mann, a nephew of the Honorable John Wrathall, the president of Rhodesia, built a superlative camp on the island, and this became home for the season. Our vehicles, the maintenance area, the skinning sheds, and other essential facilities for our hunting operation were all on the mainland in the former Chete Parks and Wildlife Lands which, until a fairly short while before, had been a game reserve and off-limits to all hunting. The three Land Rovers were all over twenty years old and were kept going because of our camp staff's dexterity with the welding torch. The age of the vehicles and the rocky terrain often meant patch-up jobs at night. Sanctions made life extremely uncomfortable when it came to spares. They also made one careful and inventive when it came to vehicle maintenance.

Chete was completely uncontaminated wilderness, undeveloped and unfenced. According to the resident game warden, it was also home to approximately 250 black rhino. I would see some of them almost every day for the entire hunting season. They have long since been slaughtered by poachers and other parties. The few remaining members of that highly endangered species have been dehorned and relocated inland under twenty-four-hour guard. What a commentary on postindependence Africa which has seen the unprecedented massacre of elephant and black rhino in particular to satisfy greed and also the superstitions of those who do not care if Africa's game disappears! Foreign-based syndicates are behind this tragedy. Traditional beliefs in the Far East, in particular, about the supposed aphrodisiac and medicinal properties of ground rhino horn account for its allure. North Yemen's ancient tradition of presenting a boy with a *djambia,* an elaborate dagger sporting a rhino-horn hilt, to mark his entry into adulthood, is the other major factor in the decimation of the rhino in Africa.

With back-to-back safaris booked, I had no time to brood. Quite apart from good hunting, there was fishing on Lake Kariba, especially for tigerfish, and rich game-viewing as well as photographic safari opportunities. The hotels downstream at Victoria Falls, where the atmosphere was redolent of "old Africa" and a gracious way of life, offered after-safari relaxation with slick casinos as a bonus. This should have been an idyllic spot, but the constant threat of guerrilla attacks never dissipated. While I never spoke in any detail of the military/political situation with my clients, they were nonetheless aware that they were in a "hot" area.

Most days, as we left Masuko Island by outboard for the mainland to hunt, a Rhodesian air force helicopter would circle overhead as we nosed into Chete Gorge, worryingly close to Chete Island and its less-than-cordial inhabitants. The chopper would check that we were safe and then, out of nowhere, a Rhodesian army river patrol outboard with its 7.62 mm machine gun mounted on the prow would come roaring up behind us, churning up the Zambezi into a furious wake as the soldiers escorted us out of the narrow gorge and into safer waters. We could not have survived as we did without the Rhodesian army's backup and, in turn, we hunters were another deterrent force and source of information on the ground. To be totally frank, most days, it was heart-in-the-throat stuff.

Today my Chete information sheet makes curious and nostalgic reading to see that a twenty-one-day safari for one hunter and one professional hunter cost a mere $7,635. An elephant game license went for $300, lion and leopard for $400, and buffalo for only $100. The glamor sable and kudu could be hunted for $150 and eland for $100. Hyena licenses were $10, although I never had a client request one. They were usually protected game. I had bad memories of hyena, anyway.

As a youngster in my trading-store days in Mozambique, I unthinkingly shot two hyenas, which were close to the camp and creating such a terrible din that night that I could hardly think coherently. The reaction from the local women was swift and hostile because they believed in transmogrification, that their dead entered the bodies of hyenas which, therefore, were their relatives. After explaining my actions to them and showing that I had acted out of ignorance, not malice, calm returned. But it was a bitter lesson about how one can cause deep offense through sheer lack of knowledge. That incident made me more cautious and observant in rural Africa.

There was soon evidence that the guerrilla threat was worsening. On some days, I would be alerted by the Rhodesians not to hunt on land but rather to hunt along the banks of Lake Kariba, where quite impressive numbers of animals would be encountered. Signs of guerrillas had been found and until they were checked out, we had to keep away. Then the all-clear would come and we could resume hunting on the mainland until the next alert. The Rhodesians had *sticks* all over the place who were very efficient. We had a comradely arrangement with them by leaving beers under a stone in a certain spot which the troops would find at the end of patrols.

The day was fated to dawn when even the ever-vigilant, skilled Rhodesian forces, who had their hearts and minds on the job because it was their country they were fighting to protect, would slip up. I had been hunting with a French entrepreneur and, after a very successful safari, he decided to leave a little ahead of schedule because his wife was expecting a baby and he was anxious to get back home. That is why I am alive today to tell the story.

We had been trying for a kudu and when we finally came across a fine old bull, my French client simply could not locate the animal. He could not "see" to shoot it, although that handsome old white-chevroned bull with generous horns spiraling upwards was facing us full-on, its large ears flicking, aware that something was afoot. The more I indicated its position, the less the client was able to locate it. Then, it was gone, gray-ghosting back into the scrub and another day of life. The client, with every other species obtained and well satisfied, despite the kudu, decided to return home a little earlier than anticipated. As I had a gap of a week or so until the arrival of the next clients, I decided to accept the offer to leave by charter aircraft with the Frenchman and see my family in Salisbury for the first time in over three months. I had had an exhausting, but safe and successful time so far, and was already making mental notes for the coming year's safari season.

Fred Rademeyer had with him two Spanish clients, José Antonio Moreno and Carlos Melgarejo Osborne. They were not my clients, as such, having arrived unannounced in Rhodesia and hoping to be squeezed in for a couple of species on the Chete concession. José had been an assistant hunter in Mozambique with another company, where his right arm had to be amputated below the elbow after a client's rifle discharged accidentally.

It was a weird accident. He insisted on going into a particular area near Gorongosa Mountain which the trackers regarded as off-limits because of tribal beliefs. José was warned that he would come to grief if he persisted. Then the client's rifle went off, injuring José's arm. This in no way put him off big-game hunting, so there he was, on my doorstep, with Carlos Osborne. Fred Rademeyer was able to accommodate the two Spaniards, who were particularly eager to hunt buffalo. They wanted me to come along, but I had other plans.

On August 12, 1976, the Frenchman and I flew out for Victoria Falls and then Salisbury. I had hardly had a chance to recover from my fatigue when there was an urgent knocking at my front door in Salisbury. It was Friday, August 13, in the evening, a date etched indelibly in my brain. Sidney Sawyer entered with the tragic news. Both Spaniards and one tracker were dead.

Fred Rademeyer, an apprentice professional hunter who was his nephew, and three trackers, together with the Spaniards, were returning to the mainland camp after a successful hunt for buffalo and zebra. Fred was driving the Land Rover open station wagon, his nephew seated next to him, with the Spaniards and a tracker right behind them. The other two trackers were sitting on top of the buffalo and the zebra at the back. They were coming down the track to the camp when a rear wheel hit a land mine. The Spaniards and one tracker died instantly. Fred and his nephew suffered shrapnel wounds. The other two trackers survived unscathed as the animals cushioned the impact.

I have always wondered just how much shock the human body can endure without giving way. From feelings of accomplishment and optimism, I was once again plunged into a black pit of anguish. The scene of Franco's private physician, shot dead on the landing strip at Nhamacala Camp only three years previously, came back to haunt me as I once again had to repatriate bodies to Spain after guerrilla atrocities. Naturally, unkind things were said about Adelino Serras Pires and his gift for having clients blown up on safari. I was traumatized.

In an instant, I knew that I could no longer return to the Chete concession. Nobody could conduct hunting safaris there any longer. As I went about in a daze, organizing the paperwork and making distressing calls to Spain once again, before accompanying the bodies back to Spain, my family showed me papers from the previous week, telling of a spectacular raid into Mozambique.

Guerrillas fighting against the Rhodesian government had camps in neighboring Frelimo-controlled Mozambique, which supported them in their guerrilla war. Raids into Rhodesia were launched from this Mozambican base and, conversely, the Rhodesian forces launched raids into Mozambique. The daring operation into Mozambique referred to in the newspaper clippings shown to me by my family had been organized and executed by the redoubtable Selous Scouts, as was revealed much further down the line. That operation proved to be the most extraordinary of the entire Rhodesian guerrilla war, one which would assume a dreadful importance for me and for my son. Not a single member of our family was ever remotely involved in any aspect of that operation, whatever the stories still circulating to the contrary. A few details are necessary.

The Selous Scouts, the Rhodesian army's overwhelmingly Black unconventional counterinsurgency regiment, was founded in late 1973 by the now-legendary Lieutenant-Colonel Ron Reid-Daly, the regiment's first commanding officer. The scouts had located a major guerrilla base on the Nyadzonya River, a mere 7 miles away from the Pungwe River in Manica Province, not far from our farm at Guro. The base was reliably reported to house over 5,000 guerrillas, with some 3,000 poised to infiltrate the eastern districts of Rhodesia. It was a major logistics base, a crucial target. To complicate the entire scenario and heighten the risk factor, the border with Rhodesia was sealed off on March 3, 1976.

On August 9, a few days before the Spaniards were killed, 72 Selous Scouts had managed to penetrate the Nyadzonya guerrilla base, driving in as blatantly disguised Frelimo "comrades" in appropriately painted vehicles and chanting guerrilla slogans. In an operation of spectacular ingenuity and daring—one which has an acknowledged place in the annals of unconventional warfare—1,093 guerrillas died that day. Many hundreds more were wounded. No air support had been allowed for Operation Eland, as it was code-named. Complete surprise had to be the main element. A deadly blow had been dealt to guerrilla capacity and morale. Of course, the world was falsely told that the Rhodesians had hit a refugee camp full of women and children. The demonizing of Rhodesia was gathering momentum.

The wheel turns, inevitably. In a BBC televised interview in early 1999, Edgar Tekere, a top guerrilla commander at the time, finally admitted on air to the renowned British television personality David Dimbleby, that the Nyadzonya raid, in fact, had been a "legitimate" target for the Rhodesians. I have since had the privilege of meeting Lieutenant-Colonel Reid-Daly and sharing with him my own experiences which, as will be seen, were to involve the Nyadzonya raid, albeit in totally illegitimate, hallucinatory retrospect at the hands of counterintelligence thugs of two countries.

Another event of crucial importance occurred, involving my son. As a fluent speaker of both English and Portuguese, Tim-Tim was used extensively as an interpreter and translator while with the British South Africa Police, on the border with Mozambique. One day, he was urgently summoned to interrogate a Mozambican named Andre Matade Matsangaissa. He had come across the border, ostensibly defecting from his position as a Frelimo military commander. My son had to try to establish his credentials as best he could and attempt to gauge whether Matsangaissa was a "plant," a pseudo defector sent to infiltrate the Rhodesian war machine. At the time, my son had no idea that he was making history.

Tim-Tim came to the conclusion that Matsangaissa was a genuine defector, that he belonged to the Ndau tribe of Mozambique, and that he wanted to fight against Frelimo. The Rhodesians took over. It was in their direct and vital interests to have a dissident group of Mozambicans join in the fight against their Marxist-Leninist neighbors hell bent on the destruction of Rhodesia. With Portugal's capitulation to the communists in Mozambique, a vast hostile front now gaped open on Rhodesia's eastern flank.

As historical records now show, Matsangaissa was believed to have been sent off to one of the infamous Frelimo "reeducation" camps, from where he escaped into Rhodesia to link up with a group of like-minded anti-Frelimo rebels. The Central Intelligence Organization of Rhodesia took charge of this group and formed them into what became the Mozambican National Resistance Movement or Renamo, to use the Portuguese acronym. Matsangaissa became its first president. His deputy and chief of operations was Afonso Dhlakama, also a former Frelimo military officer, once responsible for logistics in Manica Sofala Province.

In February 1977, Renamo began its "Second War of National Liberation" by launching attacks against Frelimo, thereby igniting civil war in Mozambique. The Selous Scouts also utilized Renamo in their cross-border operations. After Matsangaissa died in a military operation in October 1979, Dhlakama succeeded him. I would eventually be associated with Renamo.

With a third forced move in as many years, it was particularly difficult in the case of Rhodesia, given the death of the Spaniards and the fact that I regarded Rhodesia as my second home, after Mozambique. Despite the warning lights flashing in my head, I had been hoping that my family and I could settle there. It was game country, and it was close to where we had grown up. It was Africa. We did not belong in Europe.

As I flew out of Salisbury in September 1976 with the bodies of the Spanish hunters, somehow I knew that it would be many years before I would be back.

The wind was shifting.

SEVEN

THE WIND SHIFTS

In Africa, things stay the same until they fall apart.

—Keith B. Richburg, *Out of America: A Black Man Confronts Africa*

The aircraft was starting its descent into Nairobi, the Cold Stream or *Ngaro N'Erobi* in the Masai language. The old adrenaline rush coursed through me at the prospect of new challenges and of being back on the only continent I shall ever call home. It was early 1977 and I was returning to Africa, addicted to the uncertainties and the dangers. This time it was the former British colony of Kenya, covering nearly 225,000 square miles. It derives its name from *Kirinyaga,* as the Kikuyu people called Mount Kenya, Africa's second-highest mountain. With the Rhodesian land-mine death of the Spanish hunters and a tracker the previous year, I had decided to cease all hunting operations in Africa. That tragedy had shaken me, and I needed a break from African wars and the destruction they bring. I was battle fatigued.

When I was approached with a very attractive offer to assume control as managing director of the Safari Park Hotel/Casino just outside Nairobi, I never hesitated. It was not only Africa, but a part of Africa

I had long wished to experience but could not in previous years because of political antipathy toward Portuguese passport holders. The country still had a highly organized, prestigious hunting-safari industry which, indeed, was always in my subconscious. It was the cradle of the big-game-hunting safari. I had met many of the most prominent Kenyan safari operators at safari conventions in the States such as at Game Conservation International (Game COIN) and at the very first conventions staged by Safari Club International. Fate saw us meet again, this time in Kenya.

I loved Kenya, where I felt very comfortable in the Anglo culture. The champagne air of the highlands and the unfenced sweep of the plains and valleys reminded me strongly of Mozambique, the sunsets often resembling a child's paintbox splashed across the world. Down on the warm Indian Ocean, the turquoise and blue-green waters washed onto wide, surf-fringed beaches. The coastline was dotted with historic places such as Lamu, Malindi, and Mombasa, with strong links to Arab and Portuguese history. I remember standing in the shadow of the forbidding Fort Jesus on Mombasa, completed by the Portuguese in 1593, and thinking of Vasco da Gama and his men who, in 1498, were the first Europeans to set foot on that coastline. It was a surreal experience for me as I thought back on Portugal's once-overwhelming dominance of the Indian Ocean littoral. The loss of Mozambique signified the end of the Portuguese along the East African coastline. They had long since retreated to their tiny Atlantic motherland, shadows of what they once were.

The hotel/casino on the Thika road was set in thirty acres of beautifully landscaped tropical gardens abounding in bird life and lush vegetation and exuding that unhurried atmosphere of Kenyan country living. Swimming, riding, tennis, dancing under the stars to one of our two dance orchestras, game-viewing excursions, and a casino operation made our complex a very attractive destination. Apart from our hosting air crews, we hosted members of the Kenyan government regularly. There I met Daniel arap Moi, then vice-president of the country, serving under Jomo Kenyatta. Moi and Kenya would feature years later in Mozambican resistance politics.

Kenya was a pleasant place in 1977, especially for those of us possessing expatriate benefits. I visited such landmarks as the Tree Tops Hotel, immortalized by Princess Elizabeth in 1952, and the Mount Kenya Safari Club, with its spectacular setting, meeting a very wide range of interesting people. I played tennis at the renowned Muthaiga Club with all its historic, colonial associations and had a taste of the beauty pageant business when I was invited onto the panel to judge Miss Mombasa! Now, *that* was a challenge!

The stress of managing a hotel/casino is ongoing, especially when attempting to control theft. The Korean co-owners introduced me to the wonders of the pure ginseng root and its energy-boosting propensities, which kept me going as I tried to train staff, keep tabs on the casino, and promote our complex. I already knew, however, that I could not continue living this sort of life indefinitely.

My son spent some time with me in Kenya, where we were all victims of a potentially fatal incident. The casino was raided in broad daylight one Sunday when five very flashy individuals gained access to the office safes at gunpoint. Peter Economides, the casino's chief executive, was busy opening the safes during that mid-afternoon, in preparation for the evening session, when the gang burst in. After emptying the safes of a considerable sum, they brazenly walked into the slot-machine room, smacked a gambler on the face with the flat side of a Masai *simi* sword, manhandled several other guests, and snatched their rings and watches. One guest resisted and had his neck slashed. Then, as if it were a peaceful Sunday outing, the gang ambled past a troupe of traditional dancers from the Akamba tribe who entertained guests on Sundays, and made their getaway in a Mercedes-Benz hijacked from the Czechoslovakian chargé d'affaires!

I was in another section of the hotel and, on hearing the commotion, raced outside to see my son, accompanied by the assistant hotel manager and the security officer, roaring out of the hotel grounds in hot pursuit. They caught up with the Mercedes, which stopped. One gang member leaped out and came up to my son's vehicle, pistol drawn. He asked what the hell they thought they were doing, following them, before suddenly demanding that one of the other men hand over his watch! Then the Mercedes sped off.

No arrests were ever made, and the valuables were never recovered. Neither my son nor the other two men had firearms with them, and I wondered what prevented the gang that day from simply opening up and killing them all. Incidentally, the casino's official name, in fractured French, was the Casino de Paradise! Having lived through three guerrilla wars, the Great Casino Heist was warfare with a difference. Unfortunately, crime has escalated in Kenya and elsewhere in Africa where poverty, disease, rampant unemployment, equally rampant high-level corruption, tribal-based strife, lack of effective policing, and mind-numbing levels of indifference to social and political decay are the norm. I experienced it all.

My heart was not in the hotel/casino business. After a lifetime in the wilds, the confines of bricks and mortar, however lush and comfortable, were no substitute. The stress was corrosive. I was ripe for change, which came in the form of well-known professional hunter Freddie Seed. He and I became very friendly and, one day in May, after much thought, I decided to return to my first passion, the African bush and the promotion of big-game-hunting safaris. I was anxious to break out of my casino cage.

As we drove down the Thika road into Nairobi, a radio news bulletin came on the air. It stunned us. That day—May 20, 1977—the Kenyan government had decided to prohibit all hunting in Kenya immediately. The safari season was in full swing, clients from all over the world, at considerable expense, were in the field, in the middle of their safaris, when the police and army were deployed to the farthest corners of the country to enforce the new decree. The Kenyan safari industry, probably the best organized in Africa at the time, and the most effective policing mechanism to control poaching, to provide steady employment, and to generate funds for the true conservation of Africa's unique wildlife heritage, was no more.

Everything was an instant shambles as safaris were obliged to pack up in the field. We could not believe our ears. There had been no warning, no intimation of this latest insanity in African affairs. Large-scale poaching, especially of ivory and rhino horn, took off after that because the eyes and ears of the safari industry were forced out, leaving vast tracts of bush underpoliced, if policed at all. The wildlife was at the mercy of highly organized poaching entities as never before. Even President Kenyatta's wife became closely involved in the "movement" of wildlife products.

After almost a quarter of a century, the balance sheet in Kenya since that decision is not a happy one. The black rhino population is a specter of its former status, having been poached to near-extinction in that country. The elephant suffered a similar fate, and all the stage-managed demonstrations of pyres of tusks going up in smoke do not alter one fact: Controlled hunting, as epitomized by the once-thriving Kenyan hunting industry, was the most dynamic and cost-effective, community-friendly way of ensuring the survival of Africa's wildlife.

Poaching, fueled by top-level corruption, has reduced Africa's once-thriving game populations, and the exploding human population is steadily encroaching on the remaining habitat. The demise of the hunting industry in Kenya has affected game management, although individual landowners are making laudable efforts to breed species such as the black rhino in an attempt to conserve game and heighten awareness.

I felt that the May 1977 decision was shortsighted. The whole issue has long since become highly politicized. The Kenyan old hands in the safari business and enlightened individuals involved in wildlife management and conservation know the value of the controlled-hunting industry and the foreign exchange it generates, but their hands are tied by politicians, by foreign-funded nongovernmental organizations, and by do-gooders living elsewhere in the world whose gullibility, ignorance, and often, arrogance, are endangering the very creatures they profess to love so much. The sport hunter was never the problem. Rampant poaching is.

A while after this, I started receiving calls from America, spearheaded by my longtime friend and still highly active international safari promoter, Bert Klineburger. An extremely challenging opportunity was being offered to me to take over the entire management of a hunting operation in the Central African Empire, the domain of Emperor Jean-Bédel Bokassa I.

Cheers Kenya!

Stars in their billions reflected so densely on the Aouk River, between the Central African Empire and the Republic of Chad, that I literally could not see the water for their brilliance. Luminous streaks of stars, overlapping one another shone over the waters from bank to bank. I had never had such an astounding experience anywhere else in Africa and I have not seen its like again. I arrived in the Central African Empire in February 1978 to assume control of a large safari operation and resurrect it after a disastrous previous year. I was familiarizing myself with the enormous concessions we had. Hence that extraordinary night on the Aouk River, a hop and a skip away from highly unstable neighboring Chad.

The Central African Empire, independent since 1960, was once the French colony of Ubangi-Chari, named after the two rivers in the region, previously forming part of French Equatorial Africa with Chad, Gabon, and the French Congo. It straddles the Chad-Congo watershed, Chad to the north, Cameroon to the west, Congo Brazzaville and the Democratic Republic of Congo, formerly Zaire, to the south, and Sudan, Africa's largest country, to the east. It is the steaming heart of the entire continent. The southern part merges into dense equatorial forest while, in the north, it becomes moist savanna woodland, the forest along the eastern border blending with those of the Bahr-el-Ghazal and equatorial regions of Sudan. Ravaged for centuries by slave and ivory raiders, this sparsely populated country is over 240,000 square miles in extent, roughly two-and-a-half times the size of Great Britain and Northern Ireland. A very primitive country, it still had robust populations of game and outstanding 100-pounder elephant in the late 1970s. It also had diamonds—a recipe for eventual disaster.

Bokassa, who was chief of the army, staged a military coup in December 1965 and, by the time I arrived in his country, had already made himself president for life, marshal of the republic and, in 1976, self-appointed emperor. He subsequently announced his intention to convert to Islam and change his name to Salah-addin Ahmad Bokassa.

I had entered a one-party state.

From the Egyptian revolution in 1952 until 1990, single-party authoritarian systems were the norm in most of Africa. Coups, some violent, bloody affairs of one or another sort were common. Today, the much-vaunted democratization process in Africa remains very fragile and, as I soon discovered in Bokassa's "empire," the former colonial power was still calling the shots. The safari client and tourist are not usually able to perceive this. It was a question of independence on paper and something very different in real life. The wildlife was at increasing risk in this central African jungle. Managing a safari operation there was going to be more of an adventure than even I had bargained for.

Unlike the majority of sub-Saharan countries, most of the inhabitants of the Central African Empire belonged to the same ethnolinguistic Ubangian group, and therefore the country was quiet. My first day in the humid capital, Bangui, on the Ubangi River, immediately revealed that the French dominated the commercial life of the country, as indeed they did pretty much everything else. This meant that we ate very well, and French wine was freely available in the supermarkets.

When it came to availability of spares and fuel for our hunting vehicles, not to mention aviation fuel as well as all sorts of other commodities we take for granted in First World countries, the picture was very different. It was an expensive battle from the outset to keep operational. My initial impression was that the Central African Empire was by far the most underdeveloped and primitive African country I had been to until that point in my life. I thought I was long since Africa-proof, but more shocks were in store for me.

The American-backed company was called SACAF, the French acronym for the American Central African Company for Wildlife Management. SACAF had four concessions in the savanna country on the Aouk River border with Chad, with camps at Golongosso, Njoko, and Djangara. Airstrips serviced the first two camps. These concessions offered a range of antelope, as well as lion and the distinctive northern or Nile buffalo with its modest horns. The main attraction was giant eland, known as the Lord Derby Eland, named after the thirteenth Earl of Derby. Africa's largest antelope, the huge-bodied males with their equally huge spiral horns, chocolate-colored forelocks and impressive throat dewlaps were much sought after by our SACAF clients. The meat is some of the finest in all safari cuisine. Although eland hunting can be extremely tough and frustrating, SACAF's hunters soon developed an enviable record for trophy eland hunts. The savanna season was from December to May, and the rain-forest season from January to July.

To the east, we had four concessions in the rain forest, with the main camp and airstrip at Baroua. Elephant and bongo were the prime species, in addition to such exotics as giant forest hog and yellow-backed duiker. In the late 1970s, impressive ivory could still be found in the rain forests, one of the last frontiers of big tuskers in Africa. I was soon to discover the ominous extent of poaching by locals and by neighboring countries such as Sudan. Later, the airstrip at the Baroua camp would feature in a highly risky escape drama in which I became involved.

Bangui was our headquarters, where we also had a comfortable lodge for our staff and myself. We coordinated the entire operation from here. It was a typically ramshackle African town, replete with shanties, noisy bazaars, badly potholed streets, and the occasional well-kept building. Everything needed a coat of paint, and the battle against mildew was ongoing. The French, Lebanese, and Portuguese shared the commercial side of things but, clearly, the French were still in control. This steaming town on the banks of the sluggish and muddy Ubangi River had a couple of very good restaurants, a few hotels, and fair medical facilities for Africa. The supermarkets were well stocked with French goods and, if you had money, you lived well. There was no lack of domestic servants, either.

I found the people pleasant, but it was soon clear that the French were not overly enthusiastic at any foreign intrusion on "their" turf. Bert Klineburger's American tenacity and can-do optimism broke through this "French resistance," and SACAF went on to enjoy many outstanding safaris. The French have managed to retain a control over their former colonies which no other colonial power has succeeded in doing. I often wondered whether the backwardness and underdevelopment to this day of former French colonies, despite their natural riches in timber, minerals, precious stones, and petroleum, is not part of a deliberate strategy by the French. They exploit and export the natural resources, but the former colonies continue to struggle, remaining continuously dependent. Pliable, corrupt politicians only exacerbate this dependency. It is the masses who continue to endure and whose lives have hardly changed for the better in well over two generations since the first winds of *uhuru* started howling through Africa. As I would learn first-hand, elephants would be caught in this net of exploitation.

Aircraft were our lifeline in a country with appalling "roads," except for the forty miles of tarmac which led from Bangui to Emperor Bokassa's palace! We did the occasional truck supply run but, to this day, one truck sent out to the rain-forest concessions, a one-month journey, is still there, having broken down. Telephones and telexes were another learning curve in Bangui. The local technicians would come to the lodge and inquire whether these facilities were working. No sooner had we assured the solicitous locals that indeed they were when, with no warning, the lines would go on the blink, paralyzing our business. Back would come the same locals, anxiously inquiring if all was well with our lines, clearly knowing the answer. In order to restore contact with civilization, we had to pay. Working or not, we paid . . . and paid. *C'est l'Afrique.*

As I was finding my feet, I heard of an incident in Chad, just opposite one of our camps on the Aouk River, where a French safari company was operating. The hunter and client came across poachers belonging to the local tribe, easily identified by their alarming facial scarring. They were armed with bows and arrows, and the client and hunter fired over their heads to scare them off, which it apparently did. That night, as the client was relaxing around the campfire with his hunter, an arrow came whizzing out of the darkness and struck the client in the neck. Despite being rushed to medical facilities in the regional capital of Sahr, the client died very quickly. The arrow had been poisoned. It takes only one incident such as this to jolt one back to the reality of Africa.

We brought in several of the old hands from Mozambique. They eventually included my brother, José Augusto, and my son, Tim-Tim.

Captain John Brandt, the renowned and pioneering American hunter who came on safari with SACAF, affectionately called us the "Mozambique Mafia." That he is still around to enthrall readers with his often-exotic hunting experiences is one of the miracle stories in decades to come out of the safari industry.

John, with fellow Americans Bob Ward, Cisco Urrea, and Bill Worley, were scheduled to fly up to our concessions on the Aouk in SACAF's twin-engine Piper Seneca, piloted by Spaniard Javier Soler, a veteran bush pilot. One fine morning, I saw the party off at Bangui Airport and got on with the next task. Not ten minutes after takeoff, one of the aircraft's engines seized. Soler apparently barked at the passengers to throw out whatever baggage and possessions they could to the forest below in an effort to lighten the load. He immediately informed Bangui that they were returning. A full-blown Mayday then developed as the other engine, for whatever reason, could not cope. So much for twin engines!

Bangui tower received the initial message that the aircraft was returning because of the engine failure. The Mayday alarm, however, was never transmitted. All I know of that frightening morning was that our other pilot/aircraft mechanic, who happened to be at the airport and who had been told by the tower that the aircraft was returning, waited in vain for the Piper Seneca. When it did not come back, he contacted me. I went out to the airport, where we spent the next several hours in a state of rising terror at the nonappearance of the aircraft. I had already had several experiences of clients dying on safari, whether from diabetic coma or from guerrilla bullets and landmines. Now this! I thought my heart would certainly stop this time round. There are limits!

As John relates in detail in his book, *Soul of the Hunter: A Half Century of Big-Game Hunting*, the pilot was quite brilliant in managing to crash-land near the M'Boko River, in ten-foot-tall elephant grass, amid trees, and termite heaps. The aircraft broke in two as a tree came crashing down on what remained of the fuselage. To cap it all, nobody was killed. The worst injury was a couple of cracked ribs suffered by Bill Worley. Several rifles were wrecked, and the rest were damaged by battery acid. The group scattered away from the wreck, fearing a fuel explosion and fire, which surely would have killed them all.

Local tribesmen heard the noise of the crash and came upon the group. Brandt and the pilot were guided on a nine-mile trek through the forest to a bush road, where they hitched a ride in a truck, eventually arriving back in Bangui, where they reported to the military command post at Bangui Airport. Two French choppers had arrived quite by chance. I was consulting maps with the French helicopter pilots on the airstrip, wondering how in heaven we were ever going to be able to locate the crash site and recover the bodies in dense forest where the canopy cover was often well over eighty feet high. Suddenly a voice called out, "Hi, Adelino!" There was John, striding towards us on the airstrip, sporting his characteristic bandanna, looking bush-worn but fine, with Soler, the pilot, none the worse for this near-death experience. What a relief! I felt I had aged by a century!

The French went back in a chopper with John and the pilot, accompanied by paramedics, and quickly located the rest of the group. Before nightfall, they were all back in Bangui. Only those who have traveled in a truly primitive country can appreciate how phenomenally lucky Brandt and his group had been. Bangui had very limited aviation-fuel supplies and, apart from the French military choppers, which were there that day by sheer coincidence, the country had no search-and-rescue air capability to speak of. If you came down in the forest and were severely injured, you would probably die of your injuries long before anyone was able to find you and get you out.

John and his pals have always wondered what the reaction was of the simple forest tribesmen when clothing, footwear, ammo, cameras, binoculars, and medical supplies they could never have recognized came raining down from the skies, through the forest canopy to the ground.

Soler, the pilot, remained in Bangui, his nerves intact. Like the seasoned bush pilot he was, he continued flying. But his luck finally ran out and he crashed to his death. The industry lost a good man that day.

We had had a fine first season in the Central African Empire, with clients from the Americas and Europe, many of them old friends from former days elsewhere in Africa. There is no better recommendation than repeat business and, in the safari industry, it is word of mouth all the way. The record books list several 100-pounder elephant, taken with SACAF under arduous and fair chase conditions. It was not at all unusual for our hunters and clients to come across 90- and 80-pounders. SACAF was also particularly successful with giant eland and, to a lesser extent, with the elusive bongo, which were not very plentiful.

Speaking of elephant, my brother, José Augusto, and fellow Portuguese hunter, Luiz Pedro, had a bad scare out in the field when they received a warning that a caravan of about twenty ivory poachers, possibly Somalis, had crossed into the Central African Empire from Sudan. My brother and Luiz Pedro were threatened that if they valued their lives, they would leave the area immediately because the poachers were bristling with automatic rifles and would shoot dead anyone attempting to impede their poaching expedition. Word was out that the poachers were also after diamonds. My brother and his colleague radioed me in Bangui and, after consultation, we decided to move our camp to another area.

It was becoming apparent that it was useless alerting the authorities in Bangui. When I went to considerable lengths to warn them of poaching operations near the Chad border, even succeeding in having officials fly up to see for themselves, the minister back in Bangui remained inert, even berating me for stirring things up. The more I tried to explain that, as a safari organization, operating in his country, it was our absolute duty to report any illegitimate activities threatening their wildlife, the more aggressive and deaf the minister became. The message was simple: Keep your nose out of our animal affairs. Clearly, the minister had a vested interest somewhere and did not want anyone rocking this "cottage industry" boat.

I had work to do and had the wisdom to accept what I could not alter by myself—namely, corrupt, slothful bureaucrats. They did not remotely share our vision of Africa's wildlife heritage and how it should be managed.

A lion hunt with a difference took place on the Aouk River when the male managed to escape across the river, where it was shot. The problem was that it died in the Republic of Chad. Now what? Professional hunters have to use their initiative and be prepared to take decisions quickly and responsibly. Our man managed to persuade some local fishermen to lend their dugout for an undocumented crossing into Chad, where the dead lion was loaded into the canoe and paddled back to us. The client was impressed at SACAF's ability to go the extra mile. Why leave a trophy animal, which had cost a great deal of money to hunt, to Africa's scavengers?

While in the Central African Empire and, certainly, in later years, I heard all the usual stories about Bokassa's alleged brutality, cannibalism, alcoholism, misappropriation of state funds, and profligate lifestyle, as epitomized by his obscenely lavish self-coronation in December 1976. I never met the man and never had any direct evidence of the more outrageous accusations, such as cannibalism. That he was a typical one-party-state African dictator who ruled with an iron fist, enjoying the total backing of the French, is fact.

Bokassa, never interfered in SACAF's operations. We experienced no trouble at all from that quarter. In fact, I was approached at fairly regular intervals by a member of the imperial household staff with a request to provide porcupine meat, one of the emperor's favorite delicacies. I would put the word out to our hunters about the emperor's gastronomic requirements, and dead porcupines would be delivered to the imperial kitchens by SACAF, whenever we could manage it, thereby enhancing our already-sound working relationship.

At the beginning of the safari season in 1979, 1 was told in Bangui that an ex-Kenyan hunter named Alfi von Auersperg—actually, Prince von Auersperg, an Austrian blueblood—had just arrived in town, was staying at the only decent hotel, and that he had plans to go into operation. My ears pricked up at this news. I had not met the prince in Kenya when I was there in 1977, so I picked up the phone and got through to him, introducing myself as the SACAF manager and welcoming him to the Central African Empire. I suggested we meet and that we cooperate as fellow foreigners in an essentially French preserve. He sounded quite touched at this and agreed to come over to the SACAF lodge for lunch and have a chance to familiarize himself with local conditions.

Alfi was a very engaging, good-looking, and pleasant man with considerable hunting experience in Kenya, Sudan, Tanzania, Uganda, and Zaire. We got on very well from the outset. Alfi expressed some surprise at my willingness to befriend him and show him the ropes in a business noted for its extreme competitiveness and professional jealousies. I explained that SACAF had superb concessions and all the clients it could possible handle, and that it never serves to make unnecessary enemies among fellow safari operators. Africa was an unforgiving environment. The day could well dawn when we may need each other's assistance to cope with a situation. It was as simple as that. The French safari operators had offices in Bangui, but never made contact with us or attempted in any way to acknowledge our existence.

With Alfi was his wife, Bea, who has long since made Spain her home. Alfi was accompanied by Jens Hessel, a Dane, a fellow ex-Kenyan hunter and highly experienced bush pilot who had piloted the second aircraft into Bangui. Alfi had piloted the other one. We came to an arrangement whereby they would feel free to come over to the SACAF lodge whenever they liked. I subsequently learned from a good friend of mine in Bangui, a Frenchman named Maurice Alquier, who spoke fluent Spanish and who ran the finest restaurant in town, that Alfi had leased a concession from him in the rain forest.

Alfi told me how he had met Bokassa in Europe and had explained that he wished to be allowed to come over from Sudan to set up a hunting company in his country. Apparently, Bokassa gave the nod but, in the glow of the social moment, I wonder if Bokassa and Alfi actually put pen to paper and concluded a contract—not that that means much in Africa. The next thing that happened was that Alfi's trucks, loaded with safari equipment, crossed the border from Sudan into the Central African Empire, with thirteen Black Kenyan safari staff and a man named Rolf Trappe in charge. Rolf was the son of the redoubtable Margarete Trappe. A Tanganyikan pioneer hunter and the only woman ever admitted to the East African Professional Hunters Association, she had been a transport rider for Von Lettow-

Vorbeck's forces during the East African Campaign of the First World War. The safari business is full of unusual people.

Trappe set up camp with modern radio equipment in the rain forest. Alfi had a radio installed in the SACAF offices for convenience and I can clearly remember his communicating with Trappe in their rain-forest concession. This preparatory period lasted for a month or so as they tried to get things organized. Alfi and his wife made the hotel their base in Bangui and settled in.

Very early one morning, everything came to a sudden, ominous halt. I was already at my desk, dealing with the daily problems, when Jens Hessel came to the lodge, clearly alarmed. He said, "Adelino, we have a serious problem. The police have surrounded our hotel and they handed over documents to Alfi, ordering us all out of the country within twenty-four hours or face arrest. We don't have enough fuel for our aircraft to reach Sudan. Rolf has to be warned in the rain forest to get out and head for Sudan immediately by road. We need your help."

Apparently, no reason was given for this imperial decree for Alfi and his entire operation to shut down and get out of the country. My local assistant, a Black man named Marcel, warned me not to get involved with the Kenyans. Clearly he knew something I did not know, but I was not about to turn my back on this drama. I quickly checked our own fuel supplies and saw that we had some avgas (aviation gas) in our own rain-forest concession, enough fuel to get Alfi's group out of the country. We, however, would be left with nothing and our business relied exclusively on avgas in order to be able to function in that terrain. I was also meddling in dictatorship politics and, as an outsider, this could be exceedingly dangerous. People have disappeared for lesser transgressions in such countries. I could not help wondering who or what was behind this alarming development. To this day, I have not discovered the actual reason why Bokassa kicked out Alfi and his group, and I do not believe anyone else has, either.

Speaking in rapid Portuguese, I got hold of our camp in the rain forest and told them to expect visitors the next morning, to give them absolutely everything they requested, and that absolutely no questions were to be asked. Jessel then radioed Trappe and instructed him to pack up the entire camp and drive to Sudan immediately. I took Alfi and Jessel aside, telling them to observe the strictest confidence in what I was about to tell them: The next morning, they were to head for our airstrip at Baroua, where the staff would refuel their aircraft with all that we had on the ground and that they were then to leave immediately. I gave them the coordinates, and we parted.

At the crack of dawn the next day, the police looking on but not interfering, Alfi, Bea, and Jens left the hotel. We headed for the airport, all of us very tense. Once there, and with the usual crowd of police and officials standing about, but keeping their distance, I saw them off. The two aircraft became fast-disappearing dots in the increasingly hot morning air as they banked to head east and, hopefully, safety.

Back at the lodge, there was no reaction from Marcel or the other locals who knew I was somehow involved with Alfi's group. This is probably the appropriate place to say that it was known that I was on personal good terms with President Giscard d'Estaing of France. There is no doubt that this gave me a certain leeway in the empire. I did not trade on this association.

As I settled in and started juggling other issues, the radio eventually crackled out the news that the party had landed, had been accommodated by our camp staff, and had left. So far, so good.

Then another shock. Alfi radioed me from Sudan, stating that Trappe and the entire Kenyan crew had been intercepted by the police at a place called Rafai, on the Ubangi River border with Zaire, on their way to Sudan. They were being forced back to Bangui. They were under arrest. Could I see what I could do? God almighty! When was this going to end? It was an infringement of radio law to communicate with Sudan. At this rate, my luck would surely run out.

Trappe and his group eventually arrived in Bangui and were placed in the police compound with its mango trees and little else because the local jail was already bursting at the seams. Marcel, my assistant, who happened to be the nephew of the current president of that country, Angel Patassé, warned me again to stay out of the Alfi affair. How could I when I went over to the police compound and was informed that there was no food for the men? This is par for the course in many African jails. Often family members have to feed their relatives—or they will starve. The Red Cross is not the welcome guest in African jails the world fondly imagines it to be. I speak as an insider who has been detained in several African jails under horrendous circumstances. I remember turning to Marcel and explaining that there was no way I could simply stand by and do nothing for fellow hunters under such circumstances because I would wish them to assist me, should I ever be in a similar situation.

I fed Trappe and his thirteen Kenyan Blacks for about one month, giving them money and cigarettes as well. Nobody lifted a finger to help them or me. I worked out a crude code with Alfi and, using the radio equipment he had installed in our office, I let "Alpha" know that all was well in "Bravo"—that is, Bangui—and that the men were being taken care of, but that this could not go on indefinitely. I had a company to manage and was being run ragged by all these complications.

Then—just as suddenly as they had been rounded up—Trappe and his men were released on orders from Bokassa and were accommodated in a seedy hotel. Ah, but who would pay the bill? Again I stepped in and made myself responsible, but not before getting hold of the French involved and telling them that they now had to take responsibility. Matters were eventually sorted out but, when Trappe and his men left the country, I was out of pocket and taken aback by the graceless behavior of people who should have known better.

There is no point in indulging in petty bookkeeping squabbles after all these years. Suffice it to say that I was stunned speechless in February 1985, in San Antonio, at the Game COIN Convention, soon after surviving a personal ordeal which became an international scandal, when I saw Alfi again. He was lukewarm and distant. I saw Trappe in Tanzania in early 1984. His reaction was—shall we say—detached. And people wonder at my cynicism!

As the hunting and jet-set world knows, Alfi eventually had a car accident in Austria and lay in a coma for years before dying, an eerie echo of what befell his ex-wife, Sunny von Bulow, who lies in a coma to this day in the States.

The 1979 season progressed as smoothly as could be expected, and I suffered no repercussions from the Alfi affair that I knew of. What I was becoming increasingly aware of was the alarming number of elephants being shot in the country. I say "shot," as opposed to hunted on legitimate safari licenses. We had a very strict quota, but it soon became apparent that no such restriction existed for certain entities in the country who were slaughtering elephant, however immature, to get the ivory which was then airfreighted from Bangui to Paris at regular intervals.

This was the beginning of the end of the once-flourishing herds of elephant in the country. In 1979, a total of 66 elephant were hunted legally by the three safari companies operating in the country. This brought in a considerable amount of foreign currency. In the same year, however, literally thousands of elephant were slaughtered. This was evident from official statistics pertaining to ivory exports for that year. In Bangui, there was a place called Ivory Village where all sorts of ivory products could be bought. All this occurred under the auspices of a state-owned company called La Couronne (The Crown). It was owned by Bokassa, of course. This company also controlled all exports of diamonds and was closely allied with a group of Spanish businessmen.

Bokassa's excesses resulted in schoolchildren rioting in April that year. Many were arrested and killed. The unrest resulted in a coup by the army on September 29, 1979, backed by French troops who had flown in from Gabon and Chad. Bokassa, who was in Libya at the time to request aid, fled to France where he was not even allowed to disembark from the aircraft. He was given asylum in the Ivory Coast, where he proceeded to tell the world press, especially the French press, about his generosity and his gifts of diamonds to international personalities. Clearly, Bokassa had revenge on his mind and was bent on causing embarrassment in high places.

He succeeded.

Meanwhile, the Central African Empire reverted to the name Central African Republic and once again came under the presidency of David Dacko, the country's first president when it achieved independence from France in 1960. He was ousted in a coup by Bokassa in 1965 and was thrown into jail. When released, he was put in charge of a "cement company"—except that there was no such thing in the entire country. Whenever cement did arrive, it came from Zaire, and it came infrequently.

I needed fifteen bags of cement for the SACAF lodge and placed my order, paying in advance. A month later, still no cement, so I went over to confront Dacko in his shabby little office to demand reimbursement in full. He said he no longer had the money. I called the chief of police, who forced Dacko to repay me every cent. Imagine my reaction when, in the emergency that ensued Bokassa's ousting, the French appointed Dacko to head the country.

That year, on my birthday, in mid-November, I flew to Lisbon for the wedding of my elder daughter, Palucha. My mother was also there. She had been living in Rhodesia with my sister, Lucinda, and had also been spending some time with her sister in Portugal.

I was saddened to see the change that had come over my mother. The forced departure from Mozambique four years earlier and the loss of an entire way of life had had a corrosive effect on her spirit. She was no longer the robust, cheerful, and dynamic woman we had all known all our lives. She had withered inside, and it had little to do with her age. Memories weighed on her soul, and her conversation told me that she now felt marooned. She could not return to Mozambique and she was very unhappy in Portugal.

Not one week after Palucha's wedding, news reached me in Bangui that my mother had suffered a massive heart attack in Lisbon, where she lay in a coma for a week before dying. I was able to get back to Lisbon only a day after her death.

The funeral was particularly distressing for all of us. We knew that our mother had always expressly wished to be buried alongside our father on the farm at Guro, under the giant blue gum trees overlooking the wide horizons she had called her home for nearly three decades. I felt a profound sense of loss and renewed anger at those entities who had been responsible for my mother's sorrow during those last few years of her life. She had tried so hard for all of us.

In January 1980, giving no reasons, the government suddenly banned lion hunting. I immediately went to see the Minister of Water and Forests under whom such matters resorted to request an explanation. The conversation that ensued was ludicrous. The minister said, "We have to conserve our lions. Why do you people shoot lions? People don't eat lions!"

This from a minister! How, with all the goodwill in the world, does one get through the message of controlled hunting as a vital conservation tool to the masses when a presumably educated man cannot even grasp the rudiments of the portfolio he is supposed to manage? I did my best to explain and even spoke of the incidents of cattle-killing lion and of man-eaters. I spoke of the license fees and the role that hunting safaris played to generate money and employment for the country. I may as well have been speaking Mongolian that day for all the impression I made. This incident also underscores a fact about Africa: Game is perceived as meat, food. The idea of trophy hunting, of paying impressive sums of money to endure all sorts of hardships in order to obtain an animal one cannot eat made no sense. It was viewed as the strange behavior of the White man.

I then challenged the venerable minister to kindly explain what was going on with the indiscriminate slaughter of elephant, of the tons of ivory leaving the country by air for France every month, of the seeming lack of control and any thought for the future of elephants in the Central African Republic. SACAF personnel had officially reported sighting two camps of Sudanese Arab poachers, for example, close to SACAF's camp at Vovodo in the rain forest. I wanted to know what—if anything—the government was doing to counteract this looming disaster for the country's elephants. I also wanted to know what the minister intended doing about the widespread corruption in the country's police force and in his own ministry concerning people who were being paid off by poachers to be their wildlife pimps.

The minister became flustered and angry, accusing me of meddling in his country's politics. One-party-state types regard any such questioning as an affront to their authority, the act of an enemy. They are used to obsequious behavior, of underlings ingratiating themselves for favors. The interview was halted abruptly and I was told to leave. I remember telling the minister that I would be back. As I left his tatty offices, I knew in my bones that morning that trouble was brewing—for me personally and for the safari industry in general in that country.

At that juncture, I received a letter from Stu Roosa, the *Apollo 14* commander who had hunted with me in Mozambique, warning me that the American shareholders were "up to their tricks" and that I had better watch my back. I valued this from an old friend and as straight a man as you could wish to meet. I was told that a hunter-guide from America was in association with the shareholders and that the group was planning to come out to the country with a Piper Super Cub aircraft, the kind that can land and take off in tough terrain. I was also tipped off that the prime motivation was elephant.

Knowing that two of the shareholders were in no physical condition to undertake an elephant safari, and bearing in mind the news of the Super Cub, I put two and two together very quickly. Stu's next bit of information that those shareholders were anxious to replace me, giving me the identity of the person, was also no surprise. Bert Klineburger had already been a victim of these people during his three-year stint managing SACAF.

In February 1980, Marc Pechenart, a well-known French businessman who held several concessions in the rain forest adjacent to SACAF's areas, came out to hunt elephant. He got on the radio, telling me that he had come across the carcasses of many elephant which had clearly been mowed down by poachers for whatever ivory they carried, however immature. The stench overwhelmed the countryside.

Quite soon after this, at midday on March 23, to be precise, Radio

Bangui suddenly announced that all elephant hunting in the country had been banned. The tragedy is that this well-intentioned act did not stop the slaughter, which has continued to this day. The once-robust herds of elephant have all but vanished; the sport hunter is not remotely to blame. The criminals are the organized and violent poaching gangs operating out of places like Sudan, Chad, Zaire, and Somalia, the cat's-paws for their wealthy, faceless foreign masters. The other factor contributing to this slaughter is the ongoing extreme poverty of the rural masses, who are easily intimidated and exploited by the poachers and the syndicate bosses.

I subsequently fell seriously ill with amebic dysentery and also underwent surgery in Houston. While I was in the States, the ban on elephant hunting occurred. Given the unhealthy atmosphere among the shareholders and their less-than-clear intentions, I decided to call it a day and move on. With my resignation, the company became a shambles. The shareholders started fighting one another, accusations and counteraccusations flying around. They effectively abandoned SACAF. The two aircraft belonging to them—one being the Super Cub—were flown out of the country, but the Super Cub disappeared over Angola which was—and remains—in a state of civil war. Neither the pilot nor the aircraft has ever been traced.

After I left, those who stayed behind and who thought they could manage the company, failed. They also failed to pay the requisite trophy fees to the government. The result was that some of the clients' trophies were impounded and, as I knew the people concerned, I felt an overriding moral obligation to return to the Central African Republic in my private capacity to do everything possible to have the trophies released and shipped out to their rightful owners. I did just that, flying into Bangui on August 30, 1980. As they say, it's not over until the fat lady sings!

At the SACAF offices, I set about trying to sort out the trophy drama and began making progress. On September 3, I woke to the interesting sight of some fifty-odd soldiers of the Central African Republic's army surrounding the lodge, machine guns at the ready. I was under house arrest, on the orders of the president of the republic, the venerable David Dacko, with whom I had not been able to "cement" any understanding! In strode a Mr. Yollot, the comptroller-general of the state, and a Mr. Guerrela, inspector-general of finance, to carry out a thorough audit of SACAF's books.

These two gentlemen were hostile to me and refused to give any reason for the mini-siege around the lodge. I turned over every scrap of paper I could find, with the proviso that I assumed responsibility strictly for the period during which I managed SACAF and for no other. While they went to work, looking for evidence of malfeasance on my part, I managed to send a telex to Marc Pechenart, a copy of which I have retained, alerting him to the situation. I also managed to smuggle out a letter to President Giscard d'Estaing's wife, Anne-Aymone, asking that she put the word of my predicament out in the right places.

Suddenly, my two auditor friends changed their tune, becoming positively friendly. On September 15, the audit was completed, the only fault being the lack of a receipt for a telegram I had sent. The two men then said, "Mr. Pires, all is in order. We did not realize SACAF brought in so many FCFA [the currency of the former French colonies] and that you gave so much work to our country." I remember saying, very clearly "Well, it's too late now, my friends."

The next morning, as I was preparing to leave for the airport, having long since put in place all possible mechanisms to get clients' trophies released, in came one of SACAF's most trusted employees. He had managed to drive back from the rain-forest concessions and was in a very excited state, saying over and over, "*Patron, patron*, I have all the ivory! I have all the ivory." Among the clients who received their ivory was the late Bob Chisholm of Pizza Hut fame. He was a grand gentleman to the end, and I value his personal letter of thanks to me.

Fifteen years later, in 1995, I was approached by a very influential English group to go back to the Central African Republic to manage a huge ecotourism project. I replied, "You people continue to be ignorant about the realities of African politics. Do the French know about this? Do you honestly think they are going to let you English play in their backyard?"

Adieu, Empire/République Centre-Africaine!

When President Valéry Giscard d'Estaing was the guest of King Hassan II of Morocco at his hunting estate, he turned to his host and said that it was a pity that His Majesty had not been able to fully exploit the potential of his estate. The reply was that "the right man" had not yet been found for the job. D'Estaing said he had just the person in mind and, on October 4, 1980, I received a letter from Maurice Patry, a long-standing friend of the president and a hunter who had spent decades in Gabon running a hunting operation there. I knew Maurice from Mozambique days. He often accompanied D'Estaing on his hunts. I was asked to contact the Elysée Palace and to be in Paris by the end of that month to discuss the Morocco proposal with the president.

Paris. One of my favorite cities. The presidential limo picked me up from my hotel, and off we went to the Elysée Palace. D'Estaing gave me details of the protocol, date, place, and time to be observed for my forthcoming audience with the king of Morocco in order to discuss how best to develop and sustain the hunting potential in his country of nearly 175,000 square miles.

Rabat was different. The Arab world was something quite new to me. I had installed myself at the hotel, made the necessary initial contacts to announce my arrival, and was told to wait for the palace to get back to me and bring me over for an audience with King Hassan II to pursue the project initiated by President d'Estaing.

After five days, not a word from the palace. I let it be known that I could no longer wait around. Hiring a car, I drove to Tangier and, from there, I crossed into Spain on the ferry. On being informed of what had happened, D'Estaing was ever philosophical and invited me to the hunting estate at the Château de Rambouillet shortly after that. King Hassan was to be the guest of honor at a pheasant hunt, followed by a luncheon. It was hoped that we could tackle the project afresh.

The king stood up President d'Estaing at Rambouillet. He was in good company on this score. None other than Queen Elizabeth II of Great Britain was kept waiting by King Hassan. Who was I to complain? Glancing at the menu I have retained of that special luncheon, I remember D'Estaing raising his glass somewhere between the lobster Romanoff and the strawberry sorbet, and proposing a toast to "our absent guest."

Sub-Saharan politics are one thing, Moorish maneuverings another. I bid my fond salaams to Morocco and have not been back.

The fly-blown camel had been dead for a couple of days in front of the minister's residence in Khartoum. The khamsin, a vicious sandstorm, was stinging its way through the untarred streets, late that February in 1981, darkening the sky and making the heat even more oppressive. It was in the 100s that day as we sat down to a lunch of camel meat and couscous. The stench from the camel outside and the appalling heat were such that I begged off, blaming recent stomach surgery for my indisposition. My Spanish colleagues from the Madrid-based Sudan Safaris took things in their stride. We were on a major reconnaissance trip, and the minister was an important personage.

Sudan, Africa's largest country at about 2,000,000 square miles, had beckoned. It is part of a semiarid region which extends from the Red Sea to the Atlantic Ocean and which was known in ancient times by the Arabs as Bilad as Sudan, the Land of the Blacks. Sudan itself is flanked by the Red Sea, Egypt, Libya, Chad, the Central African Republic, the Democratic Republic of Congo, which was Zaire at the time, Uganda, Kenya, and Ethiopia. As the sable Nubian servant in his white robes moved noiselessly from place to place with the next delicacy, his Arab master indicating his wishes silently, I immediately saw that the Sudan meant at least two worlds with several miniworlds in between.

There is the dominant Arabic-speaking, Muslim northern and central world and, south of the Bahr-al-Ghazal and Sobat rivers, in the remote southern provinces, the predominantly Nilotic, Christian, and animist world of the Dinka, Nuer, Shilluk, and Bari ethnic groups. A small group living in the Nuba Mountains in the center of the country and along the southwestern border with the Central

African Republic belong to the Niger-Congo language family, while the Beja, towards the Red Sea Hills, are Cushites. Desert, immense plains, some mountains, dry and moist savanna, tropical rain forests, the Nile and its tributaries, and the notorious Sudd swamps of the south comprise this troubled country. Independent since 1956, it has experienced armed rebellion by the non-Muslim south since the mid-1950s, making this the longest postindependence conflict in all Africa. When I arrived, it was a sporadic affair, but it would not remain so.

I promoted the Sudan between 1981 and 1982, linking up with Avo Margossian, an Armenian and the principal of Wildlife Safaris which developed out of Sudan Safaris. We attended Safari Club International's 1981 convention in the States with a delegation from Sudan and had no trouble booking out our seasons. My son and several Mozambique old hands spent two years hunting in Sudan where he took clients into the rugged, heat-soaked Red Sea Hills between October and the end of February for the Nubian ibex, one of the most sought-after Sudan game animals, with its stunning semicircled, knotted horns. The Eritrean gazelle and the diminutive Salt's Dik Dik were also part of the package we offered. The hunting vehicles all bore a special official sign in Arabic, stating that they were authorized to transport alcohol. On several occasions, Tim-Tim saw locals scurry away from the vehicles the moment they had seen the sign because it offended their religious beliefs.

We promoted safaris in the savanna between December and the end of May and, in the rain forest, from December to the end of July, offering a general bag, in addition to species peculiar to Sudan. The bulk of our safaris were accommodated in the southern provinces which, at the time, had an astounding variety of game in vast, underpopulated country criss-crossed by nomadic tribes such as the Dinka, many of whom went about entirely naked. Conditions for game were ideal. Human pressure and encroachment upon habitat were not yet an issue in the south.

Sudan, a magnificent, unpolluted paradise for game, had another side to it. I caught a whiff of this that day in Khartoum, which struck me as a filthy town with a terrible climate. It was only when I got to

Juba, in the far south of the country, near the border with Uganda, that I realized how completely undeveloped the country as a whole was. We had a lodge in Juba, where it was a constant battle to obtain fresh fruit, vegetables, and perishables, and to keep supplies of commodities we all take for granted in even a half-civilized place. Everything was flown in once a week from Nairobi, but the problem was that sometimes the aircraft would not arrive or, when circling over what passed for a landing strip, it would refuse to land. Either the apology passing for a fire engine was absent because it had no fuel, or the pilot simply did not feel like flying in to Juba.

I once asked a visiting minister in Juba why, with the waters of the Nile right there and very fertile soil to boot, the people did not grow their own vegetables and fruit. The minister replied that there were so many goats that they would eat everything. I countered this by stating that there was plenty of appropriate natural material with which to build barricades to protect the produce. Ah, but the minister then told me that the problem really was that the police and army would steal everything anyway—so what was the use of starting in the first place!

As I learned firsthand over the decades, Africa is home to this mental torpor, an inertia which goes hand in hand with a fatalistic outlook, hamstringing initiative, and stunting prospects for growth fueled by Africans themselves. Marry that outlook to a one-party mentality where graft is the favorite sport, and you have one of the explanations as to why the continent continues to languish in the backwaters of progress. First World outsiders are continuously frustrated in their efforts to transfer the work ethic. Ideas are fine, but unless they are executed and the end product maintained, the whole exercise is fruitless. Given the realities of Sudan at the time, maybe the minister was right.

I disliked Sudan. The enervating climate, the filth, the ineptitude got to me so that I refused to be based full-time in the country. It was a superb destination for hunters, but I was not eager to plunge back into a primitive environment in order to assume all the headaches of managing a safari operation. I would visit, but I would promote from the outside, where the clients were.

My son thrived in Sudan and had some special experiences. Being an amateur history buff, he welcomed the opportunity to go to a place called Suakin on the Red Sea, opposite and slightly to the south of Jidda and Mecca in Saudi Arabia. There, half-submerged in sand, was a gigantic palace, centuries old and boasting hundreds of rooms. Why it was abandoned remains a mystery. Clearly, the local potentate had been threatened and, unable to control the situation, had had to flee, emptying his harem in the process.

Before accompanying his Sudanese guide to Suakin, my son was warned not to reveal that he was a Portuguese national because, in that region, the people bore a grudge against the Portuguese for their exploits in the area over four hundred years previously! Oral tradition had kept alive the clashes between the local tribes and the Portuguese. This referred to the sixteenth century, when Turks and Arabs attacked the Christian Abyssinians along the Red Sea coast and into the country itself, scimitar in one hand and the Koran in the other. A Portuguese fleet, carrying some four-hundred and fifty musketeers, arrived at that crucial time under the command of Vasco da Gama's brother, Dom Cristóvão, to aid the Christian Abyssinians. Much blood flowed between Christians and Muslims along the Red Sea and, as my son discovered, bitter memories were handed down from generation to generation.

While on things Muslim, the mosque in Juba was very close to the lodge and well before dawn each day, the mosque would blare out for miles around a taped muezzin, calling the faithful to the first of the five mandatory prayer sessions per day every Muslim observes. One of the hunters, reacted very badly to the heat, the mosquitoes, and the daily frustrations, as we all did. The mosque's loudspeakers finally snapped something in his mind and, unbeknown to the rest of the lodge, he dressed up in authentic Arab gear and hied himself off to the mosque to join in the morning prayers. Despite his swarthiness, he was soon spotted as an infidel intruder and was chased out of the mosque at top speed to the accompaniment of dire curses by the faithful. There was a devil of an uproar over this. The hunter somehow managed to leave Sudan without being apprehended.

During those couple of years of promotion for Sudan, hunters would come across a fair number of Blacks in the southern provinces toting AK-47s. They were the Anya Nya rebels, who have since been consolidated into the Sudanese People's Liberation Movement and the Sudanese People's Liberation Army. A military coup in 1989 further muddied the political waters of Sudan, and the rebel movements have fragmented even further. The pockets of unrest eventually developed into renewed civil war of such vengeance against the Muslim north, that Sudan shut down all hunting by early 1984. The world media has long since transmitted pictures of famine in Sudan and of bloody guerrilla warfare. Reports of persecution being perpetrated against the south and of accusations of slave-trafficking by the Muslim north, countered by Khartoum's furious denials, mean that in this cauldron of human misery, Sudan's wildlife counts for nothing. It is food. People have to eat. How can anyone speak of game laws, conservation, and quotas when people are dying, for whatever reason? How can safari clients be accommodated safely in a country awash with gun-toting fighters and an equally determined and well-equipped Muslim north, imbued with the fire of jihad and the dictates of sharia law, determined to root out all talk of secession and southern independence?

The closure of Sudan was a tragedy. The wildlife of that country occupies a special place in hunting literature, and there is no way of knowing if the country will ever reopen to the international sport hunter and the dynamic role he plays in funding conservation. If it does, what will have survived nearly a half century of unrest and outright civil war? Do hundreds of thousands of game animals still migrate annually in the southeast—the white-eared kob, the gazelle, the eland, and the tiang, a member of the hartebeest family, closely followed by the predators, other usually nonmigratory species such as buffalo, zebra, giraffe and beisa oryx, with the scimitar horns of the gemsbuck family, joining in this wave of African wildlife as it washes over the plains to the foothills of neighboring Ethiopia? The shadow of the AK-47 has long been cast over this once-idyllic country for wildlife.

There is a proverb which says that he who drinks of Nile waters returns to drink but, for me, it was salaam to Sudan. Houston, Texas called.

My old friend, Frank Green, had asked me to join him in a new venture as he had sold his top safari-booking organization in Houston to Tom Friedkin, the well-known businessman and hunter. The new company was called Sporting International, and I became a hunting consultant in 1982, sending clients all over the world. Houston and the Texans were a very pleasant break.

My restless character resurged as news came my way that Zaire was reopening for hunting. I thought of one man with a direct line to President Mobutu Sese Seko and contacted him. Like a powerful magnet, Africa was once again drawing me back.

It would be the calm before the storm.

EIGHT

CALM BEFORE THE STORM

Its autocratic leader, President Mobutu, is said to be the fifth richest man in the world. He certainly bled the Congo of its wealth far more efficiently than King Leopold.

—Thomas Packenham, *The Scramble for Africa*

Portuguese explorers arrived on the Atlantic coast at the mouth of the Congo River in the 1480s and named the region Zaire, from the word *Zadi*, meaning "Big Water." They never penetrated the far interior, and therefore had no concept of the gigantic Congo basin, with its vast network of rivers, rapids, and marshes, dense equatorial and deciduous forests, savanna vegetation, highlands, mountains, and lakes. They could only have had an inkling of the richness of the wildlife as they established relations with the kingdom of *Kongo* at the Congo River estuary, a kingdom which extended its influence far beyond its center at the river mouth.

The Portuguese came initially as missionary zealots, but were soon sidetracked into the slave trade, particularly to supply the colony of Brazil, from the 1530s onward. The pages of Congo basin history are fraught with tragedy. Little has changed on the eve of the new millennium in colossal, mineral-rich Zaire, now the Democratic Republic of Congo. In excess of 900,000 square miles, this country is well over four and a half times the size of France, and is flanked by nine other countries. It is in a state of absolute decay, and is in the grip of long-standing civil unrest, which is escalating daily.

Going on 500 years after the arrival of the Portuguese, fate saw me heading back to Africa, to Zaire with a handwritten letter of introduction and recommendation from former President Valéry Giscard d'Estaing of France to President Mobutu Sese Seko of Zaire, who had good reason to be beholden to D'Estaing.

A few facts about Zaire are essential here in order to understand what happened to our operation later on.

D'Estaing had saved the Zairean dictator on two occasions when French paratroopers, aided by Belgium and the United States, were flown in during 1977 and 1978 to put down anti-Mobutu invasions of mineral-rich Shaba Province from neighboring Angola and Zambia. Shaba was the former Katanga Province, which had seceded from the rest of the country from 1960 to 1963. The secession was eventually suppressed by a United Nations task force, which did battle with several hundred foreign mercenaries from many nations. Rivers of blood flowed, and reports of atrocities went out all over the world.

The troubles were far from over when leftist rebels called the Simbas then went on the rampage and ended up controlling about half of the entire country before Belgian and American paratroopers rescued the trapped European residents on November 24, 1965 in the heroic Stanleyville operation, and helped crush the Simba rebellion. The very next day, Joseph-Désiré Mobutu, the chief of staff of the Congolese army, deposed the head of state in a coup and seized power.

Between then and his death in September 1997, a solid thirty-two years down the line, Mobutu raped the country of its resources in a merciless, kleptomaniac orgy of one-party lunacy. He changed the name of the country in 1971 from the Democratic Republic of Congo to the Republic of Zaire and launched a policy of "Zairianization," meaning "indigenization." A policy of "authenticity" was introduced, in which Mobutu changed place names and discouraged Western dress, obliging people to discard their Western first names. Mobutu led the way; his full name, *Mobutu Sese Seko Kuku Ngebendu*

Waza Banga, means "the cock who jumps on anything that moves," an apparent allusion to his unflagging interest in the opposite sex.

The economy was nationalized, a process already well under way by 1967, with the expropriation of the Belgian-owned copper mines. All opposition was crushed, and the country started the steep slide into a bottomless chasm of patronage, corruption, destitution, and suffering which eventually erupted like a suppurating boil in late 1996, but not before Mobutu became one of the richest individuals in the entire world. The country remains chaotic and dangerous. It also remains fabulously rich in natural resources.

Major Western powers poured financial aid and sophisticated military assistance into Mobutu's regime because he readily supported Western strategic objectives in Africa, and because Western powers were closely involved in the exploitation of his country's underground wealth. An example of this was the use of Zairean territory by certain Western powers, among them the United States of America, to supply logistical support to the UNITA opposition forces in neighboring Angola in the 1980s. All this began to change, of course, with the official end to the Cold War in December 1989 and the subsequent disintegration of the Soviet Union. Countries have interests—never friends—as UNITA's leader, Jonas Savimbi, found out at the hands of South Africa and the United States, and as Mobutu also found out. On a personal level, I was to rediscover this truth all over again.

D'Estaing expressed his reservations about Zaire and about Africa as a whole when I approached him in early 1983 to facilitate an introduction to Mobutu. He knew what he was talking about, but I was restless and wanted to get back to Africa. I knew from direct experience that in Africa, if you want something to even half-work, you need a jump start from the top. I also knew that Mobutu was from the Ngabandi tribe from the extreme north of Zaire, bordering on the Central African Republic. I was interested in the far northern Uélé region because my information told of outstanding populations of elephant which would be the main attraction for the international sport hunter.

The chances were reasonable that the population would easily support a small annual quota of elephant, but a feasibility study would first have to be undertaken. With Mobutu as head of state and with tribal links to the far north, I stood a chance of being able to establish a safari operation if D'Estaing was able to assist me with a personal note. To quote Keith Richburg again in his illuminating *Out of America: A Black Man Confronts Africa*: "In Africa . . . it *is* all about tribes." This is fact, not foreign paternalistic fable.

I flew into Kinshasa, a city I would see again and again during the preparatory phase of our operation. I never met President Mobutu. He was either constantly absent, at one of his overseas mansions, or he was taking a breather at his sumptuous presidential palace at Gbadolite on the Ubangi River in the extreme north, very close to the Central African border. D'Estaing's letter, however, opened essential doors. It was not long before my son, my nephew Caju, and our relative, Rui Monteiro, came out to form the nucleus of a prospecting team to fly up north and establish the viability of our envisaged operation. We made the small town of Bondo on the Uélé River, east of Gbadolite, our base and we all began brushing up our bush French.

My son began acclimatizing very soon after his arrival in Kinshasa to the way things were done in that country. He was driving a brand new 4×4 vehicle in downtown Kinshasa, trying to avoid the potholes, when he was caught in a traffic jam to end all traffic jams. Being a patient person who is very slow to anger, Tim-Tim edged his vehicle forward whenever he could, and simply waited for the traffic jam to dissolve.

It did not. Suddenly, a traffic policeman came up to my son, gesticulating to him to stop. When asked for the reason, Tim-Tim was told that he had broken a traffic law—for speeding! Clearly, the traffic policeman was looking for a bribe to ease the vicissitudes of his daily existence in that chaotic environment. Bemused at the patent absurdity of the charge, my son declined to play along. Switching off the ignition, he removed the key and abandoned the 4×4 in the middle of the massive traffic jam. Horns blared, tempers rose, people swore, and the traffic policeman ran after Tim-Tim, imploring him to take pity and not make his life more complicated than it already was.

Tim-Tim kept walking. The vehicle was fetched later on by a friend, who greased no palms in the process. We were not bothered again by any traffic policemen. At this stage, I contacted Bert Klineburger, my most trusted friend in the safari business, to pool ideas about the Zairean venture. He was pivotal in bringing American finance into the deal which enabled us, eventually, to buy suitable boats, tents, brand-new vehicles, and all the rest of the equipment needed for a first-class hunting operation. The remoteness of the dense equatorial forest region proved to be an expensive logistical exercise because everything had to be flown in from Kinshasa. It was tough terrain, heat soaked, humid, insect-ridden, and very primitive. These factors also explained why there were still healthy populations of big elephant left. The logistics were so daunting that they impeded even the most dedicated poachers.

We were able to negotiate a ten-year written contract with the Zairean government, authorizing us to open up a concession on the Uélé River. My son, nephew, and Rui had been able to establish that the region indeed harbored some outstanding trophy elephant, as well as other highly-sought-after species such as bongo and, indeed, animals that we had had on quota in the Central African Republic a few years previously.

Bert Klineburger flew back with me to Zaire for a personal on-the-spot inspection of our area up north, of our written undertaking with the Zairean government and all related facilities. We met Bemba Saolona, President Mobutu's right-hand man. He owned a huge aircraft company equipped with C-130s, a variety of Boeings and smaller aircraft. Once Bert had had a chance to satisfy himself as to the viability of the undertaking, we then went ahead with the full-scale equipping of our operation and used Saolona's cargo aircraft to transport everything to our northern area. We had no trouble at all in signing up clients. Zaire had been closed for years, and its novelty, together with a wide base of clients, many of whom were long-standing safari clients of mine and of Bert Klineburger, meant that our 1984 season was soon fully booked.

Then the telex came. I was in Mexico in early January 1984, signing up the last client, when I was informed by a member of our staff in Kinshasa that the Zairean government had just announced a complete ban on all hunting operations, to take effect immediately. No warning. No explanation. There I sat, with a full season and my first client for elephant, Bill Quimby, the esteemed former editor of Safari Club International's flagship magazine, already having had all his shots and ready to leave on his elephant hunt. He was due out in a matter of weeks.

All sorts of theories have made the rounds about why Mobutu suddenly banned hunting in Zaire. One was that he was intimately involved in large-scale ivory poaching, and that hunting operations would get in the way and pose a risk for him. Hunting companies were in the way of this presidential pursuit.

Another theory, told to me in confidence at the time by one of Mobutu's ministers, involved Colonel Muammar el-Qaddafi of Libya, who was helping the Arab northerners of Chad in their armed fight against the non-Arab southerners of the country. Mobutu was believed to be helping the southerners and felt threatened at the prospect of armed outsiders, be they safari clients or not, coming into his country with firearms.

I never swallowed this explanation. My experience in Africa has taught me that many African heads of state, especially in one-party dispensations as was the case with Zaire, typically view their country's resources, including wildlife, as their personal fiefdom to dispose of as, when, and how they see fit. Mobutu was not one to make way for operations which would play by the book, be accountable and, in the process, keep an eye on wildlife resources in his country.

Yet another theory concerned a crowd of East African hunters who were hunting in the northeastern part of Zaire and who were flying into their hunting area directly, circumventing all immigration and customs formalities.

Whatever the real reason or reasons may have been, we were left high and dry and chronically embarrassed by this latest example of African perfidy. All our brand-new equipment, from vehicles to rubber boats and everything in between, was stolen by Mobutu and his associates. Bemba Saolona is now in the cabinet of Mobutu's successor, President Laurent Kabila, whereas his son, Jean-Pierre, heads one of the main rebel factions intent on toppling Kabila. The civil war continues as the country is in the grip of foreign troops, local armed forces, and countless petty warlords. They all have to eat. The carnage of the country's wildlife continues.

No legitimate hunting operation was allowed to resume in Mobutu's country after 1984. Today, the prospect is fainter than ever. Cease-fires on paper remain unenforceable. The United Nations has learned once more that high-sounding words and expensive conferences have failed to exert any influence on the situation, and tribal hatreds are as deep as they ever were. The country will remain a no-go zone for the international hunting community and for ecotourism in general. This will mean a greater and greater threat to what remains of renamed Democratic Republic of Congo's wildlife. The situation is hopeless.

Africa makes you resilient. With Mozambique now an irretrievable personal loss, all ties cut and my entire family long since living in several other countries, I faced the unknown future head-on once more. With my list of clients and contacts in my briefcase, I flew over to the States to Safari Club International's convention, the greatest marketplace in the safari world, whose birth I had attended back in 1972. There, I met Gordon Cundill, fourth-generation South African and highly experienced hunter, who was examining ways of buying out a company in Tanzania called the Monterrey Big Game Hunting Club. It was owned by a group of Mexican industrialists and had about thirty members.

The owners of Hunters Africa were American, and Gordon was the manager for the operations in Botswana and Zambia. If a deal could be struck and the Monterrey outfit purchased, Hunters Africa would be expanded significantly. I had an impressive list of long-standing clients, and an agreement was soon concluded. My son, nephew, and Rui were all absorbed into the Hunters Africa family as experienced big-game hunters. I was taken on board to soon replace Theodorus Potgieter, a fellow in Arusha. South African–born but carrying a British passport, he had been managing the Monterrey Big

Game Hunting Club for his Mexican bosses. There were already extremely serious misgivings about him.

But first things first.

The immediate future was bright as Gordon and I flew to Paris to conclude details for Giscard d'Estaing's Tanzanian safari with me. It was wonderful to be organized again, to have the solid backing of a large organization like Hunters Africa, and to be able to plan ahead. It was also a relief to be out of the Congo shambles. I had taken a tremendous financial hammering over that fiasco.

In Paris, our good fortune was sustained as D'Estaing, his wife, and daughter concluded plans to come out in July 1984 for a fourteen-day safari with me in the Ugalla concession. He was still a key figure in French political life and, as the immediate former president of France, certain protocol niceties had to be observed on the ground in Tanzania. I then flew out to Tanzania, connecting for Arusha, in the shadow of Mount Kilimanjaro, Africa's highest mountain, where the company had its main office for the Tanzanian operation.

Hunters Africa had three concessions in the country, divided among Masailand in the far north, straddling the Tanzania-Kenya border, the Ugalla River region in the southwest and, of course, the Selous Reserve in the southeast, where the great English naturalist/hunter, Frederick Courteney Selous, lies buried. He had been shot dead by a German sniper in January 1917, during the East African Campaign of the First World War. I thought back on Selous House of my boarding school days in Southern Rhodesia, of how my path through life has been signposted by significant names and places destined to find an echo down the years.

At nearly 365,000 square miles, Tanzania is just a whisker short of three times the size of the state of New Mexico. Flanked by eight countries, among them Mozambique in the extreme south, and with an Indian Ocean coastline over 850 miles long in which the exotic Tanzanian islands of Zanzibar, Pemba, Mafia, and Kilwa are situated, it is bold open country. With lakes, mountains, endless plateau country, savanna wilderness, the highlands around Mount Kilimanjaro and Mount Meru, and the steaming tropical coast, Tanzania boasts three World Heritage Sites: the Selous Game Reserve, the Serengeti

National Park, and the Ngorongoro Crater. Some of the most significant fossils of our ancestors have been found in Tanzania, too. It is also home to perhaps the most stunning annual animal migration spectacle still to be seen. It occurs in the Serengeti, where Thomson's gazelle, wildebeest, and other creatures blanket the countryside in undulating wave after wave as they respond to ancient instincts to move on.

As I settled in, I thought back on the Portuguese links with Tanzania. I always liked to know something of a country's history because it gave insight. Portugal had been the first Western power to settle along that part of the Indian Ocean littoral, which had been part of a trade network for more than 2,000 years. The Arabs eventually predominated and Islam took root. By the early sixteenth century, Portuguese navigators established rule over the coastal settlements, and Mombasa emerged as the main center of trade. This ushered in a two-hundred-year period of conflict between the Portuguese and their enemies. Trade involved beads, cotton, and metal implements from India and the Middle East in exchange for slaves, gold, ivory, and even commodities such as wax. The Portuguese eventually withdrew south of the Rovuma River to what became Mozambique.

Tanzania was still very rich in game when I arrived. It was also a one-party, impoverished state ruled by Executive President Julius Nyerere, who was in the forefront of support for the various guerrilla movements in Southern Africa at the time and for long afterward. No matter, I now had a fresh chance to be back in Africa on a more solid footing, to be able to live close to truly wild country, to hunt upon occasion, and to promote safaris in the international marketplace. As a whole, Hunters Africa felt buoyant about our future prospects. The potential for success was high for a well-run safari company with an A-list clientele.

The 1984 season began in May and would last until late November. My son, nephew, and Rui preceded me; I arrived eventually in July. With everything in place for the D'Estaing safari, I flew down to the Ugalla concession later that month and readied the camp and staff for the D'Estaing party's imminent arrival. We had two camps in that region, about 20 miles apart. I was at Ugalla One, as it was called. The visit was being kept low-key, except for a formal dinner in Arusha at the end of the safari, hosted by Anna Nyerere, daughter of the head of state.

The aircraft buzzed our camp with its classic East African *manyara* tents set on the banks of the croc-and hippo-filled Ugalla River in typically open savanna country. The staff were all on the alert as I drove out to the airstrip for the group's arrival. Maurice Patry, D'Estaing's longtime hunting companion, was also in the party. It was important that this particular safari proceed well, as it is a word-of-mouth business, and Hunters Africa stood to benefit enormously from prestigious references. We were making progress with a fairly drastic overhaul of the company we had taken over. I had already unearthed worrying problems and was poised to make a blunt report to the new owners as to what we had to do to get our business in order and to maintain it. The chance to hunt and relax with the D'Estaing party recharged me for the task ahead.

D'Estaing had a highly satisfying and successful safari with Hunters Africa. He managed to obtain superb lion, leopard, and buffalo as well as other species such as a particularly handsome sable antelope. In fact, the Ugalla region was noted for its sable.

Back in Arusha, we all attended a reception for D'Estaing and his family, with Anna Nyerere presiding. I saw D'Estaing and his family off at Arusha Airport and returned to my hotel to unwind for a day or two and to review increasingly disturbing issues surrounding the Monterrey company Hunters Africa had acquired and the less-than-clear activities of Potgieter. Apparently, there were two companies registered in Tanzania using the name "Monterrey." One of those companies was in the name of Potgieter. I discovered that he was also very friendly with a Mr. Ndolanga who was the general manager of TAWICO, the Tanzanian Wildlife Corporation, based in Arusha, which controlled all hunting in the country. I also discovered that Potgieter was very chummy indeed with Anna Nyerere.

I was not alone in my growing unease at what was afoot with the acquisition of the Monterrey company. Lew Games, one of the most experienced professional hunters in the business and on the staff of Hunters Africa, came out to Tanzania to feel out the situation. He was not happy, either.

A picture was emerging of illicit plans to take over Hunters Africa's equipment and operations, with the second company in Potgieter's name being the envisaged vehicle. Ndolanga was in cahoots with Potgieter in his private capacity. At that stage, non-Tanzanian Whites were "camp managers" but, in effect, they were doing the actual professional hunting. Clearly, Potgieter was preparing some kind of "coup" with the help of Ndolanga.

Another disturbing incident occurred. I was suddenly requested to hand in my passport and those of my son, nephew, and Rui for some or other "stamp" concerning visas to work in Tanzania. We were in Tanzania legally and had long since complied with all the necessary formalities. What was this? While I pondered this development, Potgieter asked me just before the end of the D'Estaing safari if I would please delay my trip back to Europe by a week as he had to go somewhere and the business could not be left unattended. I was supposed to have returned with the D'Estaings to Europe for client-related matters.

Potgieter knew something was afoot. He knew we were all suspicious of him, but I had not said anything yet. I was awaiting more tangible evidence of unethical practices before reporting back to Gordon Cundill and the American owners of Hunters Africa. This was imminent. Potgieter's last-minute request for me to stay back in Tanzania was a trap, deliberately thought out and prepared. But I did not know this at the time.

At 7:00 P.M. on August 25, I radioed the Ugalla One camp, where my son was based. It was his thirtieth birthday. He was out on safari with Jeff Rann, the well-known American pro hunter. My son sounded tense. He told me that Tanzanian police had suddenly showed up, asking for him and saying they wanted his passport. As he was not in camp and all the Portuguese passports were with me in Arusha anyway, the police had my nephew, Caju, and Rui follow them all the way back to a place called Tabora, which was a solid five hours' drive away. Once there, they were suddenly told at the police station that there was no problem and they could return to their hunting concession, another five hours' drive back, and that they could present their passports at a more convenient time.

Caju and Rui went over to my son's camp at Ugalla One to alert him when they noticed that they were being followed by two military vehicles all the way from Tabora. These military types then demanded passports from everyone in camp, including the clients. The Tanzanians then told my son that he and his fellow Portuguese were the very people they had been looking for and that they were to return with them to Tabora. When it was explained that Caju and Rui had just returned from Tabora, they were curtly told, "this is a different conversation," and that they were to return with them the next day. You do not argue with AK-47s toted by hostile locals.

I was alarmed. Decades in the African bush had helped me develop an acute sixth sense for impending danger. I contacted the camp again early on Sunday, August 26, and Jeff Rann came on the air. He was also alarmed, saying that something very serious was afoot. My son, Caju, and Rui had all been forced to pack and to abandon their clients in the middle of a safari as they were put into the military Land Rovers for the five-hour drive back to Tabora, and whatever it was that awaited them there.

Something ominous was developing.

As fate would have it, there was an American couple, Jim and Vicki Ray from Dallas, hunting out of Ugalla Two, with Bob Brown, also of Dallas. He had shot a splendid lion, and the Rays were busy videotaping the return of the lion to camp when the Tanzanians show up. The Rays captured the whole arrest on film. This was no gentlemanly request. The Tanzanians came across as secret-service types, thugs who brooked no argument and who would use force if opposed in any way. The Rays were greatly alarmed, and for good reason. Clients paying that kind of money do not expect a sudden sinister disruption in the middle of the bush.

My son and his group were now somewhere between the concession and Tabora, the administrative center for western Tanzania. My instincts told me that I was going to be rounded up before the day was out. I could smell the danger that Sunday afternoon when there was a belligerent banging at my hotel bedroom door.

Havoc was about to engulf all our lives.

NINE

HAVOC

May my enemies die before their time;
May they go down alive into the world of the dead!
Evil is in their homes and in their hearts.

—Psalm 55

Two Black men in civilian dress stood at the door. It was in the late afternoon of August 27, 1984, and I knew they had come for me. I was asked to identify myself and was then told to accompany them immediately. No chance to take a single thing with me. These were secret-police types, an impression strengthened by the one-way dark glasses and their thuggish gait. I was not surprised by this turn of events.

A short-wheelbase Land Rover was parked outside the hotel. I was told to sit at the back, and a dark blue cloth blindfold was suddenly produced. I was blindfolded, but not handcuffed. With a man on either side of me and my son, nephew, and Rui already detained, there was no point in trying to escape, anyway. The Land Rover set off. Nobody spoke at all. We drove for about half an hour before pulling up.

My blindfold was removed, and I could see that we had arrived at what looked like a military compound with some houses. I was taken to one and shown a room with bathroom—all fairly comfortable—but the thick bars on the windows and guards outside my door and around the house clearly indicated that I was under arrest, that this was no ordinary house.

I was well treated, given a meager dinner of sandwiches, and went to sleep. Nobody spoke to me at all. It was a kind of solitary confinement, a softening up for what was to come. The entire next day was the same. Reasonable food and silence. Always the silence. And gut-mauling anxiety. Where was my son? Where were the others? What were the Tanzanians doing to them? We were completely legal in all our activities, so what was all this? My instincts kept linking these ominous events with our investigations into Theo Potgieter and his less-than-clear intentions in Tanzania and the fact that I was spearheading these investigations.

My supper was brought in—meat sandwiches and coffee. There were always at least two men who were always in civilian clothes—counterintelligence types. There was one, in particular, with oddly slanted eyes in a cruel face. That night, the same procedure, until I had finished my supper. While I was drinking my coffee, the door opened suddenly and in came the slant-eyed man with his very short companion, who carried a box.

I sat watching as the box was opened and strips of black rubber bicycle inner tubing were taken out. I was pushed to my feet, in perfect silence, as the short man grabbed my arms, forced them behind my back, lacing them together tightly with strips of the rubber tubing. I started screaming with pain, saying that I was not a criminal. Silence as the tubing was tightened even further.

The short man then shoved me onto the bed and grabbed my feet, lashing my ankles together with more strips of the rubber tubing. They left without uttering a word slamming and locking the door behind them, despite the guards posted outside day and night. I was already in great pain as I felt the blood flow to my extremities being restricted more and more.

The bed was next to the wall, so I started banging my arms against the wall as best I could to try to boost the circulation past the tubing.

I struggled to move my legs for the same reason, but it felt as if the rubber vises were tightening by the minute. I screamed, I shouted, I banged, I yelled. The tubing tightened as the flesh started bulging around the bands. And night had not yet fallen.

I spent approximately twelve hours in that room, alone, in the pitch dark and in agony. There is no point at all in trying to search for words to describe the vomit-inducing torture, the stench of soiled clothing, the waves of sheer terror that engulfed my mind at the thought that I was going to lose my hands and feet to gangrene before the day was out. Where would they be amputated? Would I survive? How would I live afterward? Would I *want* to go on living afterward? Who would know? How could my family or close friends be alerted as to what had happened to us? How many more minutes of this unspeakable torment would I survive? Why had we been rounded up?

And the laughter of the guards outside my door, the smell of their cheap tobacco as they puffed away in comfort, listening to a voice on the radio, jabbering away in Swahili, and listening to their captive yowling throughout the night like a dog having its claws pulled out, one by one, followed by its teeth, also one by one. Let nobody dare dispute the truth of these ghoulish details. It happened—and the repercussions were eventually going to be felt in high government circles of several countries, involving heads of state.

As my stomach rose into my throat yet again with what remained in what remained of my stomach, a car skidded to a stop outside my window. Doors were opened and slammed shut as a series of feet marched to the front door and down to my bedroom, the door being roughly unlocked and pushed open. The same slant-eyed swine with his overpowering body odor was there with his short sidekick. Again, silence from them. I became quite excited at the thought that I was now going to be dragged outside and shot. Death was a most attractive prospect. I hoped against hope that I would be dying soon. My thoughts, such as they were in between the burning rushes of agony in my wrists and ankles, centered on my three children, especially on my only son. What were they doing to him? Where was he?

I was dragged upright and can remember screaming as weight was put on the balloons where I once had normal feet. I was stricken with terror when I looked down at the bulbous, blackening mounds of flesh. Obviously, I could not see my hands, but they had to look the same. In an instant, I could see nothing as I was blindfolded again and half-shoved half-dragged to what felt like a Land Rover—maybe the same one which had brought me to the compound an interminable two days previously.

I remember making a strange, unbroken moaning sound throughout the ride over rough and then potholed tarred roads. Every jolt, every bump was fresh agony for me. How any human could have willingly sat alongside another human and contemplated—indeed, added to such bestial treatment, such suffering, without a murmur can only indicate psychopathic personalities, bred in a psychopathic environment. We bumped along until I heard the whine of aircraft engines and could smell avgas. Clearly, we were about to board an aircraft. My thoughts then seemed to go comatose.

The rubber tubing was then cut off my ankles. I screamed afresh, my throat already raw from the previous night. The rough fumbling for the rubber, hidden by the folds of blackening flesh around my ballooned ankles was beyond imagining. The sensation of dammed-up blood as it struggled to trickle through the constricted veins was even worse. I prayed to a nonexistent deity to stop breathing right there. Several sets of hands pushed me up the steps of an aircraft. Inside, I was bumped into a seat and my blindfold removed.

It was a deluxe private jet with small tables between the seats. Opposite me was my son, unshaven, gaunt, traumatized. I shall always be haunted by the look in his eyes when he saw me. He was handcuffed. Next to him sat Caju, my nephew, also handcuffed and sick-looking. To my left was Rui, handcuffed and in a very distressed state. I started howling in pain as the blood struggled into my feet. My hands, lashed behind my back for about fourteen hours, ballooned further. My son and the others created such an uproar over my din that one of the unwashed thugs cut the rubber tubing off my hands and released my son and the others from their handcuffs. Where the hell could we run to anyway? I could not walk at all. I remember swimming in and out of blackness as my son grabbed the grotesque blue-black mounds where I once had hands and began rubbing, shouting at me that he had to do this to save my hands from gangrene. I was alternately yelling and moaning. My son held a cigarette to my lips so that I could take a puff. My hands were unusable.

The aircraft taxied and took off. Rui was able to inform us that he had seen the letters CCM on the tailfin of this F28 executive jet. They stood for Chama Cha Mapinduzi (Revolutionary Party), the Swahili name of the only political party allowed in Tanzania, headed by President Julius Nyerere. This was a presidential aircraft. The CCM is the ruling party there even today, despite the eventual appearance of a multiparty system in 1992.

By the position of the sun, it was mid-morning. We had no energy and were all in a state of profound shock and exhaustion. Our Tanzanian thugs and, as I learned subsequently, some of their Mozambican buddies in the same business, were on board anyway. They never spoke a word throughout the flight. Where were we headed? I was facing the rear of the jet which, on top of everything, made me even queasier, but I noticed that the sun was on my right. We all thought we were going to Dar es Salaam, which lay east of Arusha. But we had been in the air for too long now. Then my son noticed that the sun was still on the left of the aircraft, my right. Clearly, we were heading south and, even more clearly, we were being delivered to Mozambique. This was a grotesque violation of international law. As it turned out, we had been abducted by the Tanzanians at the specific request of the Mozambican government.

After a blurred and interminable period in the air, we started losing height. We were over Maputo, the former Lourenço Marques, and capital of the one-party socialist-Marxist state of Mozambique. After nearly forty years of living in Mozambique and a forced absence of almost ten years, here I was, back there, abducted from Tanzania for no reason I could fathom and tormented by the thought that it would be too late by the time anyone in our family or in our circle of influential friends discovered what had happened and had attempted to have us freed. There is only so much ill treatment the body can tolerate.

We landed at Maputo Airport on August 29, next to a hangar and away from the usual passenger terminal. Two Blacks boarded the aircraft and demanded that we identify ourselves. Then blindfolds again for all of us, and my being shoved/dragged into a vehicle for a fairly lengthy ride through busy streets. As the nightmare progressed, I felt as if I were floating outside of myself, that nothing was real. The new arrivals had wanted to handcuff me, but the cuffs could not fit around where my wrists once were. The vehicle then stopped in front of what was obviously a fortified entrance of some sort before being allowed in. We soon came to a complete stop and were bundled out of the vehicle and separated, the blindfolds once again being removed. I managed to mutter to my son and the others not to lose hope. This was Machava Prison in Maputo.

The entire afternoon was spent being fingerprinted, a fresh torment for me, and "processed" by a bunch of lethargic, expressionless prison officials. I was given a prison uniform: dark blue trousers with a red stripe down the outer sides and a matching short-sleeved top. No shower, no soap, no way to wash off the caked filth. I was kept barefoot. This was part of the dehumanizing technique. No force, however, could get inside my head and chain my spirit. I would retain my sanity. I would survive. I would remember all this horror. I would bear witness one day to this terror-filled time.

Guards propelled me down a dank passage which I remember because of the constant sound of clanging metal doors and the pervasive smell of urine. In the passage, next to a grille leading outside, I noticed a White man with a heavy beard and blond hair speaking Portuguese with a thick accent. Our eyes met, but he motioned not to recognize him. The guards shoved me forward and into a tiny cell with a filthy piece of rubber matting in one corner. Nothing else except for a tiny, barred window high up on the dark walls. I was pushed onto the floor.

"Adelino, Adelino! Are you all right?"

It was the White man I had seen in the passage. It was the voice of

Dion Hamilton, a British citizen, whom I had last seen in Beira over ten years previously. He had been arrested and convicted for alleged sabotage of oil tanks in Beira in 1982. He still had another eighteen years of imprisonment.

"Read this note and then destroy it immediately. Another thing: Expect to be blindfolded for at least forty days. You are now in the hands of counterintelligence. Be strong!"

And then he was gone.

I struggled over to the door, and found a tiny piece of paper with a scribbled message on it, imploring me not to ever admit to my interrogators that Dion had been associated with me in sanctions busting for the old Rhodesia. I could not imagine why he would worry about something the whole world had known about for years, when he had been imprisoned for alleged sabotage of a national key point. Clearly he had reason to be freshly alarmed when he saw me.

In the 1960s, Dion once worked for Cory-Mann George, a freight-forwarding company in Beira, where we met. Very soon after Rhodesia's unilateral declaration of independence in November 1965, Dion, my brother Jacinto, and an Englishman from Beira, joined me in an aircraft piloted by Dion and we headed for Tete. There we established a facility in the name of the Serras Pires family, to bust sanctions big time for the Rhodesians. This we did, very successfully, until 1974. I took a certain satisfaction in the irony of the British link.

I managed to take the piece of paper in my mouth and nudge it into a crevice of the foul sponge mat. I did not sleep. I could not sleep. I had not slept since the night, thirty-six hours previously, when I was tied up with the rubber tubing in Arusha. The next morning, when I was brought a cup of water and some bread, I ate from the floor like a dog because I could not use my hands. I noticed that boils had erupted along both my forearms. I had a better look at them when I asked to be taken to the toilet—a filthy hole in the ground, surrounded by excrement and no water. Certainly, no toilet paper. All part of the same pattern to break the human spirit.

A guard took me to a first-aid station, where an orderly poured Mercurochrome onto my hands and along my arms before bandaging them. Back in the cell, Dion Hamilton came by and gave me a puff from a cigarette, again whispering to me that I was to expect to be blindfolded, handcuffed when possible, and kept on a bare concrete floor and deprived of sleep for at least forty days. SNASP—the acronym for the Mozambican secret police—would be interrogating me, and I could expect no mercy. I did not see Dion Hamilton again after that. He has since died.

Minutes later, guards blindfolded me and took me to a vehicle for a short ride out of the prison compound to a building where I was again put in a bare room, made to sit on a chair, and to remain in that position without food or water until the next morning. I could not lie down. I could not stand. I was not allowed to try to sleep. I knew eyes were watching to see when I would crack. I decided in my head to survive, but I did not know how then.

August 31 dawned. Sick with fatigue and unable to sleep because of the pain and because someone was there, ready to slap me awake if I showed signs of losing consciousness, I was moved again very early that day, nudged along outside and into a vehicle, blindfolded. I knew immediately that the others were in the same vehicle. We were driven some distance to what was clearly an airfield because of the noise of aircraft engines. When the vehicle stopped, my nephew managed to shift his blindfold and peep when it became clear that our guards were distracted by the presence of helicopters. I then rapidly whispered to them what Dion Hamilton had warned me to expect at the hands of SNASP. I told them to have courage, to be patient, that we had done nothing wrong at all.

Into the chopper and a ten- to fifteen-minute ride before we landed. I shall always remember the sensation of beach sand against the throbbing soles of my feet as I was hustled out of the helicopter. We were clearly on an island—either Inhaca or Xefina, both of which lay off the Maputo stretch of coast. It turned out to be Xefina, a tiny islet with dungeons which had been used by PIDE and long before that. I immediately knew one thing: The Mozambicans were moving us around because they wished to keep our whereabouts secret. By then, a solid seventy-two hours after I had been rounded up in Arusha and even longer since my son and the others had been abducted at the Ugalla concession, the word would have got out via fellow hunters and our American clients, the Rays and Bob Brown, all of Texas.

We were photographed and put into individual tiny, dark, totally bare cells for the night, lying on a freezing cement floor. The mosquitoes were a particular torment for me as I could not use my hands or arms to swat them off me. A bowl of dry sadza, the maize meal staple food of all southern Africa, was shoved through the door and I continued to eat from the bowl like a dog.

Sleep was out of the question. I was blindfolded, as were all the others, and I spent another interminable night huddled in a corner, being bitten alive.

The disorientating, demoralizing intimidation process continued the next morning with the first interrogation session. Blindfolded, I was asked to give my full name, date of birth, address in Portugal, details of immediate family members, and so on before being taken back to my cell, expecting to spend another terrible night. I then heard the rotor blades of a chopper growing louder and louder until I heard it land and the engine shut down. My cell door was opened and I was taken to the chopper—blindfolded, of course.

After a somewhat longer flight than previously, the chopper landed on what was clearly the Mozambican mainland again. The routine was now familiar. We were all driven in a vehicle for a short while from the airfield to what I presumed was one of SNASP's safe-house facilities in the vicinity of Maputo with bare cells and cement floors. I spent another night in pain, feeling the cold and having had no sleep for over five days. The bandages on my hands and arms had not been changed since Machava, and I did not know what was happening to them—just that I was in constant pain and that there was a peculiar smell, over and above my pretty terrible body odor.

I believed we were being moved around for two reasons: to break us down and to keep our whereabouts secret. Clearly, the Mozambicans were after some information, and they wanted all the time possible to extract it from us before any outside interference could disturb them. Even more clearly, they had been put up to this whole demonic exercise. But by whom and why?

A few blurred days later, the interrogations proper started. Cold, hungry, a little thirsty, caked in filth, unshaven, and in pain, I was shoved out of the cell and into an apparently big room. I could tell by the different voice patterns that there were four people present, waiting to interrogate me. They belonged to Blacks, a White, and a mulatto. I was made to stand for hours as the insults and the same questions were hurled at me over and over and over. Everything that first day centered on Giscard d'Estaing, former president of France, now leader of the main French opposition party.

But first an entrée of insults about my fascist colonial family, my upper-class exploitation of "the people," my intention to overthrow the "revolution," my plans to bring back the suppressors of Salazar's days, rob the country, bring suffering to "the proletariat," and much more. The voices snarled, yelled, spat, and hissed to my left, to my right, suddenly from behind my head, then two inches from my face so that I could smell one interrogator's decaying teeth. Blindfolded, I could not look anyone in the eye. I had no control over where the noise was coming from. This, of course, was a classic tactic of interrogation to unnerve and disorient the captive.

I was immediately accused of being a member of Renamo, the prohibited Mozambican National Resistance Movement, which I was not. I was accused of being involved in the building of airstrips in Tanzania on behalf of Renamo in order to create a supply infrastructure to ferry in weapons and attack Mozambique which was run entirely by the Marxist Frelimo party. It is as well to point out here that our concessions were well over 1,000 miles from the Mozambican border. I was accused of using the Hunters Africa job as a cover for these nefarious activities against the people of Mozambique.

My son, nephew, and Rui were all accused of being in on this plot, of posing as hunters. I was the ringleader for Hunters Africa, a front organization, which, I was told, was really a Central Intelligence Agency front. The CIA, I was told, was working hand in hand with Renamo and with South African Intelligence to overthrow "the new order" in Mozambique. The Hunters Africa principal was an American millionaire, wasn't he? And I was the mastermind, the interrogators stated. I was a son-of-a-bitch fascist, an enemy of the people, and much, much more. Oddly enough, I noticed that the effect of the words was wearing off because of the sheer repetition.

I was grilled all day about Giscard d'Estaing and his role in my presence in Tanzania. The four voices knew we went back a long way, saying that he had hunted with me in "fascist" Mozambique days. They wanted to know whom he spoke to in Tanzania during our recent hunt. What did we speak about together? What were we planning together? Constant insults and threats were blasted at me about my being closely involved with the South African intelligence apparatus, about my being an operative for the Central Intelligence Agency, known enemies of the Mozambican state, about my close friendships in the "G7 clique" of countries. Reference was made here to my former clients from the great winemaking families of Europe. I was accused, in particular, of being in cahoots with D'Estaing in plans to overthrow the Mozambican government. Each time I opened my mouth to deny this hallucinatory rubbish of the first magnitude, I was shouted down and threatened afresh by the four voices. I was a capitalist, an enemy of the revolution.

Specific questions were shouted at me concerning my frequent trips to the United States of America. What was I *really* up to over there? Whom was I *really* seeing, and why? Gross and often obscene insults peppered the questions. The most zealous and demeaning of the four voices belonged to the White man.

The voices tried to grill me about Gordon Cundill and the "South African connection." I was battered verbally with questions and accusations, which became more outrageous as the day wore on and I was kept standing on exceptionally painful feet. My group and I were the "Lisbon terrorism connection," ready to unseat the Mozambican government. At the end of that terrible day, I was assured that I would talk in the end, that I would "sing" as loudly as I could. "They all do!" hissed one of the voices, as I was pushed out of the room and back to my cell, my bladder about to burst.

On the second day, after terrible food, no washing facilities, forcing me to use my cell as a latrine which was never cleaned, and a night in which I was again deprived of any sleep by a guard with a loud radio blaring away outside my door, and by other guards who kept opening and slamming my cell door, I was hauled back into the interrogation room to face the four voices again—blindfolded, of course.

The same constant yelled grilling about Giscard d'Estaing and our role in plotting against Mozambique from Tanzania. My constant denials. Then one of the voices shouted suddenly, "Right! You don't want to talk about your French friend and his Yankee fascist friends and what you are all up to? Now we are going to make you talk."

With that, I heard the voice of my nephew, Caju, outside. He was being thrashed mercilessly with some instrument and was bellowing in pain as each blow fell. In between the blows, I was asked if I still wanted to keep silent about my friends and our subversive activities against the state of Mozambique and her people. I kept asking them not to beat the others because they were innocent of all the accusations, and that they could beat me for what it was worth—but that it would change nothing.

This went on for several days, although the beatings of Caju stopped. I immediately noticed that there were new voices in the room, one belonging to a Spanish speaker, a Cuban, from what I could detect. The same accusations, the same threats—and a new one, reminding me that my son was also a captive. I could not admit to what was vicious nonsense. Of course I became anti-Frelimo. Of course I was filled with hatred for what had befallen my parents, my family, our friends, an entire generation—not to mention the country and the wildlife—but my group and I were blameless of everything being hurled at me.

This would not prevent whatever it was these four voices and their pals wanted to do to me, to my son or to anyone else for that matter. I was in a semicomatose state and was trying to mentally switch off the pain, the mental anguish, the filth, the indescribable fatigue, the hunger, the cold at night, and the fear that my son and the others would be killed to make me "talk." I kept telling myself that something was preventing our captors from killing us and that gave me sufficient mental fuel to hang on for another day. And another. And one more after that. My instincts told me to hang on to my sanity, to hang on to hope, to detach. Like a recovering alcoholic, I forced myself to cope with one day at a time. This, too, would end.

They moved me again, at dawn one morning. I was taken some distance over bad roads to what turned out to be another SNASP facility of sorts, I was put into a small room with a tiny barred window—converted servant's quarters, by the looks of things.

I managed to see this by pushing up an edge of the blindfold with my thumbs when my guard took me out into the bushes to relieve myself. I could not use my fingers at all. There were no toilet facilities, certainly no shower facilities. The guard saw me do this and threatened to gouge out my eyes if I ever tried to do that again. Somehow, deep in my gut, I just knew this was bluster. They—whoever they were—did not want me dead. A mere guard would beat and kick and insult, but he would not take more drastic action without a go-ahead from his bosses.

I lived on *sadza*, the maize meal diet of the locals. Sometimes I would have a piece of bread and tea with sugar in the mornings, but not always. I never once ate any greens or protein of any sort in the first fifty-three days of my captivity. One or two of the guards would feed me with a spoon because I could not use my hands at all for over six weeks after the rubber-tubing ordeal. Even a tiny act of helpfulness like that gave me moral strength. Most of the time, I fed myself like a dog, lapping at the bowl on the floor. I was going to stay alive. I was going to bear witness about this, especially to those who did not want to hear, and who still don't. To do this, I had to eat, whatever the circumstances. My spirit would not be broken.

Another interesting turn gave me hope. After I had been in this fresh location of solitary confinement for a few days, a male nurse, who never once spoke at all, would visit me at that place at fairly regular intervals. He changed my bandages and washed my arms and hands. The pain was still bad in my extremities, and I suffered an itching infection of my eyes because of the blindfold, which was never removed. I learned that the human body can get used to anything if it goes on long enough. My eyes itched and burned, but I could not scratch them. Then the male nurse medicated my eyes and I recovered. The swelling in my hands and feet was still very bad, but it was starting to subside. I no longer feared I would lose them and die of gangrene. The Mozambicans and their Tanzanian friends did not want me dead.

I was left in that state of solitary confinement for more than forty days. This was also supposed to break me because of my anguish over the fate of the others—of my only son, in particular. This abandonment was supposed to force me to eventually go off my head and start babbling anything my tormentors wanted to hear, followed by a "signed confession"—in true commie fashion, of course. Then I remembered Dion Hamilton's warning about being blindfolded and maltreated for at least forty days. After about thirty days, something happened to help me survive. One of my guards whispered to me that he had spoken to another guard who told him that Senhor Monteiro, Senhor Caju and Senhor Tim-Tim were alive. They were "fine." That simple act of kindness gave me mental strength to continue.

In all that time, I was never allowed to sit out in the sunshine, to hobble about and get some exercise in the fresh air. I lived in my cell, a tiny, dark room, twenty-four hours a day, except for when I was taken out into the bushes to relieve myself. From dawn until dawn, the radio outside the door was never turned off. The people's socialist revolutionary programs blared away without a break to alleviate the boredom of the guards and to prevent my falling asleep. The cell door would open and shut, open and shut, open and shut for the same purpose.

I do not remember waking up from sleep, but I must have lost consciousness from time to time. I must have had comalike catnaps for a few minutes at a time. I was always awake every time the door opened. What I do know is that I was kept on a bare cement floor with no blankets or mattress.

Not being able to open my eyes at will, to blink normally, to see—even if it was a somber wall and bars on the window—dispossessed me of a basic body function: control over my life. But this was the whole point of the exercise: to wear me down until I howled what they wanted to hear.

One morning, about forty-five days into our ordeal, I had visitors—the "voices," with one or two new ones. The interrogations resumed. Had I had time to rethink my situation? Was I now prepared to admit my guilt and direct involvement with the CIA, with Renamo, with the South African intelligence community, with my rich and famous friends from Europe and their complicity in this plot to destroy the people's revolution of Mozambique? I reiterated what I had stated from the first day: that we were innocent of all these accusations.

"Right," say the voices. Listen carefully to this tape recording. It is of your son, who has already confessed. The tape played and I heard my son being beaten senseless with either a hippo-hide whip, known as a *sjambok,* or a rubber hose. Of course, I knew my son had nothing to confess because we had done nothing wrong. As I learned later, he was made to stand for days, surrounded by guards who would belt him if he faltered and tried to sit or lie down. He was stretched out on the floor and beaten. The same was done to my nephew, Caju, and to Rui, who was the victim of appalling mental torture. We were all told at various stages that one or other of the group had already died. When I was told that my son was dead, I decided, more resolutely than ever, that I would never admit to all these crazed accusations. Neither would I willingly die.

After that terror-filled day, I was back in my cell, blindfolded, exhausted, cold, in still considerable discomfort, and sitting in a corner when the door opened and one of the guards came in. He apologized that he had no tea or coffee, but had brought me a mug of hot sugared water to warm me up. It was the same guard who had given me news about the others. That humane gesture by someone who had taken a great risk by coming in to me and speaking, let alone giving me anything, even a mug of hot water, affected me and, for the first time in many years, perhaps since the death of my baby daughter, Margarida, in the 1950s, I sobbed. All the pain, horror, and anxiety burst inside me. The guard was alone. Nobody else knew about this. I recovered, felt a strange relief and a fresh determination to stay alive and remember. I have never forgotten that guard. He would also share the remains of his food when he dared to—a little rice, extra tea. Even the blackest hole has a chink of light.

There was a sudden flurry of activity one morning. Guards were sweeping, sluicing, cleaning up. A table and some chairs were crammed into my cell and I could hear what sounded like recording equipment being installed. I had a premonition right there—all this preparation could only mean one thing, a high-ranking visitor. Who would that be?

"Adelino!" A mocking voice called out my name.

I knew instantaneously. It was Sérgio Maria Castelo Branco da Silva Vieira, the Minister of Security and the head of SNASP. He was the ideal person to head the security organ of Marxist-Leninist Mozambique. You have to have certain characteristics to run an apparatus cloned along the lines of the Soviet KGB and the infamous East German STASI and which was operating in constant and close liaison with both. Vieira had been handpicked by President Samora Machel.

What irony, to meet under those circumstances! As this chief of the most feared organization in the country settled into a chair while I sat blindfolded on the floor, essential memories crowded into my fogged mind. His family, of Goanese Indian, black, and mulatto origin, and mine had been good neighbors in Tete where his grandfather had been the clerk of the court and a friend of my father. My sister, Lucinda, became godmother to Vieira's sister, Gabriella, known as Gaby. The families were on good terms always and, over the years, the families had remained in touch in one way or the other. Lucinda met Vieira again in Portugal in 1961 where he was a student. We have a photograph showing my parents with his parents, Dr. Delgado, the local medical doctor, and Vieira when he left Tete as a youngster to attend one of the most prestigious "Salazar establishment" educational institutions in Portugal, the Cclegio Santo Tirso. My cousin, José Luiz Serras Lopes, attended this school at the same time. Only the very best was considered for the young Vieira who was about thirteen years my junior.

Vieira did not complete his law studies in Portugal. He eventually went to Paris at a time of radical political ferment in Western Europe. Among the fellow students who were with Vieira in Paris was Joaquím Chissano, the current President of Mozambique. When I was in Paris on safari business at one stage, I looked up several old contacts from Mozambique, some of whom had been very closely associated with Vieira during his sojourn in France before he left for the Soviet Union, Algeria and like-minded countries. Snippets of some of the utterly chilling conversations these contacts had had with me were cut off as Vieira's voice suddenly sliced into my thoughts like a bloodied scalpel.

The interrogation became more and more menacing but not before the SNASP boss spoke of our Tete days and of the Eduardo Baptista Coelho Primary school we had both attended at different stages in those far off and very happy times when our families had been next-door neighbors. It is quite extraordinary what the voice reveals about the essence of a person's character through tone, cadence of speech, the use of emphasis, of silence and of dark word pictures as tools to intimidate, and the manner in which hate stains and distorts the voice. Vieira, eloquent defender of the Marxist-Leninist revolution, was always at pains to speak the same cultured Portuguese of the now departed Portuguese colonial ruling elite. Once again, I had the impression that I was detached, that I was floating outside of my painful, exhausted body, looking down on this extraordinary scene.

Although I was undoubtedly extremely debilitated, I clearly remember making myself speak in a muttered, barely audible whisper, feigning even greater malaise as the verbal attacks gathered and grew. I was threatened that I was done for unless I came to my senses and confessed. One thing became apparent to me straight away. If the Minister of Security and SNASP boss himself, a man whose reputation preceded him wherever he went, was taking a personal interest in our case—a totally trumped up case of quite frightening dimensions by now—it was a clear indication that pressure from outside was being exerted on the Mozambican government in some way concerning us. By not being treated as "ordinary" prisoners, like the faceless, anonymous, wretched thousands who disappeared into

SNASP's "mental decolonization camps" beginning in 1975, there was a measure of hope, of protection for us that we would get out alive some day. I knew in my battered bones I was right. The more I was shouted at and buffeted by threats, the more I knew in my innermost self that something or, more likely, someone from outside was preventing our summary execution. I would only learn quite a bit later on how right my instincts had been that day in that cold, dank cell where the stench of malevolence hung like the stench of burned flesh.

Something was up.

Those last few days smudged into one another as trick after trick was tried. The "voices" told me that my mother had supported Frelimo, so what was the point of my holding out. When I heard them mention my mother, I felt a fresh rage. Yes, she knew that Frelimo was passing through our Guro farm and she instructed the staff not to seek confrontation. The area was infested with these guerrillas, and the staff always reported back to us any strange presence on our huge property. I had inherited her indomitable will, and we sometimes clashed because of our similar personalities. That day, hearing her name in the mouths of those "voices" gave me a strange new strength to survive, to defend her in death, to remember for her. If my mother was supposed to be a Frelimo enthusiast, why did the party take away our farm and all we owned? Why were we not still living in Mozambique, a country none of us ever wanted to leave, but from which we were driven because of the madness which had swept away all order, all stability and hope from 1974 onward. I let the "voices" rant on. I would survive. I would speak for my mother and, symbolically, for all those who had been rendered silent by the new masters.

Then the "voices" started on a topic I had secretly feared. What was this "group" all about which had been attached to the Safrique operation? It was Portuguese army, wasn't it? This was a reference to Carnaval and the Mandioca group with whom I fought our secret war against Frelimo for almost two years. Much to my great relief, Carnaval's name did not come up at all. Although he had died in

South-West Africa eight years previously, I did not wish to be drawn into any talk about our activities. I merely said that the bank owners of Safrique were trying to boost the security of their hunting concessions in the light of the prevailing bush war. And the topic was dropped.

With Vieira's brusque departure amid dire threats to my continued existence, I was moved yet again. Around the fifty-first day or so, I was guided onto what appeared to be a bus by the sounds of the engine and the steepness of the steps into the interior of the vehicle. I sensed I was not alone and had renewed hope that my son, Caju, and Rui were all still alive.

The bus bumped over poor roads to what I assumed was an airport because of the sounds of jet engines and of aircraft taking off or landing. As I found out later, my son was indeed on the bus. He was able to hear the pilots of a Russian Antonov aircraft onto which we were all taken. It took off, and we flew for about an hour before landing, whereupon we were bundled out, pushed into a vehicle, and taken to some other destination. This time it was a jail proper. I was put into a cell, where I felt two cement bunks and a tap with no water in it. Then I heard Rui shouting for the guards. He was alive! I had been allowed to hear him. We were together.

Something was up. Where were we? I learned much later that we were back in Maputo, that I was in the jail now, where my son and the others had been all the time that I had been kept in isolation elsewhere in the Maputo region. We had all been taken to that airport for a flight somewhere, only to have been obliged to return to the same airport from which I was taken with the others to the jail. They had been imprisoned there for the entire time that I had been kept in isolation elsewhere.

About two days later, on the fifty-third day of our incarceration, we were again taken out of the jail and put into a vehicle and then onto yet another aircraft. It was painfully slow. After several hours or so, we landed for a refueling stop. It was probably Beira. Not long afterward, we took off and the flight droned on interminably. The thought crossed my mind that we were being flown into the far interior of Mozambique, to one of those "reeducation camps," to disappear and be left to die.

But this flight was too lengthy. We landed. From what I could distinguish, it was a busy airport. Sounds of several aircraft engines, the noise of small vehicles driving about, hoists working. Dar es Salaam? Then off we went again, flying for less than one hour. Another airport, another vehicle, another ride. I was brought into a building and was able to push up the bandages of the blindfold and peep. What I saw—and I was given a deep shock at how poorly my eye seemed to focus—convinced me we were back in a compound like the one in Arusha, where I had first been abducted over seven weeks previously. The sound of other pairs of feet told me that I was not alone in this fortified house. If we were out of Mozambique, there had been some fresh development. Something must have gone wrong—otherwise why would the Mozambicans let us leave Mozambican territory? If I was out, hopefully, the others were out, too, and with me.

I perceived a shift in the wind of this latest havoc in our lives. This feeling overrode my filthy physical condition and the weeks of caked dirt and odor, my still-sensitive extremities, the total lack of any control over my life, the lack of sight. Except for my head. Even after all this, I could still control my mind.

Someone pushed me onto a chair and, before I could sit down properly, an open flat hand cracked across my face and a Black man's voice shouted at me simultaneously in English, "Do you still want to fight me, White man?"

"Stop that!"

Another Black man's voice, speaking English. The "good-guy, bad-guy" routine? Whatever, we were back in Tanzania. I was so stunned by the blow across my face, so weak and physically shaky, that I did not react as this new person took me by the arm and helped me to my feet, apologizing as he guided me down a passage and into a room. There, he removed my blindfold. I struggled to cope with the daylight, which I had not seen for fifty-three days—almost eight weeks.

I was equally stunned to see a proper bed with sheets and blankets, a decent room with the essentials. My escort was very pleasant to me, indicating that I would be able to shower or take a bath and get clean when I said that I could not even lie on the bed in such a state of personal filth. Now I knew something had gone badly wrong with this Tanzanian/Mozambican exercise. That could only mean that news of our plight had reached the outside, and that people of real influence outside were rocking the boat, fit to capsize it. I could smell approaching freedom the way I used to smell the approach of the first, lifesaving rains on the Manica Sofala savanna.

I had a bathroom with soap and hot water and a flush toilet with plenty of toilet paper. Nobody who has not been deprived of such basic facilities we all take for granted every day of our lives can understand at all what it means to again be able to shower, take a bath, to be clean, to have access to a proper toilet at any time, to have some kind of control over personal dignity again. My entire body was covered in blue dye from the Machava prison uniform. It took three changes of water to get off most of the dye. The water ran dark with dirt until the geyser ran out of hot water. I was shocked at the pitted marks in my arms, the terrible scars on my wrists, the emaciated, bearded face and the hollow, faintly crazed eyes. I felt disembodied, as if I did not belong to this face. I had aged twenty years, but I still had my hands and feet, and they worked. I could not see any sign of infection on my arms and legs as I shaved off nearly two months of matted growth from my face.

That night, I ate a little meat for the first time in all those weeks, but the rest was the usual *sadza.* I slept. I slept a dreamless sleep, the first proper sleep I had been allowed to have in fifty-two days. I was too emotionally drained to ponder this turn of events any further. It was enough to still be alive, to have fresh hope that this ordeal was all going to end soon. I switched off mentally, as I had tried to switch off mentally during all those traumatic weeks of pain, constant noise, constant interruptions, lengthy interrogations, abuse, threats, hunger, and rage. A Tanzanian doctor saw me and stated that I was in a bad way and that I needed rest to recover my health. He went one step further: I had to recuperate so that there would be no sign of the maltreatment I had endured when I left there!

What did that mean? Release, transference to some other jail in some other like-minded country? I heard Rui's voice. He was in the same house, but I did not know where my son or Caju were being kept. During the lengthy flight back to Tanzania, I was aware that there were several people on board. They were SNASP agents, accompanying me back to Tanzania to continue the interrogations on Tanzanian soil. I discovered this after a few days' rest when suddenly, I was blindfolded yet again and confronted once more by Portuguese-speaking interrogators. I had heard these "voices" before. They were from Mozambique. I recognized one voice, in particular. He had been in on this sordid little circus from the start.

Days of the same SNASP tactics. I continued to deny all accusations and I continued to resist succumbing to any kind of panic whenever I was told anything about the others. After all, had not the others "died" in Mozambique? I knew they were alive and that they were back in Tanzania. Although I was blindfolded, I was undoubtedly stronger. I was allowed to sleep on a bed, and I was no longer in such pain.

The Tanzanians came into my room with a fairly thick wad of papers, telling me to sign. I started reading the documents which were in Portuguese. A classic commie "confession." The Tanzanian snatched them from me, shouting, "You are not allowed to read them! Sign!" I refused. I told the Tanzanian that I was not about to sign something I had not read. Out he went. Back he came, on went the blindfold, in came the Mozambicans. "Sign!" spat that particular "voice." "Sign, or you'll never leave this place alive!"

That was the clue: "Or you'll never leave this place alive!" It was no longer on the cards that we were going to be killed. The Mozambicans had lost the initiative in this dangerous game. They did not dare kill any of us. They were no longer in their little Marxist paradise where all semblance of human rights had been jettisoned. Everything pointed to one fact: They had been pressured into returning us to Tanzania, and the Tanzanians now wanted to be rid of their southern comrades. Make the old man sign and go home! That was it! Tanzania was under pressure.

I thought about it. Maybe they could keep us for years in this state of emotional limbo. Maybe if I signed, we would all be up against a firing squad. If I refused to sign, we could all still mysteriously sicken and die. There were no guarantees from these bastards. We had no access to newspapers or radios. We could not communicate amongst ourselves. We had no idea at all of what—if anything—was being done at intergovernmental level to free us. If I signed, we were damned, and "proof" of our alleged perfidy would be paraded God knows where. If I did not sign, we were probably damned, anyway.

I signed. And as that particular "voice" came in and took the documents, he threatened me: "You're going to lose your head in this place! And if you ever leave this country, we'll find you and kill you!"

I had faced my share of mock charges by elephants, rhinos, and lions. This was a verbal mock charge. The Mozambicans were clearly anxious to get out and go home. The Tanzanians were anxious to see them go. So was I.

Now it was the Tanzanians' turn. It would go on for three and a half months. I had already been in captivity for fifty-five days.

My door opened and a Tanzanian told me to strip to my underpants. I was always barefoot. No shoes could fit my feet, anyway, as they were still misshapen and very tender. Interestingly enough, I was never blindfolded by the Tanzanians during those months of interrogation. The guard then took me to the interrogation room where two Tanzanians sat, ready to make me talk about this supposed international plot I was spearheading to wreck Mozambique. Whom do I see before anyone else at the table? The man with the slanted eyes who supervised the rubber-tubing ordeal. Was he about to order that I be trussed up again, right there? If so, that was probably it. Oddly enough, I never felt fear. It was always totally overridden by a deep loathing, which also gave me the mental fuel to survive in my head.

"Sit!" ordered one of the men.

I looked around. No chair. The Tanzanians were up to the old humiliation tactic.

"Sit!" barked the slant-eyed man.

I sat down on the cement floor and the interrogation began—from the most minute details about my childhood to the present, and what I was up to with D'Estaing and a variety of intelligence agencies to destroy Mozambique from Tanzanian soil. The slant-eyed man did not utter another word to me then or at any other stage. A tall man with glasses seemed to do all the questioning. It was often curt and mostly abusive. I never took my eyes off them, never raised my voice, and never wavered from the truth.

The underpants-on-the-cement-floor routine continued for a few days and then stopped so abruptly that I could only conclude word had been received to change tactics and be a little nicer to this subversive Portuguese fascist intent on destroying the African "scientific socialist" revolution. I was offered a chair and was allowed clothing. I was always barefoot, but I was able to sleep, and I was not hauled out in the middle of the night or made to hear tapes of my relatives being tortured. I was even given a cigarette or two every ten days or so. I would carefully hoard the butts, from which I would take the scraps of tobacco to stuff into my pipe, which had been given back to me.

"How's your friend Bob Denard? You may as well talk—the others have already told us everything."

I had never met the French mercenary leader and still have not met him. I had also never been to the Comores, where Denard was effectively in control of the Presidential Guard, was working closely with the South Africans in this regard, and was really the boss of that archipelago. Certainly, neither my relatives nor I was remotely connected with Denard. All threats about what the others had already said were rubbish. There was no truth at all in this latest Tanzanian fairy tale. The interrogators dropped this line of questioning as quickly as they had started it, never to resume it.

"Now you may as well tell us about Oscar Kambona. Talk!"

Kambona was a well-known Tanzanian opponent of Julius Nyerere's "scientific socialist" policies, whatever the hell that meant. Apart from what I had read in the media from time to time, I had no further idea of Kambona's life, activities, or whereabouts, and could not have cared less, anyway. The Tanzanians, however, kept hammering away at this point and the chief interrogator finally lost patience and told me that it was known that President d'Estaing had twice granted formal audiences to Kambona in Paris. For a one-party state, any such opposition activities were seen as a threat to the country. D'Estaing had known me for years; he had recently been hunting with me in Tanzania: I was a subversive. Therefore all this was linked. I was to hear this over and over again.

Naturally, this was further fantasy, and I denied any such nonsensical allegations. But I did manage to get their attention when grilled about Hunters Africa and the irrefutable evidence I had uncovered about the fraudulent activities of Theo Potgieter. He was busy manipulating the Tanzanian authorities in order to defraud Hunters Africa of its entire Tanzanian operation. I packed it out to the Tanzanians. As I learned eventually, Potgieter was one of the key factors behind my present ordeal because he knew I was at the point of blowing the whistle on him, which would have involved his highly placed associates. Potgieter was arrested while I was still in captivity in Tanzania, but managed to flee the country using a different passport. You cannot do that unaided under such circumstances. The last I heard, from an impeccable source in Kenya, was that Potgieter was seriously ill on the Kenyan coast, where he had been living with a local woman. Psalm 55 comes to mind.

The days dragged on into weeks, which dragged on into months. I was never allowed out into the sunshine, and the barred window in my room was curtained, blocking any view. I was told never to open the curtains, but I did so once. My defiance was immediately seen by a guard, who threatened to have me blindfolded if I ever dared touch the curtains again. I did not touch the curtains again.

Now there was a change. A Tanzanian doctor visited me quite regularly and assured me that he had seen the others in my group, and that they were all alive and coping. I knew he was not lying to me when he spoke of Caju complaining of toothache, because he had had this problem before our abduction. Further proof came when he spoke of my son having an allergy and that he had given Tim-Tim some medication for this. I would soon learn, however, that they had all been subjected to repeated physical abuse and atrocious mental torture. They were made to do push-ups until they collapsed from exhaustion, only to be beaten on the Achilles tendon. My son's back and buttocks were still very painful because of the SNASP whippings. Rui had had an AK-47 pressed against the back of his head and cocked, being threatened with imminent death if he did not talk. He could not have begun to invent any story to satisfy his tormentors and stop the torture. They eventually gave up on him when they understood he was in no way "connected." Rui had also been told repeatedly that Tim-Tim and Caju were already dead.

I did not know the whereabouts of my son and nephew, and I never asked because nobody would have told me. I presumed I was back in Arusha. It was difficult enough to cope with each day without agonizing over information nobody would give me.

The doctor also told me that the Tanzanians had wanted to release us all a long time previously but that President Machel of Mozambique and his security minion, Sergio Vieira, had requested that we be held ad infinitum. This was revenge because the Mozambicans knew damn well they had come away empty-handed from our maltreatment. The paper I had signed under duress was meaningless, concocted by SNASP and containing not a shred of proved evidence. We were not remotely involved in anything concerning their now-truly-wretched country, and they knew it. The Tanzanians had to show solidarity with their southern neighbor by continuing to incarcerate us. I was immensely grateful to the doctor for all this information.

Now it was a waiting game. The tedium, the mental and emotional limbo, can be a potent form of mental torture, but I knew this and did my best to switch off. My group and I were now becoming an increasing embarrassment to the Tanzanian government. Ironically, we would wait them out.

We had had no access to any legal representation; we had not been formally charged with anything at all; we had had no duly conducted open trial, and we had all been subjected to torture and degrading behavior by both the Tanzanians and the Mozambicans. We had all been in solitary confinement for what was now well over four months.

Another factor fed my hope: my international contacts with the hunting fraternity were so strong that I could not simply vanish into some bush gulag to die. It is a fraternity with immensely influential connections in many countries. My common sense told me that too many prominent people already knew of our abduction. The nature of my business meant that these same prominent people would be banging on the doors of heads of government in several countries and that they would not let up until we had been found. I had survived the nightmare so far. I could survive a few more weeks, even months. Suicide never entered my head and escape was out of the question. *My* revenge would be for me to live! White-hot hatred kept me going. I would eventually tell of our ordeal and expose our tormentors. My integrity was intact.

Every Friday, crates of beer would be delivered to the compound. I could tell by the characteristic clinking of the bottles as they were unloaded. The guards would then get plastered over the weekend, their drunken shouting and singing reverberating around the compound. Youngsters would take over the guard duties, bringing my food while their seniors slept off hangovers. Even the sadistic creature who headed the compound, and who once laughed on seeing me charging off to the toilet with stomach upsets after drinking coffee he had given me, was absent most weekends.

Early one Friday, one of the Tanzanians came to my room suddenly and said it was high time I got a breath of fresh air and came out for a "glass of beer," as I had been inside for so long! This particular Tanzanian, although he had the look of a hangman and the eyes of a vulture, turned out to be pretty humane. He would sometimes bring me fruit like oranges and papaya. My antennae now pricked up at his words. I was told to shower and shave. Even more suddenly, I was given my blazer, a clean shirt and gray slacks, clean underwear and socks, as well as ordinary shoes and told to dress for the outing. My feet managed to fit into the shoes, and my hands were not so discolored or puffy, although I struggled to shave. I was wary. Was I being taken out to be disposed of?

From the blaring Swahili of the guards' radios I had worked out that it was December 2, 1984. A blanket was tossed over my head as we drove some distance by Land Rover to a building. Once inside, I was uncovered, given a chance to comb my hair, and asked to follow my escort to a large room where a group of eight Blacks sat behind an oblong table. There was a lone White man with a beard sitting in the middle. He looked Portuguese. He smiled, stood up, and spoke my name, saying in Portuguese: "*Olà*, Adelino. I am José Gama, a member of the Portuguese Parliament for Emigration, and I have come here on behalf of Hunters Africa and your family to see you. I have just been in the United States, in Midland (the seat of Hunters Africa) and in San Antonio where I saw your friends, Bert and Brigitte Klineburger. I have cigarettes and medicine here for you."

I relaxed as it became immediately apparent that Gama was genuine. He told me that the Tanzanian government had received him well, that he now knew more about the whole situation and that I was to remain hopeful, that matters were progressing well. As it was clear that Gama wanted his hosts to understand the entire conversation, we spoke in English. I was convinced that one or two of the others, however, were from down south. Having been blindfolded throughout that time in Mozambique, I could not identify them. Nobody interrupted Gama.

Gama then told me about Potgieter, that he had been jailed in Tanzania because he had stolen a huge amount of money from Hunters Africa, and that he was to be considered the number-one suspect concerning our present situation because he had tried to use us as pawns for his own nefarious purposes. I experienced a measure of satisfaction on hearing this from the mouth of a high-ranking Portuguese parliamentarian in the presence of a bunch of Tanzanians and, no doubt at all, some SNASP agents from Mozambique. I had suspected all along that it was Potgieter who had started spreading the potentially life-threatening rumors about us to the Tanzanians in an effort to have us removed from the scene. This had nothing to do with the big-game-hunting industry but everything to do with human treachery and greed on a colossal scale. Potgieter was poison.

Gama said he had already seen my son and the others. As I found out later, they were brought into Gama's presence as they were, in a shocking state. Apparently, this made a poor impression on the Portuguese government emissary, as it should have done.

Gama took his leave after about an hour, saying that he hoped we would all be home for Christmas.

With that, he left for Dar es Salaam where he hung around for two weeks, struggling with the Tanzanian authorities to have us released. I was driven back to the compound, got back into my shorts and the Machava prison shirt, and waited. We had all become fairly good at that. I actually received a letter from Gama, posted in Dar es Salaam before Christmas, and explaining that he was trying his best to have us released soon. The letter was delivered to me intact, all interrogations having long since ceased. Christmas Day came and went, completely ignored.

A day or two after that first outing, the chief interrogator, who wore glasses, came to my room, sat down next to me on the bed, and asked that I not speak ill of Tanzania in the wake of our captivity "as we are not a cruel country."

I heard him out and then turned to him, showing my scarred wrists, and asked, "Then what's this?"

He looked away, got up, mumbled a good-bye, and left. I did not see him again. If I ever got out of that place, of course I was going to speak. How else does one begin to counteract criminal acts or keep one's self-respect? Nobody was going to silence me. To remain silent would be cowardly, to admit defeat and guilt concerning these heinous accusations.

On December 29, I was once again told to clean up and get dressed, as I was going out. The same procedure as with Gama: a blanket over my head, a short drive, into a building, off with the blanket, and into the same room where, this time, I was introduced to Luiz Barreiros, a Portuguese diplomat attached to the Portuguese embassy in Maputo, Mozambique, with jurisdiction for Tanzania as well. He was the first Portuguese embassy official I had seen since my abduction.

Barreiros was very aggressive with the Tanzanians in my presence, berating them for what was a patently illegal action and for our continued captivity. He branded the whole business *"uma palhaçada"*—a circus—explaining that the embassy had not been told of our presence in Mozambique and that when it was learned that we were in the country, no diplomat was allowed to see us. My physical condition would have been a little difficult to explain. Barreiros spoke in English and told me, "Talk, Adelino! Don't be afraid. Tell me everything!"

This was my chance to tell Barreiros that I did not believe the socialist-dominated Portuguese government would do anything for us on their own. Anything to do with the former colonies had the socialists scuttling for cover so as not to offend. Their servility was sickening. I let rip. Although I stated that the Tanzanians had since been a bit more humane than their Mozambican brothers, I condemned the lack of any formal charges, any legal representation, any due process, the solitary confinement, the terrible diet, and our gross maltreatment over a prolonged period. One of the Tanzanians then said weakly that they hoped to have something going by the next week. I laced into him, stating it was a bit late, wasn't it? There wasn't a shred of evidence, an iota of proof. The meeting ended and I returned to the compound, pessimistic. I felt nothing at all had been accomplished. The ride back to the compound was in stony silence. That was fine. I had lived through much worse. I would live through this, too. Maybe.

It crossed my mind that night that we could be sent back to Mozambique if the Tanzanians could not release us for fear of offending Machel and Vieira in Mozambique. If that was the case, I had to devise a way now in order to sabotage the aircraft and make it crash. I knew that if we returned to SNASP, it was as good as a death sentence. I stored a couple of the cigarettes I was occasionally given, together with a box of matches. If there was any clear evidence that we were going to be flown south, I would ask to be taken to the toilet in the rear of the aircraft, and I would do my utmost to set it alight and make it crash. Desperate times, desperate measures.

January 24, 1985 dawned. There was a knock at the door. A guard with my "best" clothes requested that I shower, shave, and dress. Before doing so, I secreted the two cigarettes and some matches with a side of the matchbox in the cuff of my "good" gray slacks. Out came the blanket, and off we went in a Land Rover, but this ride was quite lengthy. Then the smell of avgas and the whine of aircraft engines. Dear God! Was this the last day of my life? I was determined to end it all and take the bastards with us in a flaming crash into the Indian Ocean rather than return to Mozambique and SNASP.

I was escorted onto an aircraft and the blanket was removed. There, before me was my son, my nephew, and Rui, all looking thin, sickly, and traumatized. It was the first time we had seen one another in almost five months to the day of our abduction. The expression in their eyes when they saw me told me that I did not look very good, either. We barely spoke as we taxied onto the runway. One good sign was that it was a scheduled flight, not one of Nyerere's private jets this time. Another shock awaited me. This was Kilimanjaro Airport. I found out that Rui and I had been held captive all those months in Moshi, a town east of Arusha on the southern slopes of Mount Kilimanjaro. Tim-Tim and Caju had been held in Arusha. Where the hell were we going now?

We flew southeast for some time. I was waiting for the aircraft to reach the ocean and veer true south before attempting to set it alight, but we soon started our descent, coming in to land at Dar es Salaam Airport, where we were met by Tanzanians in dark glasses. They escorted us to what I presumed was an ordinary house, but with increased security. It was probably a military safe house of some sort. No blankets were tossed over our heads, and we were not handcuffed. Once inside the house, we were offered beer, cigarettes, and cordial treatment from some Tanzanians, who were probably from military intelligence. They informed us that we would be told what was going on and that we should just be patient. A radio was playing in the background. We did not speak much. Emotional exhaustion had set in.

After the Swahili newscast at 5:00 P.M., during which we picked up our names, an English-language radio bulletin came over the radio set the officers had turned up. It was 7 P.M. The announcer stated that we had been arrested for "subversive activities against African countries," but that we were being "released from Tanzania on humanitarian grounds," owing to the intervention of the president of Portugal, General Ramalho Eanes.

I noted the plural "countries" and was not at all surprised at the lack of any statement that we were innocent of any of the vicious accusations leveled against us and which had almost cost us our lives. As I was to discover, it was heavy, high-level international pressure, which forced the Tanzanians and their Mozambican partners in crime to release us. Had this pressure not been exerted, had we been just another anonymous group arrested on mere rumor, we would probably have disappeared without a trace and been killed. Africa is a desensitized and dangerous continent where, at any one time, more than a dozen countries are embroiled in serious armed conflict, and where human rights are often buried by unbridled brutality.

The newscast over, we were told we would be spending the night at the house and that we would be leaving Tanzania the next morning. None of us was able to open up and talk freely of our ordeal. It was sufficient to be alive and to be back together. We were surrounded by guards who were decent enough, offering us coffee, cigarettes, and quite good food. We were all silently agonizing over our final destination the next day.

Early the next morning, the cigarettes and matches still in the cuff of my gray slacks, we dressed, had breakfast, and were driven to Dar es Salaam Airport. None of us was blindfolded. Once at the airport, we were met by a number of Tanzanians in civilian dress. I asked where the chief interrogator was, the man with the glasses who had asked me not to speak of our torture to the outside world. I was told that there had been a tragedy: his little daughter, a toddler, had drowned in a swimming pool around Christmas. I expressed my sorrow at the news and asked that this be conveyed to him because, despite everything, he had been more humane than his other countrymen, let alone the SNASP thugs of Mozambique.

A distinguished-looking man came up and introduced himself in Portuguese. It was Dr. Fernando Reino, the Portuguese ambassador to the United Nations in Switzerland. He had been especially designated by President Eanes to fly out to Tanzania and personally escort us back to Lisbon via Switzerland. We all began to relax for the first time in five months. It was now clear that we were not going to be handed back to SNASP. With passport formalities completed, we were escorted onto a Swissair flight, where the cabin crew had clearly been briefed as to who we were. It was a fresh shock to the system to be treated with such deference after all the horror, and to eat the first decent English-style breakfast in months. I sat next to Ambassador Reino, the first civilized company I had had in months. The aircraft took off, gaining height rapidly as we left Tanzanian airspace and headed for Switzerland.

The aftermath of this episode in our lives would be extensive.

TEN

AFTERMATH

It was the best of times, it was the worst of times.

—Charles Dickens, *A Tale of Two Cities*

Ambassador Reino spent a good deal of our flight time between Dar es Salaam and Zurich, trying to brainwash me, albeit with diplomatic subtlety, into keeping silent about our recent horrendous experiences. He asked me to remember that Portugal's future lay in her ex-colonies, that we had sons and grandsons to think of and that they may well wish to return to those ex-colonies. The more he spoke, the more I boiled. I found it sad to see this man, an educated and traveled person, espousing the craven behavior of postcolonial Portugal.

There was a conspiracy of postcolonial silence, the sort of shame-induced muteness as was common among rape victims until very recently. Nobody had the guts to strike back, to speak the truth and confront Lisbon. My family and I and a whole generation of Mozambicans, Black and White, had been subjected to an upheaval from which many would not be able to recover because it had happened too late in life.

I was told of plans to host us at the ambassador's home in Geneva for the night where his wife would prepare a traditional Portuguese meal for us and where we could catch our breath before flying out to Lisbon the following day. We landed in Zurich that evening and were taken to the VIP lounge, where Ambassador Reino made several phone calls. I was seated near enough to overhear him. He spoke to the Presidency of Portugal, to the prime minister's office, and to the Ministry of Foreign Affairs. Ambassador Reino assured all that we had arrived safely, but admitted, "we have a problem." Reino, a pleasant man who went on to become Portugal's ambassador to Spain and whom I got to know quite well, was toeing the official diplomatic line, and I understood. I have no idea what Lisbon advised Reino to do, but he made no further attempts to raise the subject. I, for my part, had no words to waste.

My youngest brother, José Augusto, was in Geneva to meet us and to brief us in detail as to events during our five months' incarceration and what to expect in Lisbon. He and the family had kept extensive scrapbooks of newspaper clippings, notes, reports, letters, postcards, and telegrams, as well as covert documentation pertaining to our ordeal and which I have. He had appeared on Portuguese television to defend us in the face of allegations of terrorism, gunrunning, resistance activities, and whatever else the fertile and fetid imaginations of our enemies had dreamed up. We were increasingly dismayed at José Augusto's revelations.

He, Tim-Tim, Caju, and Rui were in a car ahead of us, the ambassador and I behind them as we were being driven to the diplomatic residence that night. Suddenly the front car stopped, and I saw my son tumble out of the car and collapse onto the freezing side of the road. We were all wearing only summer clothing. My son seemed to have suffered some sort of seizure in the car and had lost consciousness. That was why the driver had stopped. Tim-Tim did not respond to anything we tried, so off we raced to a hospital, where he was admitted in a state of severe shock. His condition stabilized after a couple of hours, and he was released the next morning, in time to return with all of us by air to Lisbon.

What had happened? José Augusto began by telling my son and the others in the car that one of the main reasons, in curious synchronization with the Potgieter affair, we had all been rounded up, abducted, tortured, and jailed for five months was because of the treachery of a certain Mario Ferro, a journalist working in Maputo. This stunned me. Ferro had been at school with my son and was an old friend of our family. He had elected to stay behind in Mozambique in 1975, when the majority of the Whites left.

Ferro, as was published in the media in Portugal, became an apprentice SNASP agent. In this capacity, he visited Portugal in June 1984, where he called on my sister, Maria José, Caju's mother, and saw other members of my family. He conveniently "bumped into" Tim-Tim and Caju, who were on their way to Madrid and then Tanzania, to join me in our new hunting operation. Our being ex-Mozambicans, it was only natural that we would have been pleased to see someone from Mozambique whom we had known for years. Ferro stayed late after dinner at Maria José's house and suddenly asked if the family could put him up for the night. My ex-wife gladly offered him our son's room, as he had already left for Tanzania. Naturally, Ferro heard all about our latest plans on behalf of Hunters Africa in that country. There was nothing at all to hide.

Well, in justifying his visit to Portugal to his spymasters with the zeal of the converted outsider hoping to be accepted, this Ferro character composed a secret report to President Samora Machel, dated June 24, 1984. A copy of this report was leaked from Machel's office to my family in Lisbon during our captivity by a disaffected Mozambican Black with access (to state secrets) and whose identity is known to me. It mentions a number of people branded as dangers to Mozambique, and it goes to great lengths to smear the name of the Serras Pires family.

The report is riddled with lies and inaccuracies, stating, for example, that the hunting operation in Tanzania belonged to an Italian. It states that the company's hunting concessions would be close to the border between Mozambique and Tanzania, whereas we were over 1,000 miles from that border. My son and I are accused of belonging to armed gangs, which was ludicrous.

The report states that our family was "rooted in the colonial era in the region of Guro" as if this were a crime against humanity. This is a little rich, coming from an ex-commando of the Portuguese Army who was employed by and happily accepted his monthly salary from Jorge Jardim, Salazar's man in Mozambique. Even the fact that my son obtained a private pilot's license in the United States is paraded as proof of subversion in this SNASP apprentice's fairy tale. Our family is reported to have "fled" Mozambique.

Ferro outdoes himself when he mentions my friendship with "the former president of France, Valéry Giscard d'Estaing" in language suggesting something sinister. To cap this exercise in sabotage, which damn nearly killed us all, Ferro ends his report on us by intimating that our presence in hunting concessions in Tanzania was for the purpose of "agitating Mozambicans living in Tanzania in order to recruit them."

With all this swirling around in my head, Ambassador Reino accompanied us to Geneva Airport and all the way to Lisbon.

Lisbon was another story. There was a huge crowd of family members, friends, officials, journalists, and television crews at the airport to meet us. At the first of several press interviews, I let them have the raw facts. My words about our abduction, torture, and gross maltreatment screamed out of the headlines in several newspapers the next day, overriding the highly damaging reports which had circulated about us for months—not only in Portugal but elsewhere in Europe, the United States, and, of course, in African countries.

I revealed what I had only just found out myself: that Caju had managed to smuggle out a note to his mother in Lisbon with the help of a prison guard at Machava Prison in Maputo in early September 1984, stating that we had been abducted to Mozambique, to Maputo. To add to the drama, the note was written on SNASP letterhead! And the envelope bore the postal marks of Maputo. Lisbon was immediately informed by my sister that we were being held captive in Mozambique yet the authorities did nothing. My family was left to drown in anguish as they and the international hunting community struggled to have us released before we died.

The Portuguese government was propelled into action only by the sustained tenacity of outsiders, starting with John and Vicki Ray of Dallas, Texas, who were abandoned on safari when the others were abducted in the Ugalla concession. The Rays flew to Lisbon and started rocking the boat before returning to America to continue their campaign. My son had managed to slip Vicki his mother's phone number in Lisbon as he was being shoved into a Land Rover. Vicki was a star because she alerted the world about our abduction.

Gordon Cundill of Hunters Africa took up the battle, flying to Lisbon to see my family and liaising personally and continuously with highly influential people in several countries in order to "kick ass" in Portugal, Tanzania, and Mozambique to get us out. He was a source of tremendous comfort to my entire family.

The international hunting fraternity joined the fight. At a world convention in Madrid in October 1984, hunters from every continent signed a petition en masse and, in a much-publicized effort, sent it off to Nyerere in Tanzania, proclaiming our long-standing good name and urging our release. A couple of individuals refused to sign. Here I think in particular of the blue-eyed Spaniard with an unmatched genius for self-aggrandizement, masking his profound sense of insecurity. To all the other hunters who stood by us and who never gave up on us, know that you will be valued to the end for everything you did collectively and individually to try to help us. It counted. It counted completely.

One of the second-rate stringers responsible for spreading reports during our captivity was a certain Alves Gomes, another of those who had stayed behind after 1975. He worked for the Mozambican Press Agency, AIM. Gomes had the audacity to bounce up to me like an old friend when I returned to Beira in 1995, after an absence of twenty often-very-difficult years. He is one of Frelimo's boys and his reports surfaced in *The Observer* and *The Guardian* in England, for example, and in a great variety of publications all over the world.

I was taken aback to see such completely erroneous allusions made about us in January 1985 in *Africa Notes*, published by the Center for Strategic and International Studies, Georgetown University, in Washington D.C. This is supposed to be one of the most prestigious think tanks on international affairs in the Western world. Other newspapers even invented stories of my supposed arrest in Zaire for gun trafficking before my "arrest" in Arusha.

We were suspected of being linked to alleged clandestine shipments of arms to Renamo from Saudi Arabia and Oman via Somalia and the Comores from where they were reported to have been transshipped to northern Mozambique. This was the supposed link with French mercenary Bob Denard. These allegations came during the same period that South Africa, in fact, was providing clandestine military assistance to Renamo, as was eventually revealed.

By ominous coincidence, Theo Potgieter was busy spreading rumors about us inside Tanzania for his own nefarious purposes. This resulted in a lethal witch's brew of fortuitous association of events and evil innuendo, which sucked us into the five-month ordeal.

To this day, there are individuals who still believe that I was guilty all along of the accusations flung at us. Some of those individuals sat in the Portuguese parliament. My son was also tortured in Mozambique during repeated false accusations that he had been part of the August 1976 Nyadzonya raid by the Selous Scouts into Mozambique, when over 1,000 guerrillas died. In those days immediately after our release, I was to learn more and more such shocking details pertaining to our abduction and torture.

The phone never stopped ringing for days as I paged through the voluminous amount of documentation concerning our ordeal. Anne Aymone, the wife of Giscard d'Estaing, called me to express her relief that we were alive and out of Tanzania. She had been one of the celebrities who had rallied to our cause, her husband having loomed large throughout my interrogations. The wife of President Eanes of Portugal called, as did prominent personalities from many countries as the news spread.

We owed our lives to this international, concerted effort which eventually involved the League of Red Cross and Red Crescent societies, the Paris-based International Hunting and Game Conservation Organization, and Amnesty International. The secret services of several countries were also drawn into this scandal. The office of the king of Spain took a direct and active interest in our fate because of the intervention of the Aznar family through their mother, Loli, the Marchioness de Lamiaco, to whom this book is dedicated.

We were formally invited to meet the president of Portugal, and we accepted because José Gama assured me that the president had intervened, had done all he could and had been assured of our absolute innocence in the face of the mendacious Tanzanian "communiqué" issued upon our release. We four were presented to President Eanes by José Gama. A typical presidential audience of ten minutes at most turned into one and a half hours with no other officials present.

I refused to meet Portuguese Prime Minister Mario Soares, the author of those infamous words "exemplary decolonization," and spend so much as five seconds in his company. After our trip into hell, I had no desire to shake his hand. Life was too precious now to waste going through the motions with someone who had done absolutely nothing for us. He and his socialist/communist associates had simply handed over the Portuguese colonies to communist revolutionaries, wrecking lives in the process and causing long-term damage to millions of simple people on the ground, most of them Black, who had been abandoned to their fate. I also refused to see the Minister of Foreign Affairs because he, too, had done nothing, subjecting my family and close friends to months of the blackest anguish.

I returned to the Hunters Africa headquarters in Midland, Texas for a while. Clayton Williams, the owner, was eager to have a book about my experiences published. It was not the right time for such an undertaking. I was too raw with rage to have any perspective. In any case, only someone who knew Africa from the inside, who had a seasoned interest in sub-Saharan politics and insight into the complexities of my life could tackle such a task. It had to be someone who had a feel for the subject and whom I could trust because there would be a great deal of off-the-record discussion.

Life is made up of interludes. In October 1986, I had been back in Spain for a while and was, in fact, in Barcelona when I heard the news that Samora Machel, the president of Mozambique, had been killed in an aircraft crash close to the Mozambican–South African border. The crash has never been fully explained and allegations such as that of sabotage by the South Africans, of drunken Russian flight-deck crew, and of mysterious beacons programmed to have the aircraft go off course and crash continue to resurface. There is a new theory now, coming from none other that Machel's widow, Graça, who spoke in late 1999 of certain elements within Frelimo itself suspected of having plotted her husband's death.

Well, well, well.

I decided to fly out to South Africa. I had not seen my sister, Lucinda, and her immediate family since 1979, on the occasion of my mother's funeral in Lisbon. The imminent birth of a great-niece was also good reason to have a reunion. I had passed through South Africa on many occasions and had made fleeting visits in years past, but it had been a solid decade since I was last there.

While in South Africa, a fresh opportunity presented itself when I became involved in the launching of a game-farm operation in the Orange Free State, the central part of the country. I shuttled between Spain and South Africa in this regard and was able to sign up a very healthy list of clients from Europe.

My son and Rui Monteiro became part of this operation, which involved hunting on game ranches in other parts of South Africa—from the borders with Botswana in the west and Zimbabwe in the north, down to Natal in the southeast and over to the eastern Cape. As recently as the early 1960s, South Africa would not have been considered as a hunting destination by the international sportsman. Today, thanks to a sustained, scientifically backed campaign to reclaim land from maize fields and cattle, and to reintroduce and breed back game species indigenous to the area, South Africa now boasts the best-managed game-ranching industry on the continent, attracting more hunters annually than any other African country.

After the unfenced worlds of places like Mozambique, Angola, Rhodesia, the Central African Republic, Sudan, and Zaire, for example, we found that the fenced game ranches got to us in the end. There was a "canned" element to some of the hunting, which disturbed us. For a variety of other reasons as well, I decided to return to Spain in 1988, where I ran a safari-booking agency out of Madrid but other issues were also on my mind—the Mozambique National Resistance Movement.

In the wake of the ordeal of 1984–85, any news about Mozambique was more intensely interesting to me than would probably have been the case otherwise. I set out to discover exactly what Renamo had in the way of representation abroad and was not surprised to discover that these anticommunist guerrillas lacked vigorous backing in Europe and the States. There was a presence in Kenya, Portugal, and West Germany as well as a lobby in Washington, D.C. operating as the Mozambique Research Center. Spain, for example, was socialist, and unsympathetic to a cause like Renamo, as was Portugal. British policy concerning Mozambique in the mid-1980s was molded, amongst other things, by business interests relating to Tiny Rowland and the Lonhro group's activities in Mozambique as well as by the special relationship between Mozambique and Britain after the independence of Zimbabwe in 1980. Renamo was an inconvenience. The United States was not much better but I decided to try and contact the Renamo representatives in Washington.

Tom Schaaf, Jr., an American, had worked for the Ministry of Agriculture in Rhodesia and continued in the agricultural sphere after Zimbabwe's independence in 1980. He was based on the border with Mozambique, at Mutare, opposite Manica Province, and used to enter Mozambique in connection with his work. Tom was a committed Christian and, in this capacity, became involved in missionary outreach programs, which resulted in contact with Renamo. He became aware of the brutalities of the Frelimo regime and the suffering of the people.

All this has been well documented in a variety of publications over the years: the killing of tribal authorities to break the back of traditional leaders and cow the people into submission; the institution of pass laws to restrict movement inside Mozambique; the outlawing and confiscation of religious property, the burning of villages and churches, the random killing of people and the destruction of crops, forced conscription of youngsters into the army, confiscation of livestock, forced marches to "Centres for Mental Decolonization"—Mozambique's gulag—imprisonment without trial, torture, malnourishment, manipulation of relief aid during famine to deprive those perceived as being against Frelimo, forced labor, forced collectivization, and general terrorizing of the population in order to control the people.

Tom Schaaf had taken up the cause of Renamo. During one of my visits to the States, Tom introduced me to Herman Cohen, who was National Security Africa Advisor, going on to become Assistant Secretary of State for African Affairs during the Reagan administration. I was accorded a generous one-on-one audience with Herman Cohen, whom I found attentive and interested in what I had to say.

I asked Herman Cohen who was the more authentic Mozambican? I went on to state that the fact that I was White whereas the majority of Mozambicans were Black, was not the issue. I had lived in Mozambique in an entirely multiracial situation, whatever the inherent injustices of the times. I had gone to school in Mozambique as a child, had played sports across the color lines, had worked in Mozambique and provided employment for decades to the locals. My four children—one deceased—had been born in Mozambique. All we had ever held of value had been rooted in Mozambique. I was one voice speaking for countless anonymous voices who had had their lives ruined by Frelimo.

When I warned that Renamo was not some passing phenomenon and that sooner or later, it would have to be officially included in the national life of Mozambique, Herman Cohen turned to me and said that the solution would lie in both sides sitting down together to negotiate a new future for Mozambique.

Lest there be any misconceptions, let me say I was never paid one cent by Renamo for anything I did to lobby for the movement, be it travel expenses, accommodation, or any other allied charges. I was motivated by a sense of outrage and by revenge. I wanted to see some semblance of justice done before I died, some righting of the scales. I wanted to avenge my family and all those who were voiceless and powerless under the present circumstances. I wanted to see an elimination of the Marxist-Leninist disease.

Fate stepped in yet again as I was reading one of the daily papers in Madrid. In late 1989, a fairly insignificantly placed article reported the abduction of four Spanish sailors by Renamo when their fishing vessel ran aground off the Mozambican coast in an area controlled by Renamo. Spanish fishing trawlers had long been stripping Mozambican waters in a fishing free-for-all. They still are.

The captain of the vessel had a limp and could not keep up with the other four crew members and their Renamo captors when they set out on a very lengthy trek through the bush. It was decided to free the captain, who was escorted back to the port by one of the guerrillas. The fate of his compatriots was unknown and, as I established, the Spanish agents were at a loss as to what to do.

I saw an opportunity to make political capital out of this incident and, hopefully, do something to free the Spaniards. I found out who the owner of the vessel was and had a meeting with him and with his associates in Madrid. They were very apprehensive when I introduced myself as a member of Renamo. At that stage, I had not yet been formally admitted to the opposition movement. As I spoke about a possible facilitating role I could play in having the Spaniards released, the owner of the vessel, a very prominent citizen of Madrid, stopped me short and said, "Wait a minute! I know you! You're Adelino, whom I met in Nairobi in 1977 at the Safari Park Hotel. You were the managing director, and you helped us get back another of our fishing trawlers."

That broke the ice! What a small world! Back in 1977, the Mozambicans had impounded one of their vessels while it was fishing in Mozambican waters. A heavy fine was imposed and the vessel had still not been returned to the rightful owners. My name came up as a possible help in knowing the right people inside Mozambique who could help the Spaniards. Joaquin Fernandez, the head of the Spanish fishing company and a great friend of the Aznar family, knew me and contacted me in Nairobi for help.

He and his number-two, Amador Suarez, the man now before me, flew out to Kenya, where I gave them the name of René d'Assunção, a Black Mozambican lawyer based in Beira, who often came to Portugal and whom I knew. René eventually resolved the problem for the Spaniards. Fernandez moved on and Suarez took over.

I warned him and his colleagues that the crew members of the fishing trawler would not be released immediately, but that I could assure them they would be humanely treated. I was asked to liaise with the Lisbon office of Renamo to request that they contact the head, Afonso Dhlakama, out in the bush. This was done and Dhlakama sent word that he would be prepared to meet a representative of the Spanish company as well as me in Nairobi during December 1989 to discuss the issue. In the end only I flew out with Sebastião Temporario, one of the Renamo representatives from Lisbon, who eventually became a member of the Mozambique parliament. We were received very cordially by Dhlakama, who knew exactly who I was and all about the Serras Pires family. We had lived and hunted in what became Renamo areas.

Dhlakama gave his personal word that the Spaniards would be released and that they were being well treated. The Renamo leader then asked me to join his organization which I did, there in Nairobi. I have the letter of appointment signed by Dhlakama himself and authorizing me to represent Renamo abroad. It was only then, in December 1989, that I became a member of Renamo. The leader told us that the Spanish fishermen would certainly be used to focus international attention.

Before I flew back to Madrid, Dhlakama asked me to help the Lisbon office and to promote the cause in Europe. To this end, I assisted a pro-Renamo lobby in London through my good friend, David Hoile. This lobby was able to project a more sober and honest scenario of Mozambique under Frelimo via the media and prominent British citizens. I introduced David to the Renamo hierarchy in Lisbon, during a fleeting secret visit arranged through the Portuguese Military Intelligence Service. I also was instrumental in jump-starting a similar lobby in Spain among people who were exceedingly well connected with the media and who could help give a more balanced picture of the realities of Mozambique and not the lopsided leftist stories deifying Frelimo.

The esteemed Spanish writer, Arturo Perez Reverte, was commissioned to make a documentary about Renamo on behalf of the Spanish government, a socialist government and very anti-Renamo. When he came to see me, I was blunt with him in saying that I did not wish him to go out to Mozambique in bad faith, his mind already made up, and then to produce a biased documentary that would only poison matters further in a region already savaged by years of civil war which had caused terrible suffering to the people and had decimated the wildlife. Reverte could see that I knew what I was talking about, and he undertook to show me the footage before the final editing. A fresh future can only be built on facts because the truth has a way of eventually surfacing.

Approximately two months later, Reverte and his television crew returned to Spain, and I was invited over to the studios to view the footage. It was dramatic, showing bush schools, very primitive clinics—but clinics nonetheless—to treat the wounded and sick, and all sorts of infrastructure over a vast region where Renamo dominated. There were clearly impromptu interviews with a huge variety of people who spoke very openly of their lives and what they had experienced in the years since the Portuguese had departed. It was riveting.

Reverte, an extremely fit man, spoke with awe of the physical and mental stamina of the Renamo forces he met. The Spaniards had had to walk into Mozambique from the Malawi border and they covered over 600 miles on foot into the Renamo areas, over often tough terrain. Reverte even coined a word for the cracking pace at which the forces moved, calling it the paso Renamo. He could not get over the physical strength of the female guerrilla troops who each easily shouldered 65-pound packs on these lengthy marches through the bush. They would help transport dried meat on foot, mainly buffalo, from the Marromeu Flats, about two-hundred miles away, to feed the troops and the local population.

The Spanish documentary was widely distributed and it represented a victory for Renamo, as it was the product of a socialist country. The four Spanish fishermen were released and returned to Spain, where they spoke very highly of Renamo, saying that they had been consistently well treated and had been provided with whatever Renamo had at its disposal. The news spread.

Under Daniel arap Moi, Kenya had been playing an increasingly important role as mediator in efforts to eventually have direct negotiations between Renamo and Frelimo. South Africa and Zimbabwe were also involved. Renamo's status was changing from that of "armed bandits" to an authentic indigenous opposition movement. The civil war was continuing, but so were the negotiations to try to bring an end to that war.

Renamo's second National Congress was held inside Mozambique in December 1991. I joined the Lisbon Renamo group and flew to Rome, connecting for Nairobi and continuing on to Blantyre, in Malawi. We had to be exceptionally careful in Blantyre, which was crawling with Frelimo spies. From there, we were then ferried in a Piper Aztec into a bush landing strip in one of the former Safrique hunting concessions, between Maringué and Nyamacala. The pilot was Rodney Hein, a Zimbabwean evangelical missionary, and first-rate bush pilot who was based in Blantyre. He ministered to the huge Mozambican refugee population living in Malawi, on the border with their homeland. Rodney did more for Renamo during all those years than anyone else I came across. He was extraordinarily dedicated. One did not have to share his religious beliefs to recognize this.

Flying in at a potentially lethal low altitude, we landed. I felt oddly numb at being back in my old hunting grounds under these circumstances after fifteen years. It was like bumping into someone you had once known exceedingly well but had not seen in years. The flood of memories and the sadness were overwhelming. For security reasons, we were not told the exact location of the congress, and we had to walk through the bush in midsummer heat for two solid days before reaching the site.

We were in Mozambique for one month. The congress could not start immediately because people were still on their way on foot from very distant places. In the two-day walk through the bush to the meeting place, I never so much as saw the spoor of a single wild animal. It was a deeply distressing experience for me. Weapons were used to feed the people. Times of terrible drought and ensuing famine had been experienced in the intervening years, so wildlife was massacred in the process. I understood this.

David Hoile, João Gonçalves, a dentist from Portugal, and I were the only Whites at the congress. We were accorded very courteous treatment throughout. News was relayed to me in the bush on December 3 that my daughter Palucha had just given birth in Lisbon to her third child and first daughter, to be named Margarida, in honor of my first baby daughter, who lies buried in Beira. This was an omen, the beginnings of a rebirth for Mozambique. I felt happy, all those thousands of miles away.

A Canadian television crew at the congress asked me on film if I intended returning to Mozambique to reclaim what I had lost. I shot back my reply that this was a legitimate reason to return, as Frelimo had stolen what had been legally mine and that of my entire family. The documentary was shown in Europe, in South Africa, and in the Americas.

Most of the foreign-based members of Renamo and invited observers left ahead of me upon conclusion of the congress. I was then taken on one of the three motorbikes through the bush to what remained of a little town called Canxixe, which was now a pock-marked ruin after years of guerrilla warfare. There, we waited for Rodney Hein to pick us up. His Piper Aztec duly arrived, only to break down after landing. Africa forces you to be patient.

The dead battery was removed and was taken by motorbike to the main Renamo base, where a charger was available as the base had sophisticated radios which ran on batteries. Rodney was back the next day, ready for our departure. The previous evening, as I ate my sorghum and passed on the "high" meat, I noticed that the local comandante had two tiny birds on his plate. I joked with him about his "banquet." He said, "You know what, I think these are the last birds in this area!"

I flew out, back to Blantyre and then via Paris to Lisbon. Between early 1992 and October of that year, negotiations intensified concerning a Renamo/Frelimo accord. This "General Peace Accord" was duly signed in Rome on October 4, 1992. Neither I nor any other White person who had dedicated themselves over the years at strictly private expense to helping Renamo was invited to Rome. I invited myself and arrived an hour or so after the signing. I looked about me and confronted a few sheepish individuals. In the light of this new "indigenization policy" at the heart of Renamo, I called it a day and cut my ties with the movement for good. My thoughts were with the tribal people in the bush who had placed all their trust in their representatives. It was the end of the road for me.

A clutch of Renamo personalities had developed a taste for the good life since the late 1980s as they became more and more frequent visitors to Europe. First-class air travel, fine hotels, food and drink, fancy clothes, and an inflated impression of their own importance infected these people. They became increasingly alienated from their original mission, which was to fight for the interests of the millions of simple folk on the ground who had little to nothing at all and who had borne the brunt of the suffering occasioned by civil war. A growing arrogance had taken root in the Renamo leadership.

I left Rome that October, knowing that the seduction of these Renamo representatives had already begun. They spoke to me openly of going to Maputo, of becoming part of parliament. That was where the good life was. Of course, Maputo had its place but nobody spoke to me that day of going back to Gorongosa or Maringué, in the bush, or even to Beira to fight for their people's rights in a new dispensation from within their constituencies. Gay Paris had beckoned. What I observed that day in Rome, however unpalatable it may sound now, convinced me that nothing at all would change for the millions of Renamo followers on the ground as their representatives, starting with Dhlakama, detached themselves and moved south of the Save River, where all the perks were.

Ironically, I would yet be cordially invited back to Mozambique by none other than Frelimo diplomatic representatives to witness the epilogue to this story.

EPILOGUE

> *The Wind of Change has blown and gone, and, at the end of the century, not a single African country is in bondage to any power. But hundreds of millions of Africans have been in bondage since the first day of* uhuru . . .
>
> —Jon Qwelane (prominent Black South African journalist)

The phone rang. It was Fernando Antoniotti, a voice from the distant past, with whom I had attended the same primary school in Tete almost sixty years previously. I remembered him well. His father was of Italian origin, hence the surname, and his mother was a local woman. My sister Lucinda was godmother to Fernando's sister, Elena, our families having shared many pioneering years on the Zambezi. Fernando was part of the Mozambican diplomatic mission to Portugal and had gone to some trouble to track me down. I happened to be in Lisbon, visiting my family, when we re-established contact with each other after all those decades and the collective drama of two lifetimes.

To my astonishment, Fernando invited me to the Mozambican embassy, where I was accorded red-carpet treatment and a free visa to visit Mozambique openly and freely for the first time in twenty years.

After all that had transpired, more especially concerning my active involvement with Renamo between 1989 and 1992, this was an entirely unexpected development. I spoke as frankly as I always had, saying to my hosts that it was they who had changed, not I. I still held the same values which had made me fight to the end. I know I caught the attention of the diplomats that day when I said that while I had rejected what Frelimo proved to be after 1975, I had to admit that Renamo would not have been the solution, either. In fact, they would have been just as bad.

Much had happened to Frelimo in the interim. Forced by harsh domestic and foreign economic and political realities, and paying an increasingly dramatic price for an unwinnable civil war, coupled with ever increasing pressure from the real masters of the universe, the World Bank and the International Monetary Fund, via the United States of America, Frelimo had finally had to forsake its Marxist-Leninist policies after more than fifteen disastrous years, which are often conveniently blamed exclusively on the civil war. The party had no choice but to adopt a free-market system and a multiparty political dispensation, however suspect it still is. Frelimo hardliners have had to submit to the ever-more-vigorous economic neocolonization of Mozambique through those world entities and, especially, through Mozambique's powerful neighbor, the Republic of South Africa. Maybe this was indeed the time to return and take a look at what had become of Mozambique. I hardly dared wonder what had happened to the wildlife.

Flying into Beira on a typically humid October day in 1995, I was mentally rolling back the years. Vignettes flashed past my mind's eye of my childhood, of my young manhood, of the glory days of safari, and of the eventual shameful unraveling of a lifetime at that same airport, where I was now being met with such genuine warmth. While the severe neglect of two decades was unmistakable in the peeling paint, the potholed roads, unkempt sidewalks, and general tattiness of a once-vibrant town now with its quota of street children, I could not help noticing the cordiality of the Mozambicans, which exceeded anything I had experienced anywhere else in Africa. A bitter war had been fought, there had been much suffering and death, some losses remaining irretrievable on all sides; yet, without exception, the friendliness of the locals was remarkable.

Hosted by Francisco "Chico" Brandão, a good friend from the old days who owned the Ambassador Hotel, one of the landmarks of Beira, the news spread and I was soon in touch with people who had been a meaningful part of my life for many years. In some cases, conversation and laughter resumed as if there had been no interruption. In other cases, there was an awkwardness as we tried to find words to bridge yawning chasms of two decades to cover our respective lives. Sometimes there were no words, and I found myself skirting issues rather than opening memories. I quickly learned, however, that since 1975, the ordinary Mozambican had survived terrible years of political oppression, war, ongoing privation, drought, floods, and outright famine. The scars of those years were visible. Such luxuries as the main sports grounds in Beira had become weed-filled trash heaps and open latrines, work remains scarce, especially north of the Save River, and I immediately noted an air of general disillusionment.

Despite all I heard and saw, it felt strangely comforting to be back. I visited my daughter's grave at the main Beira cemetery and noticed that it had been reasonably well cared for, indicative of the strong respect for the dead in the African cultures in general. Friends organized to take me back to the family farm and my father's grave at Guro, 275 miles from Beira, and then up to Tete, on the Zambezi, where my earliest African memories are anchored. I had a real need to reexperience the country which had shaped my life.

We drove out into the interior, crossing the Pungwe River twice as we left behind the humid coast and a thousand memories. The effects of the civil war were everywhere. The people had been forced out of their villages and closer to the roads, where shanty settlements had been cobbled together as the people tried to survive. Once-well-treed bush had been chopped bare for firewood over huge areas, severely disturbing the habitat for wildlife.

I was immediately aware of a swollen human population such as I had never seen in all those previous decades in Mozambique. Most of the people I saw were children and teenagers. Ablebodied men were away, in the towns and cities and on the mines in other countries, earning a living while the women stayed back and tried to hold together the threadbare fabric of a society long under stress. Despite all the foregoing, the population had exploded and literally doubled in my twenty-year absence. Wildlife, already decimated as a result of human suffering, would not escape the effects of this ongoing human drama. I wish it were otherwise.

As we traveled over roads in surprisingly good condition, I saw familiar landmark after familiar landmark. An unusual silence hung in the air that day as I tried to absorb what was being played out before me. I felt numb and tired at all the changes. Logic told me that you cannot go back in life. Nothing remains the same. Change is the only constant in human affairs, yet my emotions kept hoping to see a vestige of those past forty-odd years which had remained as I remembered it.

Guro Mountain rose before us. We stopped at a vantage point to look out over the valley and pick out our whitewashed farmhouse, against Guro Mountain. It had gone. So had most of the trees which had once covered the mountain. The warning bark of baboon high up in the rocky fastness could still be heard, the main attraction for them now being the haphazard patchwork of sorghum and maize plots on the valley floor. Nobody spoke as we descended into the valley and bumped along the road I had traveled countless times to reach our farm.

We were surrounded by a squatter settlement of some 60,000 people, living where the orchards and modest vineyards had once stood, where the maize, sunflower, and cotton fields had once been cultivated, where we had hacked out the airfield to save my father's life, where the big five once roamed at will, right up to the site of the farm laborers' compound. A jumble of brick and stone marked the site of our large farmhouse. It had been stripped of anything of value many years previously. I got out and looked about me, struggling to recall that enthralling sight so long ago of the pack of wild dogs, delirious with excitement, as they swooped over our lands after kudu, their high-pitched cries filling the crisp air of that magical day in my youth.

Now the woodsmoke cooking fires of thousands of people rose in the air at the foot of the stark mountain, an atmosphere of neglect hanging like a pall from horizon to horizon. The wild animals had gone. The birds, especially the raptors I always took for granted, had gone. As I made my way on foot to my father's grave, I noticed that the blue gum trees which marked the spot had not been chopped down. Instead, they were taller and broader than I remembered. I felt oddly relieved when I came up to the grave and found it undisturbed, clearly respected down the years by people, many of whom would have had no idea who the deceased had been, but who had a profound understanding of the rite of death. What I felt that day was too complex for words, too late for tears. It was sufficient to be there, to remember.

Word traveled like a flash flood that "visitors" were there and, within a short time, several former members of our farm staff appeared. Their faces, like mine, were etched with age and, in some cases, with years of ill health. It was a profoundly emotional meeting as we greeted one another and recalled times shared, times vanished. I asked that anyone who would like to see me gather at the same place three days later at an agreed-upon time, as I would be going up to Tete and would return on my way back to Beira. I wished in particular to meet anyone who had been part of our hunting staff. These simple people who had remained in the area and who, by some incredible luck, had survived war, disease, and famine, would tell me the truth about Concession No. 9, where we had had such rich animal life and such extraordinary hunting experiences.

Tete and Caroeira Hill were like a somewhat shabbily dressed older woman who had known better times—even quite successful times—but who was making an effort. If one looked more closely, traces of former beauty were discernible as once-familiar buildings came into view: the bar where I had first met John "Pondoro" Taylor, the now grubby and crumbling façade of the former governor's residence, our huge old house with its enormous wraparound veranda where the swallows from Europe would nest in the eaves, and the primary school where I made my first friends in Africa. Memories dovetailed into one another as fluidly as the flow of the river below, the Zambezi, that mighty sea of my childhood. I tried to find the spot where the paddle steamers used to dock, coming across a fine bridge which now spans the river where a pontoon was once the only means of reaching the other side. Traffic flows ever more intensely into Malawi and beyond, through these historic crossroads of my earliest days in Africa.

There were still a handful of people in town whom I had known for years and with whom I had shared life. Much remained unsaid in those three days. It was sufficient to be back among old friends, not to have to explain anything, simply to review as we saw fit, knowing that we were all now in the latter part of our lives, and that the need to remember and to be remembered was felt keenly by all of us.

Back at the site of our farm in Guro, a crowd of about thirty people had already gathered by the time I arrived. Everyone had put on their Sunday best, among them being several elderly women who had worked for my mother. It was a very touching sight as the people clustered around the food and drink I had brought with me and began telling me of the intervening twenty years and what they had survived.

It was the all-too-depressingly-familiar story of Africa: fratricide, greed, broken promises, and destruction. They asked me about members of my family and wanted to know when we would be returning to Guro. I explained that we had lost everything in Mozambique and that the land on which we were standing, where our farm had once stood and where many of those present had worked and lived for years, had been taken away from us by Frelimo and now belonged to the state, and that I could not return to start all over again. It was too late. The hyenas had been and gone. Not even the carcass of our former lives there remained. Just our memories. The crowd murmured their understanding.

Several of my former safari staff had come. Given the circumstances under which they had all had to live in those preceding decades. I was frankly amazed to see them at all. When I asked in particular about the animals in the region, especially on Concession No. 9, one of my first trackers, Moises, raised both his hands in a gesture of despair. Most of the animals had gone. There had been war. Many people had big guns. There had been hunger and even famine. Many people still had big guns. The soldiers, both Frelimo and Renamo, had killed many animals. Nobody could stop them. With that, we took our leave of one another, knowing that it would be unlikely that we would meet again.

As we drove back to Beira, I had such a sense of waste, of finality.

In Beira, I sent a messenger with money to the village of Radio, my chief tracker. I had been assured he was still alive, one of the few survivors of my original hunting crew. This was remarkable because the region where his village was located had been particularly hard hit during the civil war. I asked the messenger to bring Radio back with him. I could not leave without seeing him again. He had shared some of the most significant years of my life and had been one of the few people I could trust implicitly. Owing to my controversial recent past involving Renamo, I could not risk traveling into a stronghold of the party and perhaps causing trouble for the people there. The notion of multiparty politics is in its embryonic stage in most of Africa, and opposition parties are still the subject of suspicion and worse. Only pressure by the developed world has led to the introduction in Africa of concepts such as democracy and multiparty systems. The mindset is still largely totalitarian.

Radio came. Looking frailer but still in reasonable health, he and I were quite overcome when we saw each other again. He told me of the terrible famine in the 1980s, of the death of many people because of the famine and also because of the war. Radio had been seriously ill at one stage. One of his wives had managed to keep him and the family alive by boiling the roots of banana plants and making a type of gruel.

He spoke of the destruction of the game in the Gorongosa Game Reserve and the chopping down of its ancient trees. He described to me in detail the slaughter of the once-huge herds of elephant throughout the region for their ivory, juvenile elephants not being spared. Frelimo, Renamo, the Zimbabweans, and the South Africans were all involved. Nobody's hands were clean. The ivory was traded for weapons, in order to pursue the civil war.

Radio also confirmed the slaughter of the buffalo down on the Marromeu Flats to feed the Zimbabwean troops who had also brought trouble with them into his country. He described how the Zimbabweans used helicopters to mow down the animals from the air. He spoke with resignation. Life was worse, many people had died, and many would continue to die. Work was scarcer than ever, and the people were angry that their lives were not better after all their sacrifices. Nobody from Maputo came up there, into the bush, to talk to them, to tell them what was going on or what would be done for their region. Nobody cared. They were alone.

What could I say? I gave Radio medicines and money to return safely to his village, saying that I would always remember him and his people and that I was deeply saddened to hear of what had befallen him and our once-shared part of the world. I wondered what had happened to his hostile teenage son and, if still alive, whether he was still such a convinced revolutionary after seeing the entirely unwarranted suffering of his own family. I did not ask after him.

I have been back to Mozambique several times since 1995, going as far afield as north of Pemba, the capital of Cabo Delgado Province. It borders Tanzania, the Rovuma River separating the countries. There is still some wildlife left, especially elephant, in this Rovuma River basin region, but rampant poaching is posing a serious and continuous threat to what remains of the game.

In 1997, in an especially ironic development, my name came up for discussion once more in Maputo, the capital of Mozambique. I was asked to meet the governor of Cabo Delgado Province, who was also the vice minister for Agriculture, Fisheries, and Wildlife, to discuss plans for the conservation of wildlife in that region. I have always liked challenges. Why not one more? This led to my being directly responsible, in 1998, for introducing the top structure of Safari Club International to the governor of Cabo Delgado Province, American-educated José Pacheco.

After a series of self-funded trips to Cabo Delgado, I found myself suddenly pushed to one side, no explanation being given. Certain entities, driven by ego and greed, were more interested in hunting concessions and in making a fast buck than in establishing a viable antipoaching force on the ground or in long-term undertakings to conserve game.

Rumors and rumors of rumors about hunting from helicopters, about exceeding quotas and about smuggling ivory started doing the rounds. To date, stories continue to circulate about what transpired in the Cabo Delgado region during 1998. Apparently, investigations are still proceeding. I am unaware of anything of significance having been put in place on the ground in that area to begin combating the scourge of poaching. I have good reason to believe that nothing will now come of my initial efforts, undertaken in good faith.

As final negotiations with the publishers of this book were being concluded in New York, a fresh and terrible catastrophe hit southern Africa, when cyclones Eline and Gloria ravaged the region, causing the worst flooding in living memory. The most severely affected country by far was Mozambique, especially the southern part. Images of terror entered the living rooms of the world as television captured the fear and devastation of many hundreds of thousands of people in their pathetic attempts to escape the muddy death of rivers gone mad as they burst their banks and drowned whole villages in their ferocious flooding toward the sea. Thousands of people on the low-lying coastal plain, from babies to the frail elderly, sought higher ground or were hauled into trees where they clung to life for days, transfixed by the ever-rising water, hunger, thirst, and fear that they were being abandoned afresh to their fate.

Dehydrated, famished and at the end of labor, Rosita Pedro's mother gave birth to her in a treetop before being spotted and winched to safety by a South African helicopter. The deluge went on for days, killing people, livestock, and wildlife, wiping out food supplies and possessions, smashing infrastructure and bringing in its wake a greatly heightened threat of hunger and disease, particularly of malaria and cholera. The rain was still falling over large parts of Mozambique a solid two weeks after the cyclones had departed.

The first country to race to the assistance of Mozambique was South Africa, whose helicopter crews rescued over 12,000 people in a few days while the rest of the world watched. The once-pariah neighbor was the only African country capable of intervening immediately to assist a fellow African country patently incapable of launching any rescue mission of its own. European countries, joined by America, Canada, and a tiny sprinkling of African countries, eventually arrived en masse to assist in the rescue mission and bring some hope to a people once again pushed to the edge of a new abyss of fear and misery, forced yet again onto a muddy track to nowhere as they try to scratch a living and survive on a continent where suffering seems to remain the eternal seal of human existence.

The media, from Mozambique and many other countries, carried reports of certain Mozambican politicians and has-beens from that country's past whining at what they termed the Western world's late response to their suffering. I scanned the media for even a hint of the arrival of vigorous, visible support in the form of food, medicine, aircraft, and trained disaster-relief personnel from Mozambique's many erstwhile Eastern bloc comrades in arms who once gaily goose-stepped together under the red flag.

Reports started circulating of high-level corruption in Mozambique, where international food aid was disappearing, only to resurface on the black market at exorbitant prices. Other aid and medical supplies were not always reaching their destinations, the many bloated resettlement camps where people were falling ill, where children, in particular, were severely malnourished, where clean drinking water was at a premium, and where international aid workers, doctors, nurses, paramedics, pilots, and people of genuine goodwill from many nations were battling this faceless, lethal, and endemic corruption.

The president of the Organization of African Unity admitted to the continent's near-total lack of capacity to cope with such natural calamities. Damning reports started making the rounds in Mozambican newspapers, which I receive every day by e-mail, of certain elements in that country's armed forces who had sold, smuggled, or otherwise stolen aircraft engines and spare parts for personal gain to the point where Mozambique had no air means at all to at least launch its own rescue bid before being joined by foreign forces. The world was fobbed off with, "We are investigating." This is the country constantly being paraded before the world as Africa's success story. The Mozambican authorities also saw fit to charge high landing fees at Maputo Airport in the middle of this calamity for foreign aircraft bringing relief aid and personnel.

The effects of this tragedy will be felt for years, thereby creating new opportunities for outsiders to move in. There is undoubtedly much foreign interest in projects in Mozambique, particularly by the South Africans who have transformed their neighboring state into an economic satellite, which is just as well. Development of any significance, however, is usually south of the Save River. The north continues to be underfunded, underdeveloped, and neglected in favor of the south, which is populated by the dominant tribe of the region, which also dominates the Frelimo hierarchy. Maputo's development is in contrast to Beira's shabbiness, let alone that of all the other towns and smaller settlements in the north, and it is not by accident.

In the first months of the new millennium, many parts of Africa remain in turmoil. More than twenty countries in Africa are either in an outright war situation or are in a state of extreme stress, epitomized by Sudan and the longest civil war in Africa. Africa continues to suffer from tyrants, child soldiers, tribally driven genocide, ethnic cleansing, and population displacement. The specter of severe food shortages to outright famine hovers over large swaths of the continent, directly threatening the remaining wildlife in the process. Sub-Saharan Africa is becoming increasingly marginalized in the global economy because of the risks involved, and it is now the victim of a new form of serfdom: postindependence bondage.

The yoke of political tyranny, corruption, hunger, illiteracy, poverty, and rampant disease weighs ever more heavily. Sub-Saharan Africa is the epicenter of the AIDS pandemic, whose full force, experts assure us, is going to be felt in the next handful of years. More than 70 percent of the world's AIDS sufferers live in sub-Saharan Africa. South Africa, far and away the most advanced country in Africa on all fronts, already has an escalating nightmare concerning AIDS orphans and abandoned HIV-positive babies. The socioeconomic and sociopolitical consequences are self-evident.

Since 1960 and the beginning of the decolonization process,

Africa has suffered more coups and violent revolutions than any other part of the world. Many African countries have exchanged one form of domination and exploitation for the greater evil of domination and exploitation by their own people. Mobutu of Zaire was the classic example in the "president-for-life" mold. Millions of Africans under despotic rulers live in cocoons of fear where foreign opportunists, like jackals who have scented a kill, have moved in to exploit, grab, and run, leaving the people on the ground to face fresh ruin. Angola and the booming oil business come to mind here. Africa's mineral riches have cursed her to this fate and the wildlife in every instance, is an expendable item. Poaching has become international-crime-syndicate business, aided by widespread corruption. Soldiers and AK-47s are not a happy mix for Africa's people—or for Africa's wildlife. You cannot talk conservation to the hungry, the displaced, the diseased, and the desperate.

There is talk of an African "renaissance," of the year 2000 heralding the "African century." In the light of the foregoing, I do not share this optimism. I can merely echo the words of Wole Soyinka, the eminent Nigerian author and 1986 Nobel Prize Laureate for Literature who said in 1999: "We can no longer speak of wars on the continent, only of arenas of competitive atrocities."

The question inevitably arises: What am I still doing in Africa? At nearly seventy-two years of age, while waiting for God, I may as well wait to see if anything new at all comes out of Africa. I wait to see if Africa and the world will ever stop massaging the truth and face facts about corruption, greed, and ineptitude at the top. I wait to see if Africa will ever start looking within the continent, on a sustained basis, for solutions and break with a mentality that breeds a dependency complex on foreign donors and their conditions. I wait to see an Africa starting to clean out the rot in its leadership ranks and begin the long haul to basic self-reliance.

I wait to see the exposure of the human hyenas of opportunism who are wrecking Africa from within. I wait to see Africa begin unshackling herself and standing on her own two feet. I wait to see the draining of the cesspool of vicious self-interest and the fearless emergence in greater and greater numbers of the decent and talented sons and daughters of Africa who will help lead the continent out of this age-old muck. I wait for an end to the stale arguments about Africa always being the hapless victim and the outsider always the exploitative culprit.

While I do not believe that the AK-47s will be beaten into ploughshares or that the lion will lie down with the buck for a long time to come, there is a glimmer of hope. Nelson Mandela, who is without peer in all Africa when it comes to his moral authority and the international respect he commands, departed from his prepared speech on May 6, 2000 in Johannesburg, during the launch of the United Nations Children's Fund Global Partnership. In a clear reference to Africa's despots, he said, "The tyrants of the day can be destroyed by you [the people]. . . . We have to be ruthless in denouncing such leaders."

Although Mandela was slammed in the media the very next day by some Africans as being "un-African," his call has gone out concerning greater respect for human rights and all that this entails. Bishop Desmond Tutu, the internationally respected South African Nobel Prize Laureate for Peace, has also added his powerful voice to the condemnation of corrupt African leaders. The seeds of multiparty politics are germinating in Africa; press freedom is greater now than was the case a mere decade ago; people are becoming less fearful of speaking out and of asserting their right to a better life and to be governed by more responsible and transparent leaders; the young are increasingly better informed of what transpires elsewhere in the world, and the information-technology age is making it that much harder for tyrants to continue unnoticed and unchecked. Anything that helps stabilize the sociopolitical situation in Africa will benefit efforts at stabilizing and conserving what remains of Africa's wildlife heritage.

Many African leaders have been named openly and are currently under investigation for their bloated offshore bank accounts, funded by their looting of the national coffers while their peoples suffer. The developed donor countries have started showing signs of fatigue concerning Africa's ceaseless tragedies, the near-total inability to deal with major crises, the corruption and the ongoing abuse of donor aid. Greater and greater emphasis is now being placed on African governments to be more accountable, to start cultivating more vigorously their own abilities to survive and progress. Only when Africa as a whole becomes more self-sustaining can we start speaking of a renaissance.

Now that I am in the home straight of a full, adventurous life, I realize more clearly that my generation has surely experienced the best of Africa and its incomparable wildlife.

The true struggle for Africa's political, economic and moral regeneration has barely begun.

INDEX

B

C

D

E

F

G

H

I

J

K

L

M

P

R